The Black Seventies

DATE DUE

MAY 16 '73		
OCT 10 '73		
MAR 26 '75		
DEC 3 '75		
MAR 3 '76		
MAY 25 '76		
DEC 14 '77		
MAR 8 '78		
DEC 2 '80		
MAR 23 '82		
DEC 9 '87		

The
Black
Seventies

leading black authors look
at the present and reach
into the future

The
Black
Seventies

**Floyd B. Barbour,
editor**

An Extending Horizon Book

To those within
and those without

Foreword:

The Need For
A Dirt Path

A while back, but not too long ago, I was invited to speak on a platform with Ernest Crichlow, the painter, at a renowned New England college. Being black, we were to talk about the black cultural revolution. At that time I was considering doing a book on black culture. The college was a plush one: thick carpets and tree-lined avenues. If you are black, there is something almost incongruous about discussing anything black in such a setting. The very ease of living and manner of life seem to belie the reality of your meaning.

After the lecture, I found myself wandering about the campus. One wanders about such places trying to find something familiar to rest his history upon. Everything was paved and moon-lit. Everywhere there was more brick and cement, and grass struggling vainly to break through the cement into life. Suddenly I found myself walking along a dirt path next to what must have been the science building. Someone had left this path — an oversight, an intuition? Someone had realized that beneath the brick and cement there was a need for a dirt path. Something we could sink our boots into. Something to be remembered and cherished, beneath the brick and stone. Something true, perhaps — and real.

Now, I have never been to one of the old churches founded by the slaves, but I like to imagine what it looks like. I chart the number of rows and guess the height of the ceiling. On Sundays, a warm Southern breeze intermingles with the murmur of the brothers and sisters in their seats. The floor of this church, I like to imagine, is a dirt path.

That is what this book is about: the need for the dirt path.

I sit looking over the correspondence which has served as pathfinder for *The Black Seventies*. As I said above, I began with the idea of a book on black culture. Harold Cruse has called the shape of the black movement a triangle: politics connected to culture connected to economics. With this in mind, I wrote the following letter to Dr. Adelaide Cromwell Hill of the African Studies Center at Boston University:

September, 1968

Dear Adelaide:

I have been thinking about a new anthology. As a rule I do not like anthologies, but I like my own. An anthology should be a house whose rooms have glass partitions, each essay or contribution lending entry to every other essay or contriblution. At any given moment in the anthology, the reader should be able to perceive what has gone before and what can come after. Each author is himself and something other. Out of this can emerge a sense of unity.

A painter begins with an empty canvas; for the writer, it is a blank page. A canvas has its own limitations and possibilities. An anthology can be a collage, a landscape, a portrait in time.

The book I envision must be the thing itself. It must not be an address to the white world, but a community talking among itself. When we talk to each other there are a lot of poses we need not take. This book must re-connect the black writer to the black performer to the black teacher. To examine culture, we must break down the artificial boundaries which separate members of our black community.

A book on black culture must speak to the thing itself. A madman does not have to say he's mad; he demonstrates it. In the same way, a book on black culture must in itself demonstrate that culture. I want to explore what there is that is priceless about us right *now*. What is there that I get from walking through the Hill District in Pittsburgh or down Fourteenth Street in D. C. that I do not get from anywhere else?

I want to juxtapose the revolutionary with the poet, the visionary with the housewife. Not a book of protest only; we have gone beyond that. A book about what we are up to now: a practical account of things as they are, here. The thing in itself . . .

My initial idea altered as I began to talk to people. I began to see that the subject of black culture was too broad for a single volume. Besides, much of this work was being researched by others. I wanted a black book which would explore those areas which have never really been looked into. For me, for obvious reasons, black can not be a fad, an American phase. It is life and blood.

I sent this letter to Lance Jeffers, noted poet and teacher, in California:

November, 1969

Dear Lance:

I should write one day about the anthology as "work of art." Or rather, as an accident which must stand on its own. The book I project will not be the book which will eventually evolve. One has got to get to the point where he appreciates the accidents that produce a book or a satisfying walk in the park!

For some time I have felt there should be a book which complements *The Black Power Revolt*. I thought the book would be one thing. Now I see it can be something else.

I want to present for the new decade a collection of writings by black authors. I am asking each author to address himself to what he would like for the 70's and how he suggests we achieve what he cites. Such an essay would implicitly carry an analysis of the present and a projection for the future. A book with vision. The working title is *The Black*

Seventies. What we want and how we think we should get what we want.

I hope you will consider this letter an invitation to join my list of authors. I hope the new book becomes a reality and that it can carry some meaning and truth . . .

About this time, I had begun to sense the shape of my book. My job was to convince my authors of this fact. I wrote to my friend Henry Martin, teacher and art critic, in Milan, Italy:

January, 1970

Henry, greetings —

The Black Seventies is an attempt to open spaces for us in the new decade. The essays look at the present and future in the light of reality. Our confusions and contradictions. Our struggle. The beautiful and free thing about Federico Fellini is that he talks of embracing *all* his history. To give up anything is to give up too much, is to give up something which one day might be the foundation-stone upon which Roman survival may depend. When he talks about his movies, he talks about the mean and meaningful ways of the past. The delights and follies. The satyr and the warrior and the virgin. He doesn't leave out bits in order to justify a present mood. He is free to embrace what is true about the Roman, because he knows that all experience is ultimately about the human experience.

In the same way, I think you will find in the new book a true sense of black community and identity. In the black seventies we will not allow ourselves to be led about like puppets. *We* shall be in control. We shall not be persuaded by rhetoric or Afro or militant-stance. We want more. We want, simply, reality. Reality to move and to be ourselves. And we shall not give up any of our past. We want Malcolm and Aunt Sadie and the pimp down the block, because each of these is a celebration of what is human. We want all our black experience: the good, the bitter, the grape-time and the in-between time!

A book of open spaces. (In your letters, you are talking about the wish to redefine your own space.) Most of my book's authors suggest ways of nation-building in the 70's. They are talking about new drama and technology and automation and new images for the 21st century. It is as if we are taking a walk around ourselves. Some of the things we see, we like. Some of the things we see, we mean to change . . .

The Black Seventies is a structure which takes its nature from the community within. I see this volume as a house of new black thought. Each essay is a room and each room is a means of conveying a truth about blackness. If you inhabit a house, you can either look outward or look inward. I have divided the present volume into three sections. Writings dealing with the *future as memory* are in the first section: Outward. Writings dealing with the *future as present reality* are in the second section: Inward. And writings dealing with the *future as projection* are in the third section: Forward.

Three sections: Outward, Inward, Forward — the *future as movement*. In the seventies we shall require not only the frontal attack on the racism which plagues American educational, cultural, and political institutions; we shall require not only the enlightened design for our future; we shall also have to regard the interior struggle which, too, is the black American's.

I have not capitalized the word 'black' because black is a state of mind which we accept. It does not have to call attention to itself. It, simply, is.

The Black Power Revolt moves from the past to the present; *The Black Seventies* moves from the present into the future. *The Black Power Revolt* opens with a letter from Benjamin Banneker to Thomas Jefferson; *The Black Seventies* concludes its postscripts with a letter from H. Rap Brown to America. In between is repetition. The question remains, what has changed? When shall we reach beneath the surface, beneath the concrete of the practical hour? How do we learn to touch those things which are real, which are ours? How do we get to that dirt path . . . ?

A book does not stand alone, but upon the goodwill of many people. I wish to acknowledge but a few of these: Mary L. Barbour, friend and mother; Michael Pollet, whose advice guided me legally; Martin Schechter and Donald Young for their support and encouragement; Margaret Burroughs who at the outset asked: Are you black? A belated thanks to Thomas Lindsay whose ideas enriched not only this book but the previous one.

My gratitude also to Elizabeth Cook and Dorothy Porter of Howard University, who answered when I called; Priscilla Long Irons and Gwen Sanders, who were there at the beginning; Sandi Mandeville, Pam Johnson, and Jan Boddie for their editorial acumen; George Kearns for the gift of enthusiam; F. Porter Sargent, the publisher; and Jennie Fonzo, who sets the book straight. And to all my authors, whose faith and trust formed the bridge that carried me across, thank you.

Floyd B. Barbour
Boston, Mass. 1970

Contents

III Forward

Postscripts

BLACK
Declaration
of
Independence

IN THE BLACK COMMUNITY, July 4, 1970 A DECLARA-
TION by concerned Black Citizens of the United States of
America in Black Churches, Schools, Homes, Community Or-
ganizations and Institutions assembled:

When in the course of Human Events, it becomes necessary for
a People who were stolen from the lands of their Fathers, trans-
ported under the most ruthless and brutal circumstances 5,000
miles to a strange land, sold into dehumanizing slavery, emascu-
lated, subjugated, exploited, and discriminated against for 351
years, to call, with finality, a halt to such indignities and genocidal practices — by virtue of the Laws of Nature and of Nature's God, a decent respect to the Opinions of Mankind requires
that they should declare their just grievances and the urgent and
necessary redress thereof.

We hold these truths to be self-evident, that all Men are not
only created equal and endowed by their Creator with certain
unalienable rights among which are Life, Liberty, and the Pursuit
of Happiness, but that when this equality and these rights are
deliberately and consistently refused, withheld or abnegated,
men are bound by self-respect and honor to rise up in righteous
indignation to secure them. Whenever any Form of Government,
or any variety of established traditions and systems of the Ma-

jority become destructive of Freedom and of legitimate Human Rights, it is the Right of the Minorities to use every necessary and accessible means to protest and to disrupt the machinery of Oppression, and so to bring such general distress and discomfort upon the oppressor as to the offended Minorities shall seem most appropriate and most likely to effect a proper adjustment of the society.

Prudence, indeed, will dictate that such bold tactics should not be initiated for light and transient Causes; and, accordingly, the Experience of White America has been that the descendants of the African citizens brought forcibly to these shores, and to the shores of the Caribbean Islands, as slaves, have been patient long past what can be expected of any human beings so affronted. But when a long train of Abuses and Violence, pursuing invariably the same Object, manifests a Design to reduce them under Absolute Racist Domination and Injustice, it is their Duty radically to confront such Government or system of traditions, and to provide, under the aegis of Legitimate Minority Power and Self Determination, for their present Relief and future Security. Such has been the patient Sufferance of Black People in the United States of America; and such is now the Necessity which constrains them to address this Declaration to Despotic White Power, and to give due notice of their determined refusal to be any longer silenced by fear or flattery, or to be denied justice. The history of the treatment of Black People in the United States is a history having in direct Object the Establishment and Maintenance of Racist Tyranny over this People. To prove this, let Facts be submitted to a candid World.

The United States has evaded Compliance to laws the most wholesome and necessary for our Children's education.

The United States has caused us to be isolated in the most dilapidated and unhealthful sections of all cities.

The United States has allowed election districts to be so gerrymandered that Black People find the right to Representation in the Legislatures almost impossible of attainment.

The United States has allowed the dissolution of school districts controlled by Blacks when Blacks opposed with manly Firmness the white man's Invasion on the Rights of our People.

The United States has erected a Multitude of Public Agencies and Offices, and sent into our ghettos Swarms of Social Workers, Officers and Investigators to harass our People, and eat out their Substance to feed the Bureaucracies.

The United States has kept in our ghettos, in Time of Peace, Standing Armies of Police, State Troopers and National Guardsmen, without the consent of our People.

The United States has imposed Taxes upon us without protecting our Constitutional Rights.

The United States has constrained our Black sons taken Captive in its Armies, to bear arms against their black, brown, and yellow Brothers, to be the Executioners of these Friends and Brethren, or to fall themselves by their Hands.

The Exploitation and Injustice of the United States have incited domestic Insurrections among us, and the United States has endeavored to bring on the Inhabitants of our ghettos, the merciless Military Establishment, whose known Rule of control is an undistinguished shooting of all Ages, Sexes, and Conditions of Black People:

For being lynched, burned, tortured, harried, harassed, and imprisoned without Just Cause.

For being gunned down in the streets, in our churches, in our homes, in our apartments, and on our campuses, by Policemen and Troops who are protected by a mock Trial, from Punishment for any Murders which they commit on the Inhabitants of our Communities.

For creating, through Racism and bigotry, an unrelenting Economic Depression in the Black Community which wreaks havoc upon our men and disheartens our youth.

For denying to most of us equal access to the better Housing and Education of the land.

For having desecrated and torn down our humblest dwelling places, under the Pretense of Urban Renewal, without replacing them at costs which we can afford.

The United States has denied our personhood by refusing to teach our heritage, and the magnificent contributions to the life, wealth, and growth of this Nation which have been made by Black People.

In every stage of these Oppressions we have Petitioned for Redress in the most humble terms: Our repeated Petitions have been answered mainly by repeated Injury. A Nation, whose Character is thus marked by every act which may define a Racially Oppressive Regime, is unfit to receive the respect of a Free People.

Nor have we been wanting in attentions of our White Brethren. We have warned them from time to time of Attempts by their Structures of Power to extend an unwarranted, Repressive Control over us. We have reminded them of the Circumstances of our Captivity and Settlement here. We have appealed to their vaunted Justice and Magnanimity, and we have abjured them by the Ties of our Common Humanity to disavow these Injustices, which, would inevitably interrupt our Connections and Correspondence. They have been deaf to the voice of Justice and of Humanity. We must, therefore, acquiesce in the Necessity, which hereby announces our Most Firm Commitment to the Liberation of Black People, and hold the Institutions, Traditions, and Systems of the United States as we hold the rest of the societies of Mankind: Enemies when Unjust and Tyrannical; when Just and Free, Friends.

We, therefore, the Black People of the United States of America, in all parts of this Nation, appealing to the Supreme Judge of the World for the Rectitude of our Intentions, do, in the Name of our good People and our own Black Heroes — Richard Allen, James Varick, Absalom Jones, Nat Turner, Frederick Douglass, Marcus Garvey, Malcolm X, Martin Luther King, Jr., and all Black People past and present, great and small — Solemnly Publish and DECLARE, that we shall be, and of Right ought to be, FREE

AND INDEPENDENT FROM THE INJUSTICE, EXPLOITA-
TIVE CONTROL, INSTITUTIONALIZED VIOLENCE AND
RACISM OF WHITE AMERICA, that unless we receive full Redress and Relief from these Inhumanities we will move to re-
nounce all Allegiance to this Nation, and will refuse, in every way,
to cooperate with the Evil which is Perpetrated upon ourselves
and our Communities. And for the support of this Declaration,
with a firm Reliance on the Protection of divine Providence, we
mutually pledge to each other our Lives, our Fortunes, and our
sacred Honor.

Signed, by Order and in behalf of Black People,

NATIONAL COMMITTEE
OF BLACK CHURCHMAN, INC.

SIGNATORIES and SPONSORS:
*Father Lawrence Lucas, Roman Catholic, New York, New York
*Bishop H. B. Shaw, A.M.E.Z. Church, Pres. NCBC-Wilmington, North
  Carolina
*The Rev. Leon W. Watts, II, Associate Executive, NCBC, Brooklyn, N. Y.
*The Rev. M. L. Wilson, Convent Avenue Baptist Church, N. Y. C.
 The Rev. J. Metz Rollins Jr., Executive NCBC, White Plains, New York
 The Rev. Charles S. Spivey, Jr., Director Dept. Social Justice N.C.C.,
  N.Y.C.
*The Rev. Edler G. Hawkins, St. Augustine Presbyterian Church, N.Y.C.
 The Rev. Albert Cleage, Shrine of Black Madonna, Detroit, Michigan
*The Rev. Tollie Caution, Episcopal Church, New York City
 The Rev. Caroll Felton, A.M.E. Zion, Chicago, Illinois
*The Rev. Will Herzfeld, Missouri-Synod Lutheran Church, Oakland,
  California
 The Rev. Oscar McCloud, Division Church and Race, United Presbyterian
 The Rev. Robert C. Chapman, Dept. Social Justice N.C.C.
 The Rev. Mance C. Jackson, C.M.E. Church, Atlanta, Georgia
 The Rev. Charles J. Sargent, Jr., American Baptist Convention, N.Y.C.
*The Rev. Gilbert H. Caldwell, Executive Ministerial Interfaith Assoc.,
  N.Y.C.
 The Rev. John P. Collier, A.M.E. Church, New York, New York
*The Rev. Calvin B. Marshall, III, Varick Memorial A.M.E.Z. Church,
  Brooklyn, N.Y.
 The Rev. Quinland Gordon, Episcopal Church, New York, New York
 The Rev. James E. Jones, Westminster Presbyterian Church, Los Angeles,
  Calif.
 The Rev. John H. Adams, Grant A.M.E. Church, Los Angeles, Calif.

Mr. Hayward Henry, Black Unitarian-Universalist Caucus, Boston, Massachusetts

The Rev. Vaughn T. Eason, A.M.E.Z. Church, Philadelphia, Pennsylvania

The Rev. R. L. Speaks, First A.M.E.Z Church, Brooklyn, New York

The Rev. Charles L. Warren, Executive, Council of Churches of Greater Washington, D.C.

The Rev. E. Wellington Butts, II, National Chairman, Black Presbyterians United, Englewood, New Jersey

The Rev. Jefferson P. Rogers, Church of the Redeemer, Presbyterian, U.S. Washington, D.C.

Miss Janet Douglas, New York, New York

Mrs. Frank E. Jones, New York, New York

The Rev. Lawrence A. Miller, A.M.E.Z. Church, Durham, North Carolina

The Rev. Bennie Whiten, New York City Mission Society, New York, N.Y.

The Rev. George McMurray, A.M.E.Z., New York, New York

The Rev. Charles Cobb, U.C.C. Commission on Racial Justice, New York, N.Y.

*The Rev. William C. Ardrey, A.M.E.Z, Detroit, Michigan

The Rev. Clarence Cave, United Presbyterian Church, Philadelphia, Pennsylvania

The Rev. J. Clinton Hoggard, A.M.E.Z Church, New York, New York

Black Economic Development Conference, Brooklyn, New York

I.F.C.O. Black Caucus, New York, New York

The Ministerial Interfaith Association, New York, New York

The Rev. W. Marcus Williams, Antioch Baptist Church North, Atlanta, Georgia 30318

The Rev. James M. Lawson, United Methodist Church, Memphis, Tenn.

*Members of Executive Committee.

I

Outward

Every house has its foundation; black America has its history. By looking at the sixties, we can perceive what to and what not to aim for in the seventies. For Neal, black consciousness is good if it allows more light and more understanding of the complex struggle ahead.

LARRY NEAL *was born in Atlanta, Georgia, and was reared in Philadelphia. He received a B.A. from Lincoln University and did graduate work at the University of Pennsylvania. He was formerly the Arts Editor of* Liberator Magazine *and a contributing editor of* Journal of Black Poetry. *He is co-editor, with LeRoi Jones, of the anthology* Black Fire. *Larry Neal and his wife live in New York City.*

Larry Neal

New Space / The Growth of Black Consciousness in the Sixties

It was a squeeze really. Sometimes, in some places, it looked like we weren't gonna make it. But we squeezed through, just like we have been squeezing through for decades. Only this time there was a little more light at the end of the tunnel. Some of us saw God, and seriously began the work of freeing ourselves. The benevolent demon imprisoned within us broke loose, and manifested himself. The Black Spirit asserted itself collectively, and with obvious effects everywhere throughout the country. We were forced, as never before, to make explicit our desire to determine the nature and course of our lives. In short, we demanded self-determination. What the full implications of this demand are, we do not know yet. One thing is clear, though. As we move into the seventies, many of the things that concerned us in the early sixties are no longer as important as we once thought they were. We fought for the right to eat a meal in some cracker restaurant in the deep South, but now that that right has been assured by the Federal Government, black people are no longer interested in such things. Perhaps it was the victory itself that turned us off. Perhaps it was the acute awareness that finally what we wanted was not the cup of coffee in the cracker restaurant, but something more substantive than that. If we could get it, we wanted the land that the restaurant was built on. We wanted reparations. We wanted power. We wanted Nationhood.

Power became the central issue. Essentially, it has always been the central issue; but for so long we were caught up in symbols.

We found ourselves reacting to the most obvious manifestations of white racism while failing very often, to penetrate the core of the problem. When we cut past the bullshit, it became evident that even though the victories of the civil rights movement were legitimate, noteworthy, and necessary, they did not address themselves to the central problem of the black man in America. We came to understand that the simple acquisition of those rights which abstractly belong to all citizens of the United States would in no fundamental manner alter the oppressive situation in which we found ourselves. And that situation is essentially one of powerlessness.

But we had to go through the civil rights movement to understand this. The integrationist cause championed by the NAACP, Urban League, early CORE, and SNCC represent significant watersheds in the history of the black liberation movement. I believe that this evaluation is indisputable even if their concerns were not necessarily the concerns of a broad segment of the black community. In spite of the short term goals of these organizations, they have contributed significantly to the growth of black consciousness. The freedom rides, sit-ins, bus boycotts, Selma March, Meredith March, Harlem rebellion, Watts rebellion, Newark rebellion, school take-overs, and the explosion of black culture all grow out of a conglomerate will towards black liberation.

It was in the midst of all of these activities that we learned the workings of the system that oppressed us. All of these struggles moved us a little closer to the goal of black self-determination which has got to be the end result of all of our labors.

The decade was one marked with fantastic changes in the concept of group leadership. New styles of leadership arose: Robert Williams, Martin Luther King, Malcolm X, Stokely Carmichael, Maulana Karenga, Rap Brown, LeRoi Jones, Huey Newton. . . . New heroes who, even in their diversities of style and contradictory methods, illuminate essential aspects of the struggle for national liberation. The point now is to perceive the whole, and glean out of this conglomerate a method that is appropriate for the tasks facing us.

For example, I was never an admirer of Rev. King. I felt that his philosophy of nonviolence was at times suicidal and detrimental to the liberation of black people. But some aspects of King's philosophy are strategically and tactically valid. A case in point is James Forman's disruption of the church services at an upper-class Riverside Drive church. This action represents one of the high points of nonviolent action; and it was carried out by one man. The thrust of the act, its psychological and moral character, resulted in the fragmentation of the white liberal's sanctimonious smugness. It was beautiful. It revealed, in very graphic terms, just how psychologically and morally insecure the northern white establishment is. The church, the weakest link in America's mythic and cultural superstructure, was tested, and found lacking in moral stamina.

James Forman's act had ramifications throughout the entire church community. Black church men who had heretofore perceived the exact relationship between the church and other racist institutions in the society were free to consolidate around the issue of a relevant church.

All the major activities that were directed towards the question of liberation and Black Power spring from an ethos, a group spirit. What we have to understand, I think, is that somewhere in the maw of this ethos which continuously manifests itself, are the techniques and means of our liberation. It is not a question of falling into one bag, tenaciously holding on to it as if there were no other. That would be the route to suicide. Rather, what we should be about is a meaningful *synthesis* of the best that our struggles have taught us. This is a more difficult task than feeling secure in our own particular, and often narrow, endeavors. What we need, above all, is a widening of our perceptions, especially in terms of our own history.

For example, take the concept of "Black Consciousness." When the thing got really going, black people in different places developed unique and often contradictory attitudes towards it; they operated out of the principle along a variety of different styles. Some people joined the Muslims. Some people stopped eating certain foods. Other people, just as sincere as the first group, began to relish those very same tabooed foods. Some people put on African clothing. Most wore naturals. Some wore brighter colors. Some raised hell in school. Some left their white wives and hus-

bands. Some joined RAM or the Black Panther Party. Some dug
B. B. King, and some dug Coltrane. But shit. *It was all good and
on time.* It was collective motion/energy that could be harnessed
and organized.

At times one would walk the streets and feel it in the air—
black people asserting that they were each the bearers of an ethos.
The beautiful became more beautiful; the black woman assumed
more of her rightful place in the psyche of black artists; brothers
greeted each other warmly. This was especially true after some
catastrophic upheaval like Newark or Watts. Black people spoke
to each other in strange tongues which they did not understand,
but yet spoke well. Harlem, blighted and dope ridden, oozed an
atmosphere of love and concrete spirituality. Black consciousness
manifested itself collectively and resolutely upon large segments
of the black community. What we are faced with now is the
mature shaping of this consciousness. That is, we long to be comfortable with it, to gird ourselves for the long struggle that certainly lies ahead. Black consciousness is necessary and good only
if it allows more light, more understanding of the complex struggles in which we find ourselves. But we must emphasize that it is
impossible for a people to struggle and win without a sense of collective consciousness.

Let me clear something up here: the term "collective consciousness" is not meant to designate a sense of ourselves that is imposed from outside of a *usable* historical past, but indicates rather
a sense of our psychic blood lines that are rooted in the *living* culture. The African past, on the other hand, is an archetypal memory. Unless that past can be shaped within the context of a living
culture, it basically has no function. That is to say: we are *an*
African people, but we are not Africans. We are slave ships,
crammed together in putrid holds, the Mali dream, Dahomey
magic transformed by the hougans of New Orleans. We are field
hollering Buddy Bolden; the night's secret sermon; the memory of
your own God and the transmutation of that God. You know
cotton and lynching. You know cities of tenement cells. What we
have got to do is to understand that there are no blues in Africa.
That is to say, the world view that created the blues is not there.
This is the immediate history that we are going to have to shape

and confront. Just as the blues confronts a specific emotional history, it is necessary, for us, to confront the folkloric as well as written past. The value system for whatever we will be must, if it is to be operational, spring first from readily available sources. *What we need to do, however, with African and other Third World references is to shape them into a new cosmological and philosophical framework. We need to shape, on the basis of our own historical imperatives, a life-centered concept of human existence that goes beyond the Western world view.* Along with the most overt forms of political and economic repression, the peoples of the Third World are dominated by the psychological attitudes of the West. Liberation for us and for them is inextricably bound up with a new set of national and global formulations, and with the erection of new moral and philosophical attitudes. These attitudes inform the following: the use of human and material resources; the idea of justice and human conduct; the relationship between Man and Nature; and the use of force as a means of national liberation.

Under the leadership of Dr. King, the civil rights struggle took place on an essentially moral plane. Black people tried to convince white people of the essentially ethical nature of the struggle. It was the ethical principle that informed the concept of nonviolence. It was the young people of SNCC who de-emphasized the ethical aspects of the concept, and began to use it as a tactical weapon. But whether or not we agree with the philosophy of nonviolence is not the question. What is important here is that this means of liberation was shaped out of the black man's spiritual legacy. Black people are the last remaining "Christians" in America. In the South, where the movement began, most of the black population are devout Christians. And the minister is very often the only form of leadership existing in many communities.

We know the historical reason for this. But we must understand that people can only work with the tools and the concepts that are available to them. Therefore, the expressive mode of the civil rights movement was spirituals, gospels, and folk songs. These modes of expression spring most immediately from southern black culture.

Had the struggle been born in the North, the modes of expression would have been quite different. In substance, the struggle would have been far more brutal and disruptive in its early phases. It would have been less concerned with the ethic preached by King and other black southern leaders. Where the black leadership in the South expressed itself in the language of Christianity, radical northern leaders expressed themselves in a quasi black nationalistic rhetoric.

King's rhetorical devices, poetic and chock full of imagery, grew primarily out of the symbology of the black church service. On the other hand, Adam Clayton Powell expressed himself in the rhetoric of the street corner speakers—speakers who were spawned by a long history of urban mass movements beginning with Marcus Garvey, and coming through to the labor movement of the thirties and forties.

In the South, the preachers have always been the leaders of a large segment of the black community. Often, they took political positions that were not always in the best interest of the community. But sometimes they were in the forefront of militant action, as it was then perceived. Many of them gave their churches over to civil rights activists, and suffered for it. Many of them were lynched or burned out for aiding in the struggle. The movement would have not been successful, on any terms, if it had not attempted to shape and utilize the living culture of the people. Those of us who are engaged in the current struggle for self-determination and for Nationhood must understand this, and move to make this consciousness of ourselves an integral part of everything that we do.

What is the point of these observations? It is simply this: that in spite of the failures of the civil rights movement and its peculiar lack of focus, it still managed to engage a great many people in the struggle. And further, unlike many of today's black organizations, it expressed itself in terms that could be easily embraced by broad segments of the black community. We say this even though we know that, in the main, the civil rights movement failed to address itself to some of the most fundamental problems confronting us. Organizations like the NAACP, Urban League, SCLC, early CORE, and SNCC were finally speaking to an individualized view of our prediciament. Hence, when an NAACP official spoke in terms of "qualifications" he spoke in white man's terms. When he spoke of integration, the term always seemed to imply the dissolution of the black community and of black culture. And finally the concept of integration strongly implied an uncritical acceptance of a white value system. You only had to look at the life-style of some of the more prominent leaders to recognize that they were pitifully enslaved to some of the worst aspects of American national life.

About 1962, many young blacks began to seek another direction, one that they believed would more militantly set about achieving true freedom for black people. These were primarily urban youth who had recognized the need for action, but were decidedly alienated from the movement in the South. Some had been involved with the radical white left where, in the process of reading Marx and Lenin, they came to realize that despite the importance of these theoreticians to late nineteenth and early twentieth century revolutionary thought, they were still confronted with the necessity of developing their own theories of social change. As a result of this observation, they found themselves squeezed between the pallid liberalism of the integrationists and the pseudo-scientific jargon of the white left. Therefore, they had to turn inward on their most immediate historical experiences in order to construct a meaningful concept of social change.

In doing so, they found that throughout Afro-American history there had always existed a persistent, though fragmented, sense of nationalism. They came to feel that somehow previous generations of black activists and radical thinkers had not fully utilized this feeling; this group ethos tugs at all black people regardless of their social standings. It was clear that, however you cut it, every person of African descent, living in America, had to at sometime come to grips with *Blackness*. And further, there was something metaphysical about it—this confrontation with ourselves.

And the questions, many questions: Who was this Marcus Garvey the old "race men" often spoke of? Why did he have so many followers? Why did his organization fail? Who was W. E. B. Du Bois? Why was he against Garvey? Why didn't Monroe Trotter join the NAACP? What is the NAACP? Who did they represent? What is Africa to me? What is my name? Why do our women straighten their hair? Where are we going? Why William Delaney, Edward Blyden, Poppa Singleton, Malcolm X? How could they exist in America? If integration was not the answer, what is? There are millions of black people in the world; what is our relationship to them? Why our music, our dance, our talk, our attitudes?

When we asked these and other questions, it became exceedingly clear there were some black men who were trying to escape their blackness; men who were drowning themselves in the culture of the West. Men who, in effect, had made a pact with oppression. We came to learn what falsehood was, and why some members of the black community were cheap, imitation white men. And were not some of them the so-called leaders of the Negro community? It was shameful watching how we raised our children to hate themselves.

> *Who's yo' pappy?*
> *Yo' hair is nappy;*
> *You sho' is a ugly child . . .*

Attacking lips, skin, hair, legs, attacking the self that we had been trained to hate. Not knowing then that the very assertion of Selfhood would engage us in the act of truly liberating ourselves.

But then there were other black men who had the vision. Men who had always upheld the sanctity of black people; men who had sought a large, profound concept of freedom, and had made no excuses for doing so. These were the men, too, that we had to reckon with.

I remember in 1961, coming to New York with a sharp, very revolutionary brother named Bill Davis. We had come up on a Saturday to go to the Muslim restaurant; to meet Jesse Gray who was organizing rent strikes; to meet Jim Houghton who was organizing black labor; to buy Marxist literature down on 12th street; and, finally, to go to Mr. Michaux's bookstore which, at that time, was located on 125th and Seventh avenue. It was Freedom Square, Garvey Square, Little Africa, Mecca, the University of Timbuctoo, the voice of Nat Turner, DuBois, Benjamin Davis, Duke Ellington, Eloise Moore, Queen Mother Moore, Charlie Parker, Shango, Black John the revelator, Buy Black, Carlos Cook Porkchop Davis (somebody oughta do a book on him), Malcolm X,

Mr. Michaux, James Lawson, Richard Wright, Kwame Nkrumah, and Ellison's Ras.

The square in front of the bookstore was a mind-blower. From here, one could feel emanating all of the necessary but conflicting strands of African-American nationalism. For more than thirty years, this corner had been the area for a community discussion on the Nature and Destiny of the Colored Peoples of the World. And behind those thirty years, this tradition reached back four hundred years. In the bars, the lodges, the Saturday morning kitchens, the church, on the job, between breaks; everywhere black people are/were/have been in the cotton fields, in the folk-lore, the spirituals, the dance; everywhere black people are/were, a group ethos is at work, trying to define the essential terms of our existence.

On that Saturday, after the speeches and the book buying, Mr. Michaux took us in the backroom of his store. It was a crowded room jammed with books and other artifacts. Photographs of Marcus Garvey, Harriet Tubman, Sojourner Truth stared down at us. There was a heaviness about the room, as if it were crowded with ghosts. The spirit that drew the people to Harlem Square every day was being manifested in the room; ghosts emanated out of old books, photos, and the sounds and rhythms of Mr. Michaux's voice. A strength and perception was there that we had never before experienced. Michaux would make some heavy observation about the contemporary state of the race.

"The *Negro* is not a man; *it's* a thing to be used, abused, accused, and confused. He is a political tool, he's an economic stool, and he's a religious fool. His politicians are picked. His economy is fixed, and his preachers are tricked. The politician pacifies; the preacher sanctifies; and the white man crucifies!"

Now that's an interesting way of looking at the world, I thought, as we all cracked up laughing in the ghost-whispering room. Then he introduced us to an old man who said that he had been a conscious nationalist ever since he could remember. He said that he was a nationalist, too, and that the whole family was for the black man, "the Original Man," "the Black Sun," "the Black Holy Ghost." Then he went into a long parable about the Eagle who had always been taught that he was a chicken:

One day a naturalist said to the owner of this magnificent bird: "That bird is an eagle, not a chicken."

"I know," said the owner, "but I have programmed it to be a chicken. It is no longer an eagle, it is a chicken even though it measures fifteen feet from tip to tip of its wings."

"Naw," the natural man said, "it is an eagle still; it has the soul of an eagle, and I will make it fly."

"No," said the owner, "it is just a dumb chicken and it will never fly." So they agreed to test the eagle. The natural man picked up the eagle and *said* with all of his power: "Eagle, you are an eagle; you belong in the sky and not to this earth, go on and fly." Well the eagle dug the other chickens hopping around like chickens do and eating their food and he jumped out of the naturalists hand back to the ground.

Then he decided to take the eagle to the top of a house. He said the same words to the eagle as he had said before. The eagle jumped right back down to the other chickens pecking in the chicken coop.

So the next day, the naturalist rose very early and took the eagle to a high mountain. The sun was just easing up, coming over the mountain top, shining, lighting up the world. He tried to get that eagle to fly again. Way up high, like that the eagle was scared; heart throbbing mad. The natural man made it look directly at the sun. The hulk of the eagle expanded, the wings flared; he screeched and rose into the sky. It truly was an eagle, and not a chicken.

I asked the man where he had heard that story. He said that it was really a well-known story, but if I wanted to read it there was an account in a book by Edwin W. Smith's *Aggrey of Africa*.[1] Aggrey was an African educator and pastor; Nkrumah had been one of his pupils. On the way out of the store, the man said: "Whatever you do. Wherever you go. No matter who you may know, and what you may see. No matter what your beliefs. One thing is fundamental, son—don't forget your nationalism. Be a nationalist always; even when you're *pretending* otherwise. Think nationalist. Live nationalist. That's what you young people gonna really need soon. But don't be no tankhead though. Learn to be swift and flexible. And remember your ancestors, all of them."

Then we began to hear Malcolm, the black voice skating and bebopping like a righteous saxophone solo—mellow truths inspired by the Honorable Elijah Muhammand, but shaped out of Malcolm's own style, a style rooted in black folk memory, and the memory of his Garveyite father. We could dig Malcolm because the essential vectors of his style were more closely related to our own urban experiences. He was the first black leader, in our generation, to resurrect all of the strains of black nationalism lurking within us.

In the precise sense of the word, his stance was radical, rooted in a long strand of flesh-filled nights, and sea deaths, and cotton deaths, and revolutionary deaths; Malcolm was the Opener, the Son of the Word made flesh, and for the first time in our lives, we had a voice to offset the weaknesses and the temptations that we saw around us.

But we refuse to accentuate Malcolm's post-Nation-Of-Islam-period while ignoring the long years he was with the Honorable Elijah Muhammad. To do that would be improper. Malcolm definitely learned his nationalism from the Muslims, who provided him with the means of expressing the latent beliefs of all black people.

What timely combination of events led to the growth of the Nation of Islam are too complex to discuss here. One thing is certain, the rise of the Nation is a significant and concrete denial of the viability of contemporary Christianity. It especially denies to Christianity the ability to liberate black people. In spite of its Eastern origins, Christianity is clearly the religion of the oppressors. Its very symbology as projected in the West is anti-black. In the history of people of African descent it has played contradictory roles. On the one hand it has taught submission to slavery and oppression; on the other it has represented the only means by which black people could express themselves spiritually. Hence, we were in a trick: the Devil and The Black Spirit contended within us. And we were shattered by the continuing struggle. We longed for a point of focus, a concrete set of references that reflected *our* view of the world, and not a view imposed from without. It was, therefore, from out of the womb of the Nation of Islam that Malcolm called us.

Through Malcolm, the Nation of Islam effected a broader and more open discussion of identity—a subject that has always been a part of our ideological continuum. But not since Garvey had anyone proposed organizing around identity on a mass scale. And most important, no one in our generation had proposed this identity to be distinct and *separate*. It was the separation part that most annoyed most black people hearing it for the first time. It was the separation part that made the Negro leadership accelerate its demands for integration; that sent them scurrying like rats to any radio or television program. On these programs they would denounce Malcolm and the Nation, while themselves claiming unbounded loyalty to America and its ideals. Most of these Negroes were jive-ass leaders who seemed to be psychically wedded to the notion that niggers ain't shit. It was really impossible to understand where they were coming from. They seemed tied to dead options like: "There is no hope unless the Negro integrates"; "A black child cannot be truly educated in an all black learning situation." All assumptions that fail to address the central problems. This Negro leadership showed no concern for black people that went beyond the bounds set by white power. That they were concerned for the good of black people is not in question here. We know they were concerned, but they were concerned with the wrong things, and had been for quite some time. They seemed to have no concept of *group* priorities.

For example, let us take the famous Supreme Court decision of 1954. The NAACP legal division, under the leadership of Thurgood Marshall, abstractly won the right to an education free of racial discrimination. But that right is implied already in the Constitution. What they failed to do was go beyond the Constitution to the question of human rights. If they had done that they would have had to demand reparations from the United States government in the form of land and other resources. Along with fighting for those rights which are supposed to be legitimate under the white man's law, they would have also demanded that discrimination in the allocation of funds to predominantly black schools be stopped. Achieving the integration of public schools could never be as important as building black institutions which address themselves specifically to the needs of black people. But the Negro leadership had so essentially based its program on integration that it failed to deal with the issue of blacks controlling the institutions that affect our lives.

For a long while, it was impossible to understand what this leadership was about. Was it simply about copping out and begging for freedom, or was it that they just didn't know what to do? Or perhaps it was because they had been conned by the idea of the American dream, a dream that saw all of the country's national groups melted and submerged into a new, more humane entity. At one time, what these leaders demanded was radical; but by the middle of the sixties they were the new conservatives. Their thinking had calcified and ceased to be inventive. They had lost style, the easy manner people have who are engaged in an important struggle. True, they were for the race, as the saying goes, but finally what they demanded from the white establishment was often against our best interests. They rarely addressed us. They always spoke to us *through* white people. And since they had groomed themselves in the craft of addressing whites, whenever they did condescend to speak to us it was only in the terms that they had perfected. All of their models of what is known as "civilized" achievement were white. In retrospect, it is this aspect of their lives that is the most tragic.

Their generation was caught in a strange set of contradictions, foremost of which is: *in order to survive America one must understand the enemy.* But our history, in the West, indicates that understanding the enemy entails, in some respect, an internalization of his values. You hate the motherfucker, the beast, the pervert, the moneylender, the general, the president, the whore, the mayor, the police, the literary critic. You hate this historical raper of peoples and of nations, but to a certain extent, you feel dependent upon him for survival. He has taught you to believe that you need him, and that you always will. And since he is the one in power, he determines the mode of the relationship. His style, as corny as it is, exudes power. The secret nigger that is locked within you whispers persistently in your ear: "Get some power like the white man has, brother, this is your secret nigger talking." The problem for the Negro leadership is the phrase, "like the white man." Like the rest of us, they long for a place that black people can control, something to call our own; but many of them have come to imitate the thing they despise. And it is at this point that they begin to be challenged by the "new" nationalism. For they are a fragmented lot of men. Except for Du Bois, who had come from among them, very few of them expressed themselves in a manner that spoke to our *collective* will for survival on our own terms. Those of us who had been filtered through Western academic culture knew that the white man would allow an occasional Negro to survive and "do his thing" individually; but we knew also that finally there is no real *sustaining* survival outside of the collective ethos. Therefore, we posited the idea that the struggle needed a nationalistic overview— an ideological construct that was based on our own emotional history. Our leaders seemed not to know or care about these things. They seemed to be perpetually caught up in a white solution to the problem; it wasn't a problem caused by us, but by white oppression. However, *we* are the ones most responsible for developing the means to our liberation.

America is in fact two nations, one Black, one White. That is what the nationalists began to say. Not only were there two nations, one was a colony:

> The American Negro shares with colonial peoples many of the socio-economic factors which form the material basis for present day revolutionary nationalism. Like these peoples of the under-developed countries, the Negro suffers in varying degree from the hunger, illiteracy, disease, ties to the land, urban and semi-urban slums, cultural starvation, and the psychological reactions to being ruled over by others not of his kind. He experiences the tyranny imposed upon the lives of those who inhabit under-developed countries. In the words of a Mexican writer, Enrique Gonzales Pedrero, under-development creates a situation where that which exists "only half exists," where countries are almost countries, fifty per cent nations, and a man who inhabits these countries, is a dependent being, a sub-man. Such a man depends "not on himself but on other men and other outside worlds that order him around, counsel and guide him like a newly born infant."

These statements are found in a remarkable essay[2] written by Harold Cruse entitled, "Revolutionary Nationalism And The Afro-American." It is significant because it provided the young nationalists organizing in SNCC and RAM (Revolutionary Action Movement) with the first theoretical explanation of why they were nationalists, non-Marxist, and anti-integration.

Further, Cruse pinpointed the particular malaise affecting the Negro leadership:

> large segments of the modern Negro bourgeoisie have played a continually regressive "non-national" role in Negro affairs. Thriving off the crumbs of integration, these bourgeois elements have become de-racialized and de-cultured, leaving the Negro working class without voice or leadership, while serving the negative role of class buffer between the deprived working class and the white ruling class elites. In this respect, such groups have become a social millstone around the necks of the Negro working class—a point which none of the militant phrases that accompany the racial integration movement down the road to "racial attrition" should be allowed to obscure.[3]

If what Cruse was saying is true, then any course to black liberation that is not nationalistically oriented is doomed to failure. It would have to imply also that the civil rights movement, so helplessly locked into the notion that America is a democracy, is finally leading black people down the path to ethnocide—leading them towards cultural annihilation. And since we had turned inward on ourselves, and glimpsed what we considered to be the inner potential of our people, we were frightened by the concepts of the integrationists. Not merely intellectually in disagreement with them but frightened, if you can dig it. So much so, that in order to preserve something of our private selves, many of us refused to even talk to white people. We had to withdraw to get this thing together that had risen before us in all of its truth:

We want a nation controlled by black people. Yeah, that's what we want. Everything else is cool: no discrimination in housing, fair employment, more black teachers and schools, greater medical aid, more blacks on television and in films, black studies programs; the whole fucking lot was all cool. But we want a *nation*. In spite of all the theories and the arguments against it. We want a nation. We want our children to see a place governed by the sensibilities and highest attitudes of black people. We don't want to rear them to utilize their blackness as a weapon against a death-centered and inhuman culture. We want them to be comfortable in the knowledge of themselves, and not a set of reactions to white people. Therefore nationalism, with all of its contradictions, proposed itself to us.

Many young black people in the sixties began to move from that point. The actions that they initiated throughout the country began to grow into what roughly constituted the "Black Power Movement," which was, in reality, a movement long before Brother Stokely shouted the words, "Black Power" on the James Meredith March. As a member of SNCC, Stokely had been an active participant in the civil rights movement. He had seen the established Negro leadership led by King compromise the movement. He, and others, remembered the deal that John Lewis had to make at the 1963 March On Washington; a deal that saw Lewis's speech censored by white leaders. Their attempts to use black and white organizers in the South proved unsuccessful. Intra-organizational strife, spiritual disunity, and operational co-option by white left wing youth were the result.

Here is Askia Muhammad Touré (Rolland Snellings) writing in the fall, 1964 issue of RAM organ, *Black America:*

Not only are the Civil Rights organizations faced with the crisis of emerging awareness and vengeful anger developing among the blacks; but now SNCC is being shaken with a new and deadly crisis within white-led offices—main and field. White liberals and radicals—it seems—have infiltrated and formed power-blocs within the decision-making structure of the group . . . thereby castrating and invalidating the potentials of this outspoken organization. The SNCC crisis now raging within the Deep South is another example of the deadliness of the astute "fifth column" of "liberal" and "radical" whites working to undermine and neutralize the black freedom struggle. . . .

Increasingly, the nationalist wing of the movement came to see the civil rights movement as one under the tight control of white liberals from the President to the American Jewish Congress. The March On Washington, for example, was almost totally co-opted and defused, with the help of white liberals. To an observer like Malcolm X, the whole thing had an unwarranted carnival atmosphere.

Therefore, one of our chief problems was that the organizations which claimed to represent us were not even finally controlled by us. The control was rooted in the white liberal establishment whose interests could not, ultimately, coincide with ours. After observing the impotence of the civil organizations, one highly significant thing the nationalists came to understand was that we needed to control our own institutions. So whites working in CORE, SNCC, and the Southern Freedom Movement were asked to leave and to organize in the white community.

Malcolm X was assassinated on February 21st, 1965, at the Audubon Ballroom in Upper Manhattan. It was a very un-February-like day; I recall a hot sun. The sister I was with was accompanied by her daughter, who was about ten or eleven years old. We each had a bundle of the magazine *Black America* under our arms. When we arrived at the Audubon there were no police cars parked in front of the place. This was quite unusual. Most of the time when Malcolm spoke at the ballroom there were policemen everywhere. But on this particular afternoon, nothing; just the weird February sun. Upstairs we walked into the Ballroom just as Brother Benjamin X was finishing his speech which, if I recall, was about the liberation movements in Africa, Asia, and Latin America. Then he said the following: "And now, without further remarks, I present to you one who is willing to put himself on the line for you, a man who would give his life for—I want you to hear, listen, to understand—one who is a *trojan* for the black man."[4]

We responded, "Wa-laikum salaam." We were sitting near the back on the left side of the aisle facing the stage; really not good seats, but we had come in late. It could have been church. There was such a very diverse grouping of black people; some of the women were matronly, but tricked up real fine in their Sunday clothes. There were many young children there. The sun was shafting through the windows. The audience had quieted down in anticipation of Malcolm; and after what seemed like two or three long minutes Malcolm came out:

"As salaam alaikum, brothers and sisters"

"Wa-laikum salaam," we answered.

Count about ten beats, after the sound of the response dies down.

An obvious commotion had started down in the front rows. Malcolm was standing at a podium. He stepped from behind the podium to quiet the commotion. He said something like, "peace, be cool, brothers." The shots came rapid fire; Malcolm fell back, his arms stretched out like wings. After it happened there seemed to be a pause, then the fear was everywhere. People scrambled for cover on the floor under the tables in the back, shouting. Security guards were trying to reach Malcolm, trying to stop the assassins who now were safely escaping in the confusion. One of the assassins leaped over chairs, and fired at a knot of black men chasing him. He twisted and turned, firing shot after shot, until they caught him at the stairway leading out of the ballroom. The whole room was a wailing woman. Men cried openly.

Malcolm's death was an awesome psychological setback to the nationalists and civil rights radicals. The established Negro leadership lamented his death, but qualified their lamentations by asserting that he "preached by the sword, now he has died by the sword." The militants and the nationalists, on the other hand, felt guilty. They felt that they had not done enough to support Malcolm while he was alive. Hence, they had not protected him, and, somehow, they felt responsible for his assassination. After all, had Malcolm not said that his life was in danger? Had not the man's home been bombed only a week before his assassination? *How we gonna build anything if we let our leaders get shot down like dogs?* We were ready to retaliate, but everything was fuzzy. The assassins were Negroes, and we really couldn't get that together. Malcolm had broken with the Muslims, and had previously accused them of trying to kill him.

But we could not understand why the Muslims would want to kill Malcolm, considering that they would be the prime suspects. No, that didn't make sense.

We considered the CIA, the right wing, the zionists, and the mafia. Lacking facts and a clear orientation, we found these considerations merely led to interminable days of agonizing arguments, and charges, and countercharges.

But even though Malcolm's death—the manner of it—emotionally fractured young black radicals, there were two central facts that *all* factions of the movement came to understand. And they are: that the struggle for black self-determination had entered a serious, more profound stage; and that for most of us, non-violence as a viable technique of social change had died with Malcolm on the stage of the Audubon.

Some of us did not survive the assassination. Strain set in. Radical black organizations came under more and more *official scrutiny*, as the saying goes. The situation made everyone paranoid, and there were often good reasons for being so. People were being set-up, framed on all kinds of conspiracy charges. There was a great deal of self-criticism, attempts to lock arms against the beast that we knew lurked outside.

Some people dropped out, rejecting organizational struggle altogether. Some ended up in hippie cults in the East Village. Some even started shooting smack again. Some joined the poverty program; some did serious work there, while others, disillusioned and, for now, weak, became corrupt poverticians.

Malcolm's organization, the OAAU (Organization of Afro-American Unity), after being taken over very briefly by Sister Ella Collins, Malcolm's sister, soon faded. But the ideas promulgated by Malcolm did not. Malcolm's ideas had touched all aspects of contemporary black nationalism: the relationship between Black America and the Third World; the development of a black cultural thrust; the right of oppressed peoples to self-defense and armed struggle; the necessity of maintaining a strong moral force in the black community; the building of autonomous black institutions; and, finally, the need for a black theory of social change.

After Malcolm's death, thousands of heretofore unorganized

black students and activists became more radically politicized.
The Black Arts Movement started in Harlem with the opening
of Black Arts Repertory Theatre/School under the direction of
Imamu Ameer Baraka (LeRoi Jones). The Black Arts school attempted to effect a union between art and politics. Not since the
thirties had such a union been attempted with such intensity.
Never before had black artists entered into such a conscious spiritual union of goal and purpose. For the first time in history there
existed a "new" constellation of symbols and images around
which to develop a group ethos. What was happening in Harlem
was being repeated all over the United States. Black people were
shaping a new concept of themselves both in the national and
international sense. Where we were going, we did not know. But
one thing was certain, we knew that, as James Brown says, we
were a "New Breed." At first we were smug and self-righteous
in this new found knowledge of ourselves. We were often arrogant and pushy. Underneath these negatives, we knew that much
of what we were about was concertedly related to the total liberation of black people. We knew that without a strong sense of
nationalism black people would not survive America. There was
no way to survive America fragmented and in general confusion
about who we were, and what we wanted.

All of the development of our remembered and unremembered
history began to weigh down on us. And the more of our memory
that returned to us, the sharper, the more acute the pain became.
The more we probed our history and the history of the Third
World, the more angry we became, the more nourished our hate
for the white world. It had to go down that way. There was a
concrete historical reason for everything that we felt. White
people deserved to be hated uncritically. Sometimes in our perception of them, they even ceased to be people. They were the
"Big White Fog" of the Ted Ward play. They became like the
snow falling in Richard Wright's *Native Son* —a dead natural
phenomenon that contaminated the entire planet. We reversed
the Manichean dualism that placed the symbolism of Blackness
on the side of Evil, and whiteness on the side of Good.

This was a necessary reversal. But it led to some contradictions, the most important of which was that our nationalism could

not exist primarily in contra-distinction to white nationalism. We could never hope to develop a viable concept of self, if that concept were purely based on hating crackers. We had to really dig each other, for each other, on our own terms and on the basis of the common emotional history and identity that we shared. The primary focus of our emotional energies would have to be black people. If we made the mistake of constantly addressing scorn and venom to white people, we would fall into the moribund category of the Negro leaders who seemed to be constantly affirming the black man's humanity to white people, and thus constantly implying that somehow black people would gain their humanity when the benevolence of white people finally asserted itself.

It did not matter the style of the address. Even if it were one of scorn and vindication, or if, as in the case of James Baldwin, it was rooted in compassion and ardent desire to make one's self felt as a human being, this approach still implicitly fortified the white man's sense of power in the world. We could historically trace this tendency among black leaders, a tendency that has blurred vision and shattered energies. We had to dig each other, for each other, on our own terms, and on the basis of the common emotional history that we shared; a history that had shaped us both positively and negatively. Somewhere in the maw of that history we will find the means of redeeming ourselves, of "vindicating the blues," as Askia says. *It has to be that way.* Accepting this reality, we can now begin to deal from a strong emotional base.

We will take a stand in the history primarily on the basis of our own emotional history. We have become synthesizers, bringing to bear upon the struggle *all* of the accumulated knowledge of the world. We can only deal realistically, if we know where we are coming from. So we *got* to start dealing with specifics/each to each. That's not an easy thing to do. Black people know how to relate to white people; that part of the survival kit is cooled out. But us relating to each other, that's another thing. We have still to get that together. Witness our Brothers in the Black Panthers struggling for liberalism like everybody else, but so caught up in addressing themselves to the white community that they, in spite of their deaths and harassments, have become objects of art for jaded folks like Leonard Bernstein and Mrs. Peter Duchin. "It's exciting," the bitch says. And all the time our brothers in the black berets know that it is not exciting. In fact, it's some rather serious shit. Even though it may have started as a dimly perceived game, when you get right down next to it, up under its skin, it ain't no game. No kind of way.

Cut loose from a unified center, we become freaks, confused, driven from without rather than from within. The Eunuch has found his balls only to become the object of wholesale masturbation. Revolution becomes a talk show, the maudlin chatterings of some Hollywood actor. You become just another object of glamor. Slick white boys manage your most private affairs. The swiftness that is you, your essence, becomes mechanized, a glib part of a dead game. Outside of the ethos, you have to become bitchy and perverted, *'cause you ain't holding on to nothing.* You are being squeezed spermless, your seed scattered among the ice and rocks.

Think about a nation, a place where, as much as natural laws will allow, you can shape your face. Like:

> *visions/all forms/actual life is the poem*
> *your song bodies/life faces*
> *your face/your child's face*
> *save something Brother/but let the dead thing go/*
> *com'on now/shape the face/and space/yes Father*
> *and space/yes/save space/give breath to words*
> *make a world/com'on now/move/give fire to deeds*
> *love your millions/make a place for all of the faces/*
> *but mostly your own/be change/love no dead things/*
> *give flesh to energy/do it with style/nigger elegance/*
> *com'on now Brother/shape a space/*
> *love your face/make a place....*

NOTES

1.   See also Mercer Cook and Stephen E. Henderson's *The Militant Black Writer in Africa and the United States* Madison, Wisc., (University of Wisconsin Press, 1969), pp. 7-9.
2.   From *Studies On the Left*, Volume 2, No. 3, 1962, p. 13. Also in *Black Fire*, edited by LeRoi Jones and Larry Neal (New York, Wm. Morrow, Apollo Editions, 1968), p. 39. In the issue of *Studies On the Left* quoted above, there is also a lengthy interview with Robert Williams, who was a major influence on revolutionary nationalist thinking. Between the Klan, the Monroe police force, the FBI, the NAACP, and the Cubans, this Brother really caught hell.
3.   *Ibid.*
4.   *Autobiography of Malcolm X*, (New York, Grove Press, 1965), p. 433.

Black nationalism represents the realization by blacks that our problems are unique. James Boggs delves into the ways in which black revolutionary nationalism can be implemented. The challenge facing blacks is that of developing programs which will revolutionize America so that politics will be put in command of economics.

JAMES BOGGS *was born in Marion Junction, Alabama. After graduating from high school in Bessamer, Alabama, he bummed his way through the western part of the country, working in the hop fields of Washington State, cutting ice in Minnesota, and finally in Detroit with the W.P.A. At the start of World War II, be became an auto worker, and has been one ever since. He is the author of* The American Revolution, *translated in Latin America, France, and Japan:* Manifesto for a Black Revolutionary Party; *and* Race and Class Struggle. *James Boggs has published in the anthology* Black Fire. *His articles on black power have been printed in Italy and Argentina.*

James Boggs

The Revolutionary Struggle for Black Power

As we enter the seventies, practically every United States citizen, black and white, recognizes that the traditional view of the United States as a melting pot is no longer valid. Many will insist, quite correctly, that it has always been a myth. It is only one of the many myths, both superficial and fundamental, which the black movement has succeeded in exploding one after another during the last sixteen years.

Today there exist two Americas: one black, one white. For some Americans, black and white, the key question now is whether, or how, these two Americans can ever live together in harmony. For others, the question has come to be whether, or how, they can peacefully co-exist as two entities, geographically and/or politically separate.

Whichever view any particular person may have arrived at, one stark naked fact is now beginning to dawn on most people: there is no simple solution.

It is this stark naked fact—that no simple solution exists—which torments United States citizens, be they black or white. The people of this country have been led to believe that if things were just left to the politicians while they pursued their own individual wants and desires, somehow, some way, some day, some leader would come up with the necessary answers. Now that the working out of solutions increasingly depends upon people themselves, there is widespread confusion and demoralization.

Even the black movement, which has been shaking up and disturbing every section of the country since 1954, has embedded
deep within it the illusion that those in power have only to push
some buttons, and *presto,* anything they want done will be done.
Prior to the eruption of the black movement, this belief in the
omnipotence of White Power in the United States took the form
of blacks not even daring to dream of doing anything more than
what whites would permit them to do.

When the Supreme Court issued its historic decision in 1954,
few blacks, North or South, could see how it could ever become
effective. Northern blacks, having left the South because they refused to put up with its daily and increasing humiliations and
intimidations, could not conceive of Southern whites ever allowing blacks to go to the same school with them. Southern blacks,
who had continued to endure this daily humiliation and intimidation, could not believe that they had the forces within themselves
or on their side to translate the court's decree from words into
fact.

Northern blacks were less optimistic, if possible, than Southern
blacks. Having fled the South, they were, like all refugees or
renegades, able to recall only the unrelieved horror of what they
had escaped. Also, they had become accustomed to accepting the
excuse of Northern liberals—that the South is to blame for all
the nation's racial ills, including the continuing misery of black
lives up North. Believing all this, Northern blacks, during the
early years of the movement (from 1954 to 1963), spent their time
mostly bemoaning the evils of the South, insisting that "if it was
me, I would have left long ago" and boasting of how, if they had
remained, they would not be taking the abuse but would be fighting back.

During these early years, movement activities up North consisted chiefly of rallies and demonstrations aimed at highlighting
conditions in the South and collecting funds to send South. The
appeal was principally to the white liberals and the labor movement for aid to Southern blacks. The sympathetic attitude of most
Northern blacks was not too different from that of the white
liberals, pricipally because they had not begun to question their
own working conditions up North. During this period Northern

whites in every category, middle, upper, and even working class, were ready to deplore the conditions in the South. And so they did, singing "We Shall Overcome" side by side with blacks and in many instances more fervently than blacks.

Blacks who lived up North were pushing for integration as much as or more than white liberals and radicals; and the more viciously the average Southern white fought against desegregation, the more infuriated Northern blacks became at the failure of the government to intervene directly to enforce it. Reliving or witnessing for the first time the brutality of the South on TV, radio, and in the newspapers, Northern blacks began to search their consciences for ways and means to become more directly involved in the Southern struggle.

The search to become involved led to the freedom rides and to formation of the Student Non-Violent Coordinating Committee in 1960-61. SNICK people were those young people who were ready to take a year or two out of school to give to the struggle. At the time it seemed a tremendous sacrifice for these students, but their timetable for involvement reflected the prevailing illusion that there was still a simple solution and that, if only more blacks would join in the struggle, pitting their bodies against the iron will of Southern whites, integration could be achieved in the South as it had been in the North, and the black problem would be resolved.

The wave of sit-ins, stand-ins, ly-ins, and jail-ins which developed at the height of SNICK activity, from 1961 to 1965, took the struggle into every state and practically every county of the South. The young people of SNICK, trying to make concrete what the law had laid down abstractly, were ready to risk their lives in the movement. At this stage the national spokesman and leader of the struggle was Dr. Martin Luther King Jr., the young preacher who had come to prominence in the Montgomery bus boycott and made the tactic of nonviolence a philosophy. King's dream was that by confronting white resistance with nonviolent black determination, he would arouse the sympathy of liberal whites. This in turn would induce the government to pass civil rights legislation which would legitimize integration as the American Way of Life. What King apparently did not foresee was that his strategy of *confrontation* would also unveil white violence and barbarism to such a degree that young blacks would reject his philosophy of nonviolence. Hence King was taken aback when, as a result of the increasing mobilization of black street youth, the black community and white police clashed in the streets of Birmingham in May 1963. The explosion transformed the black movement into a nation-wide movement.

What few people realized at the time of Birmingham was that the coming North of the movement would also explode the myth of integration as a simple solution and force the black movement to face the question of the American economic system.

Looking back at the state of the movement in 1963, we can see that nearly everybody approached the problem as if the struggle for rights up North could follow the pattern of the struggle down South. It was only after Northern blacks began to examine the issues and grievances on which to focus their struggle, that they, slowly and painfully, began to realize that *every* institution, North and South, had been structured with the clear-cut purpose of keeping blacks at the bottom, and that the role assigned to blacks in this society since colonial days has been that of the scavenger: to take the leavings in every sphere, whether it be jobs, homes, schools, churches or neighborhoods that whites had discarded or considered beneath them. The condition of blacks in the North could not and cannot therefore be blamed upon the law, as in the South. It was and is clearly grounded in the structure of the society itself. The result is that the Northern movement, since 1963, has been confronted with the dilemma of how to organize a struggle for rights when, according to law, Northern blacks already have the rights for which blacks are still struggling in the South. True, there remains discrimination in areas of public accommodations such as restaurants, swimming pools, hotels, etc., but the grievances which most directly affect the great mass of blacks in the North are clearly those in the arenas of jobs, housing, education, health and welfare, in other words, grievances involving the very structure and operations of American economic and social institutions.

In the last seven years the black movement in the North has tested and discussed many different solutions to this dilemma, from mass demonstrations to mass rebellions, from voting black to buying black. In the course of its many activities, it has produced a tremendous social force of millions of black people who formerly had been apolitical and apathetic but who are now anxious to act. At the same time the movement has rid itself of a number of illusions: for example, the illusion that integration in and of itself is the solution; or that spontaneous eruptions in and of themselves are the solution; or that militant rhetoric is the solution; or that the unity of sheer numbers is the solution. (In other words, blacks getting together is not the same thing as blacks getting themselves together.) It is now clear that the problem of black people cannot be solved by the most charismatic or most militant spokesmen for black grievances, or by economic aid from city, state, or federal government, or by massive programs for hiring the hard-core unemployed.

Faced with these realities, the black movement is now painfully evaluating its past actions and seeking a program for the future, precisely at the time when its actions have brought into the social arena a white counter-revolutionary force which feels certain that its entire way of life is threatened by the black movement and therefore that it must wipe out this movement before it acquires any more momentum.

Unlike the black revolutionary force, the white counter-forces do not have to search for an ideology before they can plot their actions. Their ideology is that of the existing society: materialism, individualism, opportunism. Even if, as white workers and white middle classes, they do not reap all the benefits from their system, even if they are powerless to affect its major decisions about what to produce or when to go to war, they still believe that it is the best system in the world because it has been the system which has enabled them, as whites, to climb up and over any blacks. It has therefore become for them a system of privilege which they are determined to defend at all costs.

The present cry for "Law and Order" and the prevailing police terror in black communities are not just some conspiracy dreamed up by a few right-wing policemen and Minutemen and then foisted upon the white masses. They are a reflection of what most whites expect and demand from their police force even if it ends up in a police state. So long as "Law and Order" preserve the American Way of Life, most whites are for it whatever the cost in social injustice.

It is because blacks can see all around them this growing counter-revolutionary force that so many tendencies have developed inside the black movement during the past period. Most of these tendencies are attempts to escape or evade the cold realities of the American economic system and the protracted struggle that is necessary to revolutionize America which is the only way that black people in this country can ever be free.

Among the various solutions which are offered or advocated at the present time to the dilemma of black people in America are: a) a return to Africa; b) the setting up of separate states; c) black control of black communities, leaving the task of changing the "mother country" to whites; d) black cultural separation; e) black capitalism. There are even large numbers of blacks who still believe that they can still be assimilated into this society as the old immigrant groups were, if only they can elect some more black politicians.

Most of these tendencies are led by and reflect the interests of various sections of the black middle classes: professionals, artists, preachers, businessmen, politicians. All of them consider themselves part of the Black Power movement which has dominated the Black Revolt in the wake of Watts, Newark, and Detroit rebellions.

Each of these "Black Power" tendencies, with its particular goal, has some support within the black community. Each one believes that if the black masses would just support its particular solution, the black problem would be solved and the black revolution would have succeeded. Meanwhile, large numbers of blacks still maintain a lingering hope for integration, despite the fact that the manifest failure of integration as a solution was what originally gave birth to the mass rebellions and the Black Power movement.

However, revolutionists cannot determine their perspectives by counting noses. We have to recognize that each of these tendencies has emerged as a sincere effort to give concreteness and specificity to the abstract slogan of Black Power. At the same time we have to recognize what all these tendencies lack and learn from an evaluation of their limitations.

Whatever may be the present shortcomings of the black movement, it has created the largest concentration of revolutionary social force that this country has ever known. It has also created an unprecedented level of mass political development and of mass efforts to find the correct solutions to real social problems. Within this unprecedented political energy, with the proper political leadership based on a realistic evaluation of the stage of the movement, there exists the potential for mass political consciousness and political struggle on a level never before achieved in this country.

The revolutionary movement of black people inside this country is presently at the Black Nationalist stage. Their conceptions of Black Power are presently still within the Black Nationalist framework. Black people have recognized that there is a uniqueness about their history and about their present conditions of life inside this country which sets them apart from the rest of the people in the United States. They have also recognized that this, which is the basis of their oppression, is also a source of strength. Such a sense of Nationalism could only have been achieved as a result of a long process of continuing struggle which has forced blacks to give up certain myths: i.e., that they can never become like white people; or that it would be desirable to become like white people; or that they will ever be free as long as they are ruled by White Power. The long protracted struggle of the last sixteen years, with its minor victories and its many failures and setbacks, has not only swelled the ranks of the black movement. It has given blacks a sense of their uniqueness and their identity as a nation of people.

Black Nationalism has been and is progressive because it has bound black people together and given them strength, although Black Nationalism in and of itself is not the sufficient answer to the problem of black people. Black Nationalism represents the realization by black people that their problems are unique and that their separation from whites can be a weapon in their struggle for freedom. In this sense Black Nationalism organizes black people into a "nation" and transforms what the enemy hoped would be a weakness into a source of strength. But black people will have to go beyond the stage of Black Nationalism into the stage of Black Revolutionary Nationalism if they are going to resolve the very real problems of black people, because only Black Revolutionary Nationalism will enable them to attack the real causes of their problem.

Black Nationalism has created a united black consciousness, but black consciousness which does not develop into a real and realistic attack on the causes of black oppression can only become false consciousness, in other words, a breeding ground for the cultism, adventurism, and opportunism which are now rampant in the movement. Black Revolutionary Nationalism involves real and realistic struggles, not only against those who control the very real institutions of this society but also a struggle to reorganize these institutions to make them serve human needs rather than the needs of the economic system for profit and technological development.

In the course of the development of Nationalism inside a colony in Africa, Asia or Latin America, the first step is usually very simple. It is to get rid of the colonial oppressor. The second step is much more difficult because it requires a rapid political development of the people, enabling them to bring about a drastic reorganization of the economic and political system. If this rapid political development does not take place simultaneously with the struggle for national independence or immediately thereafter, the new nation will soon sink back into Neo-Colonialism. This is what has happened with most of the African colonies.

In the United States the problem for blacks is much more complex because our lives and our condition are so bound up with those of the oppressor. On the one hand, we have lived a separate and distinct life. On the other, we have been organic, that is, indispensable and intrinsic, part of the development of the most highly industrialized country in history. Even while we have been systematically denied all the benfits of rapid industrialization, we have been the direct source of the profits by which the country could industrialize itself rapidly. The slave trade created the first profits for a developing commercial capitalism. Black slave labor provided the raw materials for developing manufacture. In the agricultural era we were kept as slaves on the plantations so that the whites could homestead Western lands and take the expanding industrial jobs in the North. Then as whites began moving up to white collar jobs, we were used to man the dirty jobs on the line. At every stage of economic development in this country, our super-exploitation has been a decisive factor in the country's ability to advance rapidly in the economic arena and in white mobility up the social and economic ladder.

Wherever or whenever we take a good look at ourselves, we have to recognize that in every aspect of our concrete lives and throughout our history in this country, we have been scavengers. We always took the jobs that whites thought beneath them. We have always inherited the used churches, the used schools, the used houses. We live in used communities that are passed down to us only after other groups (all white) have run them down and are ready to move on to newer, cleaner communities. Not only are we at the bottom of the social and economic ladder of American society, our bottom position on this ladder is a necessary part of the system, the part that enables those on top of us to keep climbing.

It is thus impossible to separate the development of our condition and life as blacks in this country from the development of the system itself. Nor is it possible for blacks to free themselves without turning over every institution of this society, all of which have been structured with blacks at the bottom. The climax of this development is our present situation, with 35-50 per cent of our young people unemployed and roaming the streets, each a potential victim of the organized drug traffic. With the advancing technology of automation and cybernation, the unskilled labor of our youth and women has become increasingly expendable. In the cities where we are now concentrated, we survive how we can, no longer needed as producers but constantly stimulated by the mass media to consume the abundance pouring off America's assembly lines.

It is only from this realistic appraisal of the inter-relation between our fate as black people in America and the American economic system that we can develop a positive perspective for struggle. We are no longer needed in this structure which has been created to meet the needs of rapid economic development regardless of the cost to human beings. Our only salvation is to find a way to break up this structure and replace it with a new structure whose chief purpose is the most rapid and fullest development of human beings rather than the most rapid and unlimited development of technology.

The essence of the American Way of Life has been and continues to be the organization of all institutions for the most rapid economic development as the means for resolving all the problems of the society. The result is constantly increasing investment in highly advanced technology, increasing production of highly-trained specialists to produce and handle this technology, increasing centralization of capital, and increasing concentration of economic and political power in the hands of the relatively few individuals and corporations who control this vast technological apparatus. Accompanying this rapid and systematic technological development and concentration of skills and power at one pole, there has taken place, just as systematically, at the opposite pole and on the lower rungs of the social and economic ladder, a continuing decline in skills, power, and responsibility. At the same time, in the entire society, because of the total reliance on economic development to solve all social problems, there has been a total failure to build any institutions or procedures which might develop the population politically—in social responsibility and in the political skills and procedures needed to cope with social problems.

This has been and is the essential law of development of the American Way of Life. It has resulted in the present extremely dangerous situation and contradiction: that this country is, on the one hand, the most advanced technologically and, on the other, the politically most undeveloped country in the world. With the technique at its disposal to destroy or to advance mankind, it does not have the political consciousness or will to choose one rather than the other. This system has been able to function because the vast majority of whites have accepted the philosophy of economic development as the key to social progress and because they have for the most part been able to benefit from this economic development. The chief victims have been blacks, who always stayed at the bottom, scavenging white leavings.

As long as blacks did not dream of reaching the middle or top rungs of the ladder, they were no threat to the system. But sixteen years ago, precisely at the time when the number of positions on the middle rungs of the ladder was beginning to decline because of automation and cybernation, blacks began to feel that they also had a right to climb. Competing with whites for positions on the ladder, they have aroused the fury of these whites who blame them for disturbing what has seemed to these whites a perfect society. Actually blacks have only been exposing the failure of a system which has put economics in command of politics, and which has therefore failed to develop within the population the political institutions and the political consciousness to control economic development and cope with social problems.

The challenge which faces blacks as the ones who have benefited least from American economic development, and who have now been made expendable by this development, is to revolutionize America so that politics will be put in command of economics. This must become the goal of Black Power in the seventies.

In order for blacks to achieve this goal, they must develop programs of struggle that will concretize this goal in stages and in relation to specific issues, constantly escalating the readiness of blacks to struggle against those now in control as well as maintaining their vision of the new society which only Black Power can create in the United States.

In developing programs for specific struggle, it is necessary, *first*, to choose problems which are closely related to the human needs of the masses and at the same time demonstrate the organic weakness of the system to resolve these problems, thereby exposing the system's illegitimacy. *Second*, it is necessary to propose *solutions* to these problems that involve a change in the existing power relations as well as changes in the structure of operations. These solutions should be of the kind with which people can identify and recognize as legitimate and reasonable, even if not immediately realizable. *Third*, it is necessary to propose concrete organizational steps and struggles which people can be involved in to reach these solutions. Thus every program should: 1) define the problem; 2) propose solutions; and 3) propose steps by which people can organize and struggle to reach these solutions.

There is no lack of such problems inside the black community. All of the institutions most essential in our daily living—schools, health, industry, housing, welfare, transportation— are controlled by alien elements. Under the control of these alien elements, all these institutions have failed to meet the needs of black people. Now as a result of the spontaneous mass rebellions from 1965 to 1968, all segments of the black community are united in their determination to wrest control of these institutions from whites. The collective will to struggle for Community Control is thus already far advanced inside the black community.

In the course of developing programs for Community Control of all these institutions, we must constantly be developing concepts and procedures for completely reorganizing these institutions to meet human rather than technological needs. For example, we must develop educational programs that will transform the schools from what they are today—training grounds for a professional elite and mass detention homes for the great majority—into community-centered educational institutions that will develop human beings able to govern over themselves and administer over things. We must develop programs to transform the health system from what it is now—a system for the production of specialists further and further removed from the masses and chiefly concerned with making profit, miracle drugs, and bio-technology—into a system which is primarily oriented towards preventive medicine, with medical personnel and health centers close to the people, seeking to develop the broadest self-knowledge and participation of the people themselves in their own health and the health of the community.

In the field of industry, we must struggle to make places of work into places of increased control on the part of those employed and of continuing education, instead of what they are today—virtual prisons in which the workers are robbed of any decision-making powers or any possibility of continuing development.

In the field of housing, we must recognize that housing is a No. 1 social problem for the entire United States, black and white, and that it is impossible to meet the very real needs of human beings, not only for shelter but for community living, as long as land, financing, construction, and industry remain under the control of private individuals and corporations whose only interest is profit. Whatever activity is programmed by blacks around housing must focus on helping people to understand that the housing problem will never be resolved until the government and the community together take responsibility for Land Reform and for housing construction on a socialized, non-profit basis.

The struggle for Community Control has to be seen as a stepping stone on the road to black control of the major cities of this country and ultimate control by blacks of the national government. Today blacks are already, or almost, the majority in most major cities. The City is the Black Man's Land as it is the land of no other section of the American people. Pouring into the city as an escape from the limitations of the countryside, blacks are now imprisoned in the city because racism blocks the road out. Therefore, in order to survive, blacks must now solve the crisis of the cities, the place where all the contradictions of a system dedicated to economic development at the expense of human needs have reached the point of explosion.

In totally reorganizing the city to serve human needs, Black Power will not only be resolving the problems of black people but advancing the interests of the total society. For example, what kind of transportation is needed today to keep cities from becoming asphalt jungles serving the interests only of the auto industry? Shall we produce subways, homes, and recreation areas—or more highways, parking lots, and air terminals? Shall city codes in relation to garbage, pollution, transportation, and housing be left in the hands of bureaucrats amenable to control by absentee landlords, speculators, and giant industry—or can these matters be placed under the control of popular committees in every part of the city?

Is the city itself going to remain a concentration camp for the reserve army of occasional labor which industry no longer needs —or can it be reorganized into a school for self-government where youth in particular can begin to acquire the will and the skills in identifying and solving social problems, skills which this country so urgently needs? Will the city remain a showcase of glittering consumer goods, luring young people into covetousness and crime, or can it be made into a living storehouse of human creativity in the art of living and of politics, from which people of all kinds and all ages can learn?

These questions touch on the many problems facing not only black people but everybody in this country, pointing a direction and a challenge for a society which now drifts from assassination to assassination, not knowing where it should go or how to get anywhere but to the moon. To launch this country on this new course will require painful and protracted struggles, but not to struggle to reverse its present course is to assure total disaster for all mankind.

To mount this kind of struggle will mean putting behind us forever the illusion that the masses will on some given day or days spontaneously explode and settle all issues, or that we can wait on some charismatic leader to emerge as our spokesman with a quick and simple solution. Rather we are confronted with the challenge of beginning, quietly and methodically, to form a revolutionary organization of serious, dedicated, and disciplined blacks who have recognized the need for Black Power to revolutionize America and who are prepared to work patiently among the masses to mobilize them for the struggles which will, stage by stage, create pockets of power. These blacks must have no illusion that their task will be completed in months or even in a few years; yet they must be confident that by systematic work and struggle they can develop the forces for fundamental change out of people for whom this change has become urgent but who, like masses all over the world, have been convinced that the problem is insurmountable. To build this kind of organization in the seventies, blacks will, above all, have to abandon their present practice of looking for leaders whom they can parade before the public. Instead, they will have to build the kind of unglamorous organization which makes a working leader out of every member. So long as blacks are more concerned with identifying and being identified as leaders than with gaining victory over the enemy, so long will they be unable to assume the responsibility for revolutionizing this country which, in its decline, is already well on the way to becoming a police state.

To those who remain skeptical about the possibility of Black Revolutionary Power in America, my answer was given in my *Manifesto for a Black Revolutionary Party:*

> To the question whether Black Revolutionary Power is possible, the answer is yes. Concretely American society faces only three real alternatives: 1) to continue rotting away as it is today; 2) naked counter-revolution; 3) Black Revolutionary Power. The fact that these are the only concrete alternatives makes Black Revolutionary Power as realistic a possibility as the other two.
>
> *The key to the whole question is that the United States cannot go home again.*
>
> First, the black community is rapidly approaching the point where it cannot survive unless the present system based upon the exploitation of human labor is abolished and a new society based upon the development of socially responsible human beings is established. The momentum of the black struggle to establish such a society is already well under way and cannot be reversed except by naked counter-revolution.
>
> Second, the black struggle for liberation, coinciding with the struggle of the world black revolution, has already created such turmoil and crisis in the entire society that great masses of people are searching for political leadership to restore to the country a sense of purpose and direction.
>
> Third, inside the white community we can expect increasing conflict, division and splits between a substantial minority demanding the counter-revolutionary crushing of the Black movement, a small minority who are ready to accept Black Revolutionary Power, and the overwhelming majority in the middle who will be immobilized, not because they want Black Power but because they are afraid that resistance to it will reinforce the naked counter-revolutionary repression that, once unleashed, cannot possibly stop with the black community.
>
> Finally, and never to be forgotten, the struggle for Black Revolutionary Power in the United States is developing in the context of international conflict between the world Black revolution and the white counter-revolution of American imperialism, a conflict which the United States cannot possibly win.

This conjecture of historical circumstances makes Black Revolutionary Power possible. It does not make it inevitable. To bring it into being will require a long, sustained and carefully-organized struggle. To ensure the success of this struggle, *the most important task now before the Black movement is the building of a Black Revolutionary Party.*

Education has always been a major goal for black America. The following essay examines an institution which could and should serve as an inspiration and example to all those interested in the American educational process.

ADELAIDE CROMWELL HILL *is a sociologist and teacher. Born in Washington, D.C., she attended the city's public schools before attending Smith College in Northampton, Massachusetts. She did graduate work in sociology at the University of Pennsylvania (M.A.), Bryn Mawr College, and Radcliffe College (Ph.D.). Most of Dr. Hill's professional work has been in the fields of teaching, research, and writing; although one of her first jobs was as a parole officer at a school for delinquent girls. At present, she is a faculty member and the acting director of the African Studies Center of Boston University. Among Dr. Hill's writings are many published articles on sociology and on Afro-American culture. She is the co-author with Martin Kilson of a historical anthology,* Apropos of Africa: Sentiments of American Negro Leaders on Africa, from the 1800's to the 1950's.

Adelaide Cromwell Hill

Black Education in the Seventies: A Lesson from the Past

Caught between the shrill cries of education for revolution and the less persuasive arguments of the irrelevancy of black studies, one should be hesitant to project expectations for black Americans in the next and following decades. Yet, education of some sort, based on some delineated principle, is perhaps the most crucial experience for any group of people, and in this period of history, of the most critical importance to black people. Today blacks are extremely vocal in their demands of society and of themselves as to the goals of education and other community drives. These blacks are asking themselves the familiar questions: Knowledge for what? To educate their children for a separate or for an integrated society? To play what kind of role in what kind of America? For what purposes—integration or revolution?

The most unique feature of this debate over educational goals in the black community is the fact that for the first time in his long sojourn in this country the black American is in a position to demand and indeed to acquire the kind of education he desires. One of the characteristics of being a discriminated-against minority is the fact that the majority group under these circumstances not only determines the position but dictates the kind and to a large extent the quality of education prescribed for the minority group. This in turn is designed to perpetuate the position of the minority as one characterized by inferiority and submission.

Educational policies with regard to the black man are fairly well-known: none at all as long as he was a slave, limited and restricted when he was a segregated citizen of the South, and theoretically but rarely actually equal if he were a citizen of the North. Of course there were, even during slavery and much more frequently afterwards, exceptions to these policies. Yet, as a rule, this was the kind of education the black American received because this was the kind of education white America wanted him to receive. And should he prove an exception or use the system, if and when he could, to become a different order of being, the white society was most reluctant to acknowledge the fact.

The existence of the railroad porter with the Phi Beta Kappa key unable to find an appropriate job is a familiar phenomenon to the black community, though largely unknown to white society. Or consider the brilliant black scholar or artist who was a victim of the lack of academic and artistic opportunities. These were the individual instances of persons who refused to be programmed by the system. They were personal tragedies and undoubtedly losses to the larger society. They evoked no community outrage. Such examples, however, were illustrative of the inappropriateness of the educational system in the larger society for the development of the potential of black Americans.

Faced with these tragedies of unrecognized superiority in an integrated system on the one hand and the programmed mediocrity of an isolated segregated and inferior system on the other, the black community should now examine its expectations of education and the kinds of experience it in fact has had over the last hundred years. For the black community one factor seems to be given: the correct education needed for black youngsters to enable them to play a useful role in society requires a suitable educational environment. The assumption here is that regardless of specific philosophies, no one would deny that the goal of education is to make the black child a thoroughly equal citizen. Much rhetoric can be spent on arguing whether he shall be equal within the system or equal outside the system. The fact remains, in either instance he must survive and master the system. At the very minimum, he must receive an education at least equal to that of any other child. Yet it is no simple matter to identify the components of an equal educational environment.

Certainly such an environment demands a proper curriculum, inspirational teachers, and motivated students. As members of the black community increasingly exercise their rights to determine the quality of this educational environment, it will be necessary to be familiar with the wide range of educational programs to which blacks have been exposed in the past. Within the educational pattern of the North having nominal integration but few if any black people, or in the South where blacks were educated separately but in an environment of deprivation and discrimination, there were undoubtedly positive as well as negative factors relative to the projected educational goals for the black community.

For purposes of comparison, interested members of the black community might well examine an educational setting which was controlled largely but not totally (for it was a part of a larger system) by blacks, which had black teachers, a curriculum that was competitive with that of any in the country, and which was strengthened by significant racial components and designed to educate a black elite. The very concept of elite for many blacks and almost all whites is a category that does not exist. To be black *ipso facto* means inferiority, not elitism. And in their cries for instant success many blacks merely reinforce the feeling that none can survive without help. However, it is in search of the elite or, if one prefers, Dr. Du Bois's "talented tenth," or merely our best minds, that the black community must go, if indeed it is going to achieve equality, or self-determination, or both. Endeavors must be made to create an environment which will produce black graduates able to meet and even determine the requirements of the larger society.

History does provide at least one example of such an institution: Dunbar High School in Washington, D.C. As recently as Sunday, December 28, 1969, the white press belatedly acknowledged the existence and the success of such an educational environment for blacks. In the article "Years Bring Change to Dunbar High School, Black Elite Institution Now Typical Slum Facility," Lawrence Feinberg attempted to deal with all the ramifications of this kind of educational environment.[1] Feinberg clearly had no background for the task, and therefore failed miserably to convey the real significance of Dunbar. But others, black and white, should continue the inquiry. What is or was Dunbar High School and what particularly is its relevance to the education of black youth? It would be difficult to complete this inquiry in a brief essay.

Dunbar High School was named for the famed Afro-American poet, Paul Lawrence Dunbar, and was founded as a high school for black children in the District of Columbia. As a building it was dedicated in January, 1917, worth, so it was said at the time, more than a half million dollars. This included $550,000 spent on equipment which included an auditorium with a pipe organ, a lunch-room with a modern kitchen, two gymnasiums, laboratories for botany, zoology, chemistry, and physics, a library with a capacity of more than 4000 books and accommodations for 185 students.[2] But the institutional roots of Dunbar as manifest in this building extend much further back into the fibers of the black community than 1917.

In November, 1870, in the basement of a black church in Washington, a preparatory high school was started for Afro-American youth from money raised in memory of Myrtilla Miner, a white teacher of black children. The school was planned to be an institution which would bring into one building "only those pupils pursuing advanced studies." Later it was moved to the Thaddeus Stevens School (21st Street between K and L Streets, N. W.) where it remained until 1872. In that year the school was moved to the Charles Sumner School (17th and M Streets N. W.) where it remained until 1877. In 1877 it was moved to the Myrtilla Miner School (17th and Church Streets, N. W.). In 1891 the school was again moved to a new building located on M Street, near the intersection of New York and New Jersey Avenues. Known as the M Street High School because of this location, the school was now housed in the first building constructed for the purpose of giving secondary education to Afro-Americans in Washington, and according to Mr. Feinberg, it was the first public high school, black or white, in the District. The school remained on M Street until it was moved in 1917 to the new Dunbar building, where two plaques on the auditorium walls enjoined the students, in the words of Dunbar the poet, "to keep a-pluggin' away."[3]

So much for the basic thread of a story which, on the surface, surely has little unusual about it. Though, indeed, if only the quality and quantity of the equipment already described were casually appreciated by a larger society then only dimly aware that Afro-Americans were being exposed to some kind of education, this realization should have excited an interest in, if not a curiosity about, what did in fact take place inside that building. The lack of concern or interest in what happened within Dunbar High School (or old M Street, for that matter) is a measure of the lack of knowledge on the part of the white community about—or interest in—the black community. This lack of knowledge or interest has certainly for many decades added to the hostility, surprise, and confusion that characterize the present state of affairs between the races. It is not a generation gap, but a gap of generations, that one must document.

Pursuing the specifics of Dunbar, one finds the gap can be graphically illustrated if he takes as an example the reaction of a graduate, Robert C. Weaver, former member of President Johnson's cabinet, when he says:

> Perhaps the finest tribute I can pay to Dunbar High School is the fact that, when I graduated, I went to Harvard College where many of my classmates had been trained in some of the best preparatory schools in the nation. I found myself on the whole about as well able to survive in the College as they were. My brother, who graduated from Williams College Phi Beta Kappa, had a similar experience there and subsequently at Harvard where he took his Master's Degree. The catalogue of achievements of its graduates is significant and inspiring. It is . . . another evidence of how an inspired faculty, good students, and a will to achieve can produce success.[4]

Within the walls of Dunbar and those of old M Street from 1870 to 1954 (eighty-four years) there was teaching of only black children by only black teachers. There was a respect for learning and an expectation of superiority based on knowledge and pride emanating from teachers and instilled into pupils that made Dunbar a special educational environment. It is appropriate that as Dunbar is approaching its centennial, its character and flavor dur-

next to freedom, the most highly desired goal. The black commucational planner. At this period of history, when an articulate black community seeks increasingly to control its own institutions, it becomes of paramount importance to examine an institution which, in spite of racism in American society, did in fact motivate and educate to the highest level generations of Afro-Americans. This, before the fears of the white society facilitated the achievements of the black community.

Dr. Weaver felt the success of Dunbar rested with an inspirational faculty, good students, and a will to achieve. However, for an institution to flourish, there must also be some advantages in the environment in which it is located. Washington was psychologically and geographically a southern city, and slavery existed there until the Civil War. As capital of a salvaged Union, however, a Union dedicated to emancipation, Washington became a magnet for many uprooted blacks. Washington's leaders felt it incumbent upon them to project a picture of equality as a model for the rest of the country.

The black community which evolved—called *The Secret City* by Constance McLaughlin Green—had its character determined by the larger Washington environment.[5] This environment provided sufficiently varied opportunities to draw blacks to Washington from the nearby states. And in Mrs. Green's opinion, even before the Civil War and in spite of a co-existing slave society: "with the exception of New Orleans, no other American city in which the proportion of colored people was high offered them wider opportunities than they had in ante-bellum Washington and Georgetown." Blacks were settled in many parts of the city, and as described in one of the local papers of the day, the situation did seem in 1883, relatively advantageous:

> The colored people of Washington enjoy all the social and political rights that law can give them, without protest and without annoyance. The public conveyances are open to them, the theatres, and the jury box, the spoils of party power are theirs. Many of these men are wealthy.[6]

But as expected, Washington was not entirely an Eden for the black man. The writer goes on to say:

But the color line is rigidly drawn in what is known as society; wealth, learning, official place give no colored family
the right of the privilege of entering the best of the common-
est white society on terms of equality or endurance. In this
respect the colored man lives as in the days of slavery, and as
a drop of African blood was once held to make a man a negro,
so now it taints him and makes an immutable barrier against
social recognition.[7]

Among the problems besetting Washington was that of how to
incorporate the black newcomers who were neither skilled nor
affluent. From the earliest days, apparently, the question of the
proportion of blacks to whites had been of concern to the city
fathers. Black migration was a special factor with which to be
reckoned and which from time to time seemed to disturb the previously described equilibrium between the races. Nevertheless, as
has been indicated, a sizeable group of black persons managed to
develop a style of life based on decent jobs, education, and a sense
of community. Mrs. Green refers to Washington during this period as a center for Negro civilization for the time. This was a civilization based on government employment, Howard University,
and the Bethel Literary and Historical Association, founded in
in 1881 as a forum of expression for Afro-American intellectuals.
    Gradually, however, there was a decline in the position of Afro-
Americans in Washington. In 1891, out of 23,144 federal employees in Washington, nearly 2400 were Afro-Americans. They
ranked as copyists, transcribers, and clerks. But in employment
for the city of Washington, Afro-Americans had few jobs. In
1879 there was only one black policeman on a force of fifty. There
were no black firemen. In fact during this period, outside of the
school system, Afro-Americans held only 25 positions above the
rank of messenger and day laborer in the city government. Professionally, however, the black community was growing. By 1900
there were more than 400 schoolteachers, 50 qualified physicians,
10 professionally trained dentists, over 90 ministers, and some 30
lawyers.
    It was within this socio-political setting that old 'M' Street and
Dunbar High School emerged as an institution. For black Americans throughout the country before the Civil War, education was

next to freedom, the most highly desired goal. The black community in Washington was no exception. As early as 1807 three Afro-Americans started a school with their own money and employed white teachers. By 1818, the Resolution Beneficial Society composed of black people started another school. In 1829, there was in Washington an African Education Society. The first public school for Afro-Americans was started in 1844, and M Street, Dunbar's predecessor, opened nine years before the city had a high school for white children, as Mr. Feinberg observed.

With one exception, only black teachers taught these black students, under the supervision of black principals. And what an extraordinary group of black individuals they were! The first principal was Miss Emma J. Hutchins, from New Hampshire and white; she only stayed one year. All the principals since that time have been black. Miss Mary J. Patterson, an 1862 graduate of Oberlin (taking the "gentleman's course") and the first woman of African blood to receive a college education, was followed in 1872 by Mr. Richard T. Greener, the first black graduate of Harvard College and U.S. Consul at Vladivostok, Russia. Others were of equal achievement. Mr. F. L. Cardozo, Sr., a graduate of Glasgow University and the London School of Theology, who during the Reconstruction was the Treasurer of the State of South Carolina, was followed in 1884 by Dr. W. W. Montgomery, a graduate of Dartmouth College and Howard University Medical School. Dr. Montgomery's successor was Robert H. Terrell, a graduate of Lawrence Academy and Howard University, later to be named a municipal judge in the District. The second black woman principal, Mrs. Anna J. Cooper, also an Oberlin graduate, occupied the post from 1901-1906.

When the Dunbar building was occupied, the first principal was Garnet C. Wilkinson, an Oberlin graduate and a graduate of Howard University. In sum, of the thirteen black principals during the period under discussion here, two held degrees from Harvard, four from Oberlin, one from Dartmouth, one from Western Reserve, one from Amherst, one from the University of Glasgow in Scotland, two from Howard University, and one from the University of Pittsburgh. The philosophy and teaching in M Street and Dunbar High School was therefore exemplary, with a curriculum based on courses in English, Latin, French,

Spanish, German, history, mathematics, science, art, music, physical education, and before 1920, Greek, preparing a student body in 1899 that was able to score higher in a city-wide examination than students attending the high schools for whites.

Some of the strength of Dunbar as a school came from the need to compensate for the discrimination against Afro-Americans in the city of Washington. As Mrs. Mary Gibson Hundley has indicated in her book *The Dunbar Story*, there were racial barriers in the theaters from 1913 to 1949, in amusement parks, restaurants, concert halls and other places of public accommodation. To compensate for this, the teachers of Dunbar encouraged their students to visit the federal and municipal buildings, libraries, art galleries, and museums. Distinguished speakers and successful graduates were invited to the school. Dunbar became a protection, though racial discrimination was an ever-present factor against which pupils and teachers alike had to fight. There were many forms of discrimination: large classes, rarely equal custodial services or building facilities. Dunbar's lunchroom was dark and always crowded; it took ten years of lobbying and protest to secure a stadium for Dunbar. Central High School, built the same year for whites, had its stadium as part of the original plan.

The list of teachers who served under these principals is also a missing page of Afro-American history: the grandson of Frederick Douglass; the son of the first Afro-American to receive a diplomatic post; the famous historian Carter G. Woodson; and so many others—writers and scholars. It is an impressive list of men and women who themselves had been prepared at the best colleges in this country and who in turn sent forth their students to these schools to become doctors, writers, ministers, artists, judges, politicians, a U.S. Senator, scholars, bishops, members of the diplomatic service, colonels, and hundreds of teachers of black children throughout the country. In 1920, Dunbar had many teachers with graduate training and three women teachers with Ph.D. degrees. One came from the University of Paris, one from Radcliffe, and one from the University of Chicago.

The fruits of their labors were seen of course in their students. Between 1910 and 1930, the largest number of students who went "North" to school entered Amherst, Bates, Bowdoin, Brown,

Colby, Colgate, Dartmouth, Hamilton, Harvard, Michigan, Mount Holyoke, Oberlin, Pembroke, the University of Pennsylvania, the University of Pittsburgh, Radcliffe, Smith, Syracuse University, Wellesley, Western Reserve University, Williams and the University of Wisconsin. Amherst College alone admitted thirty-four students from Dunbar (between 1892 and 1954). In those days few went to Yale and none was welcome at Bryn Mawr, Princeton, or Vassar. As Dr. Weaver has attested, the students did well. Many received Phi Beta Kappa keys. Many went on to graduate training. The inspiration, once given, did not wear off. Of the 156 Rosenwald Fellowships awarded between 1937 and 1952, twenty-one, or thirteen per cent went to Dunbar graduates.

In view of more recent history, it is interesting to note that Dunbar did not, as a rule, attempt to prepare black athletes to seek coveted athletic scholarships. During this period (or, shall we say, before Jackie Robinson?) athletic competition was hardly a channel of mobility for the college-oriented black student. For black athletes there was no future in professional baseball or professional football, and prizefighting has seldom seemed to attract college men, black or white. Dunbar graduates sought and received scholarships based on academic merit, not on athletic prowess. But this did not imply a lack of concern for or readiness to compete in the arena of physical fitness. The first black boy to attend the Naval Academy after the Reconstruction was a Dunbar graduate. West Point, too, has had a large proportion of its few black graduates from Dunbar High School. The first black general in the United States Army was a graduate of Dunbar. From 1870 to 1955, about three-fourths of the graduates of Dunbar went on to college.

After the Supreme Court decision of 1954, and after many other legislative advances in the field of civil rights, Dunbar changed, and so did the larger society. Black children were now scattered in all the schools of Washington—private and parochial as well as public. Those pupils who now attended Dunbar came exclusively from the immediate neighborhood in which Dunbar was situated. Black college graduates were no longer limited in their career choices to medicine, the ministry, and law.

Public school teaching in particular became less attractive. The best minds found alternate careers. Some teachers from the old days continued until their retirement to inspire their students to excel in their pursuit of more education. The new teachers, however, were faced with many changes in the school and in the relation of the school to the educational priorities for the city. The 1954 decision was based on the assumption that quality education could not occur in a separate, but only in an equal, or non-segregated system. At Dunbar, prior to that time, teachers attempted to provide quality education for their students because they and the students and the community thought it was possible to do so. They had not yet been told that it was not, nor were they then denied the possibility of reaching the best young black minds of the city. In this racial shift of educational assumptions, the student body has remained almost completely black, but some of the teachers (in 1969, for example, 19 out of 85) are white.

The glory of Dunbar and the value of its example rest on the careers of its graduates. It is of some importance, particularly when we remember that it is no longer necessary for black students to knock—usually unheard—on the doors of white colleges, to examine the career or educational goals of its recent graduates.

Of the 336 graduates of Dunbar in 1969, 201, or roughly one-third of the class, were going on to college. This pattern, however, was most unfamiliar for the old Dunbar. Sixty-three were going to the Federal Teacher's College, 23 to Washington Technical Institute, 16 to D. C. Teachers' College, 15 to Howard University. Not one was going to an Ivy League College, not one to a big state university, not one to a school north of Philadelphia or west of Ohio.[8] To the informed this was progress; to the knowledgeable this was retrogression. The irony of Dunbar, it seems, is that at the time when opportunities were opening, the school was unable to provide an adequate educational environment.

Is what we have been documenting the emergence of a ghetto school, a type so familiar in contemporary parlance or, as Mr. Feinberg says, "a typical slum facility"? I think not. The change in Dunbar is no consequence of blacks driving whites out of a community, or a school designed to keep blacks as second-class citizens. It is rather the evolution of an institution initially inspired by the best qualified minds in Afro-American society. Dunbar educated generations of black students, from Robert Weaver to Julian Mayfield, to meet any test. It was not just another, nor could be described as being just another, high school for black "culturally-deprived youth." What does its existence as a superior school mean and what does its decline mean to the future goals of black Americans?

Dunbar vividly illustrates the possibility of having intellectual equality within the black community. It shows, for all those who care to see, that given certain circumstances—kind of teacher, kind of students, quality of school—black youngsters can be educated to meet any standards the American system wishes to project. Acknowledging this fact, however, we must note some other points. First, the teachers who were black and could thereby provide a basis of identity did derive their intellectual, if not their emotional, strengths from having themselves achieved in the larger society. Separate though it was, and equal, Dunbar did during its fluorescence capitalize or build upon the strengths of blacks who brought knowledge and security to an educational task because they themselves had met the standards of the larger society. Secondly, and better to understand the militancy of the sixties, a point to stress is the fact that the activities and achievements of this educational institution went unrecognized and unrewarded for the most part by the larger society. We accept the truth that no institution can function to its full potential if it operates separately and is not accorded a realistic measure of recognition.

To those closely identified with Dunbar—the students and teachers and handful of admission officers in northern schools who came to know what to expect of Dunbar graduates—this lack of appreciation seems incredible, but the facts are there. Feinberg's recent "discovery" is only one example. Earlier the same year that Dr. Weaver gave his laudatory assessment of Dunbar, Edward P. Morgan, the well-known radio commentator, devoted portions of two of his programs to what he was calling *The Dunbar Story*.[9] Rather than developing such ideas as we are discussing, Mr. Morgan saw "The Dunbar Story" as centering around the endeavors of a young white teacher to acquire paper-back books from her friends to give to the deprived black students attending Dunbar!

The dilemma, if not the tragedy, of this kind of treatment is that when the black man has indeed achieved or excelled, there remains at most levels of white society a preference to deny, ignore, or explain this away. Until blacks began to demand to be heard, to demand recognition, such recognition as was patern-alistically offered came only voluntarily as a *rescue operation:* uplifting blacks from some real or imagined deprivation to the more glorious levels of culture and achievement of whites. *But what to do when they were already there?*

There is another and very important conclusion to be drawn from the Dunbar experience. Neither the students nor the teachers were handicapped by strong feelings of racial bitterness or hos-tility. Few energies were wasted on "hating the Man," all were directed towards developing superiority and pride in the indi-vidual. This is not to say that many faculty members were not fully aware that their very employment in high school teaching was a reflection of racial barriers. (How grateful and fortunate some of the now-so-interested white colleges would be to be able today to bring back to their faculties many of their own former black graduates who had to seek Dunbar if they wanted a teaching career commensurate with their education!) Nor were the stu-dents permitted to forget they were black and all that meant, both positively in terms of self-awareness and negatively in terms of the racist character of American society. The key was one of priorities. The students were to receive a first-class education so that they could go on for more, with the requisite academic and psychological preparation.

Dunbar High School was not designed to create Uncle Toms. A major hallmark of the Dunbar graduate was not only his will to achieve but his pride in the achievement of other Dunbar graduates and in the school as an institution. This strength and security made him able to face white society as an equal. This is not to say the student body did not suffer from some of the frivolity of American secondary education: military uniforms, maybe too much sports, parties for the few, too many clothes, etc. But in retrospect these activities were never really challenges to the goals of Dunbar as an educational institution. There were no "Black Studies," for in a sense there was no real need for Black Studies. Well-trained black teachers taught the subjects in ways black students with proper education understood. The black experience in terms of persons and content was ever-present. All students knew and sang with regularity and more feeling than the manner in which they saluted the American flag "The Negro National Anthem," with words penned by the black poet James Weldon Johnson and which began "Lift every voice and sing . . .". There were no high school sororities or fraternities. Extra-curricular activities were on the basis of interest, not social status: a stamp club, a Negro history club, or a tennis club; or, in competition, the National Honor Society, the glee club, a special club for outstanding athletes.

One could examine and evaluate the specifics of Dunbar in terms of modern needs for quite some time. Suffice it to say that Dunbar does seem to provide raw data on which community leaders today might wish to project some of their educational plans for the future. Here was a case of separatism, but separatism with certain qualifications, for Dunbar was not an institution committed either to separatism or integration. Both of these were and are choices determined by the larger society. Dunbar was committed to superiority which can be the choice of the black community. The Dunbar experience seems to suggest that equality does not require the coloring black of an entire curriculum or the inability to create a strong mind from "racist" texts. Actually, as has been already noted, had Dunbar preoccupied itself *exclusively* with these issues, as important and crucial as they are, the task of training its students for college and for life might well have remained undone.

This Dunbar is no more; but the lessons derived from its experience should not be ignored by blacks merely because they are unknown to whites.

Black teachers in all black schools can teach and develop superior black students, but the specific circumstances under which this can be achieved must be acknowledged. A crucial factor is that the training and exposure of the teachers be to the standards and qualifications of a fully competitive society. Furthermore, in our educational debates, more attention should be placed on how and at what ages we should place the primary emphasis on equality, even superiority. How do we prepare the black youngster not for withdrawal or isolation but for constructive confrontation? Ideally, of course, this stress on equality and identity should characterize the entire educational experience of the black child. But when this has not been or cannot be the case, when must academic security be firmly established?

If Dunbar can be informative, it would seem that the years of early adolescence spent in high school are the critical ones. Many youngsters in Washington—and bright ones, too—chose not to go to Dunbar, preferring instead (for what must have been quite human reasons) to go to one of the other two black high schools: Armstrong or Cardozo. Some could, and many did, go on to college and other careers from these schools.

Dunbar itself received many students who came from a wide variety of elementary and junior high schools, ranging from poor to good; once within the walls of Dunbar, however, all students were exposed to a special academic environment. For the majority, this meant the essential and first step on the ladder of equality with any student of similar endowment of any race. There were few failures at Dunbar, but Dunbar obviously was not meant to meet the needs of all youngsters. For those who chose not to continue, there remained the mark of exposure.

The ironic factor is that Dunbar still exists in the same building as a high school for black children taught by black teachers. Since 1954, whites have been on the faculty and in the student body, but as exceptions. Now this institution is a "slum facility," a ghetto school, and all the other names so popularly used to suggest deprivation, inadequacy, and inferiority. Surely this is a dramatic lesson. Color is not enough, yet mixture *per se* is no guarantee for improvement. The best institution must be flexible in the presence of change. Dunbar was permitted to erode and wither away rather than tool-up for change. The question remains, what was there in that institution which could (and *would*) serve as an example and inspiration to all those interested in the American educational process?

Blacks succeed or fail, as human beings always do, on the basis of the quality of their environment. No man is an island; no competitive education can be designed to be in isolation. Each community must assess its needs and demand the best of its own young, and the best is equal. Such a philosophy could perhaps ensure that the black teachers and community leaders of the 1970's will really prepare black students for the 1980's and 1990's.

This would be the glorious legacy from the tradition of Dunbar High School, that once was the pride of the race.

NOTES

1.   *The Washington Post*, December 28, 1969, pp. D1-D2.
2.   Two sources have provided most of the historical material for this article: Mary Church Terrell's "History of the High School for Negroes in Washington," *Journal of Negro History*, Vol. II, July 1917 (pp. 252-266); and Mary Gibson Hundley's *The Dunbar Story, (1870-1955)*, Washington, D.C., (The Vantage Press) 1965. Mrs. Hundley's book gives the most complete documentation yet available on Dunbar. As one of its former dedicated and inspiring teachers, Mrs. Hundley's contribution in writing this book without subsidy is in itself testament to the spirit and devotion the teachers of Dunbar had for the school and its pupils.
3.   Here is an interesting progression in the naming of public institutions designed for use by Afro-Americans exclusively. In this case, the first three persons so honored were white, but had some public identification with the problems of blacks. Myrtila Miner, for example, came to Washington from New York and opened a school for black girls. Her name, if not her fame, remained closely identified with the education of Afro-Americans. In addition to the school mentioned in the text, the first normal school, and later the first teachers' college for Afro-Americans in Washington were named in her honor.

Apparently it was not easy to get a consensus on either a name of an Afro-American or on the appropriateness of honoring a black American when the M street High School was built. The hiatus between the recognition of Charles Sumner and the agreement on Paul Lawrence Dunbar certainly suggests this. The choice of Dunbar was unanimous, but not without some competition. Mr. Francis Grimke, minister of the 15th Presbyterian Church, was a contender. The black community, it seems, must reach a certain degree of identity and assertiveness in order to demand that blacks be chosen for the names of bulidings and for public monuments.

4.   Hundley, *op. cit.*, Preface.

5.   Constance McLaughlin Green, *The Secret City*, Princeton, N.J., (Princeton University Press), 1967.

6.   *Ibid*, p. 140.

7.   *Ibid*.

8.   Correspondence from Charles S. Lofton, Executive Assistant to the Superintendent of Schools, District of Columbia, June 6, 1969.

9.   October 1964 and April 1965. Unfortunately, the research facilities of CBS, according to correspondence with the Manager of Audience Relations on October 16, 1969, could not provide me with the specific dates on which these broadcasts took place.

Citing that the slaves were the first to develop a black theology, Rev. Mr. Joseph calls for a new religious consciousness: the church must be taken out of the edifice and carried back to the people.

JAMES A. JOSEPH *is chaplain of the Claremont Colleges in Claremont, California. He received his undergraduate degree from Southern University in Baton Rouge, Louisiana, and his graduate degree in theology from Yale University. Rev. Mr. Joseph spent two years as Associate Director of the Irwin-Sweeney-Miller and Cummins foundations and also taught at Stillman College in Tuscaloosa, Alabama, where he was involved in the early civil rights movement. He has also lectured at more than twenty major colleges and universities. In the summer of 1968, he was a Visiting Fellow at the Metropolitan Applied Research Center in New York City.*

James A. Joseph

Has Black Religion Lost Its Soul?

Nat Turner, the rebellious mystic, insisted that it was the spirit of Christ which directed him toward rebellion. He saw religion as the sacred cement which binds a people together in a common commitment to liberation. Yet today's black activist is more likely to reject the black church for its past sins rather than seek to recover the spirit of "Brother Nat."

In the face of such a mood it is important to ask: What is the future of the black church? Can it survive? Should it survive?

It is now clear that the black power emphases of the last few years have had a cathartic effect on the black church and its theology. But it is not yet clear whether the Christianity which has been so infected with the ideology of preservation and permanence can be made to return to the spirit of liberation which was present at its birth. A black theology which is only black at the edges is not likely to be enough. A theology of revolution which is not grounded in concrete historical experience will prove to be only a temporary diversion.

What we need is much deeper and more pervasive than the blackening of an institutional form, or even the celebration of blackness. While these are certainly worthwhile contributions to a people's self-understanding, the black church is in a position to have a much wider impact. Its future role in the black community will depend to a large degree on whether or not it proves capable of reading the pulse of the times. Most black youth are alienated from the church not because they are immoral but because they are too moral for the static moralisms now being proclaimed. The black church can no longer simply preach what is moral without joining men in doing what is moral.

I am persuaded that the call for a new value system by the younger activists is the stuff out of which a new black theology will emerge, a theology which will be a reflection on the faith of the new moralist rather than simply an attempt to make traditional Christianity relevant to the new mood. But any consideration of what form this is likely to take cannot be a starry-eyed leap into tomorrow. It must begin with a careful consideration of the future as it is now breaking in upon us. As St. Augustine pointed out, time is a threefold present: the present as we experience it, the past as a present memory, and the future as a present expectation.

The Present as We Experience It

Every movement has its peculiar form of rhetoric. In the public rally the message often appears to be more important than the mission. Yet every serious agent of change knows that effectiveness is directly related to the degree in which slogans take on substance and rhetoric becomes reality. What we tend to forget, however, is that substance has to do not only with the content of programs but the insight of ideology.

Our necessary preoccupation with programming the revolution is in danger of blinding us to the significance of the ideology that is emerging. "Thinking black" has turned out to be neither a racist slogan nor an alien idea. Like other timely and enduring ideas, it transcends the needs of any particular people or place and provides enduring insights into the human condition. Philosophically, the emerging ideology is both classical and contemporary. Theologically, it is the natural offspring of the marriage of crisis and celebration; it is, at one and the same time, both orthodox and radically new, both Christian and secular. It provides the necessary corrective for a society which has lost its capacity to talk about God and is now losing the capacity to understand man.

What I am suggesting is that the black church as it reflects upon its faith is in a position to provide the substance beyond the present symbolism now in vogue. Black consciousness can be given a theological content. And this is the first job, although only one among many, of black theology.

What we are now coming to realize is that a black man must first be able to affirm the beauty of his own humanity before he can affirm the beauty of creation. He perceives reality through his own subjective perspective. In order to reflect on his faith he must begin where he is. To some this may seem like an excessive emphasis on contextualism, but it should be clear that I am not arguing that the reality perceived in the particularity of the black experience represents the whole of what is real. It simply represents the starting point, and in so doing is admittedly more closely in tune with Aristotle's emphasis on the particular rather than Plato's emphasis on the universal. For, as Rosemary Ruether has argued, the phrase "black is beautiful" is a contextual statement of the biblical doctrine of man. God looked at his creation and, behold, it was very beautiful. Each part was beautiful on its own terms. There was no exclusive standard of beauty to which the rest should bow in a debasing way. Each people must affirm their own integrity in affirming the beauty of the whole.[1]

Black theology, however, must be more than simply a contextual statement of the Christian doctrine of creation. For out of the black experience is emerging a disposition towards truth which questions traditional absolutes and suggests instead that truth is a process, an unfoldingness, in which today's absolutes become tomorrow's myths. Therefore, as long as truth is still in the process of being revealed, no creed dare be frozen as final; no individual dare be labeled as infallible; no institution dare be labeled as complete.

This leads to an awareness that, like Adam, today's activist is also in on the beginning of creation because creation is not a distant event, but a happening now. The God who in the beginning created, is the God who now creates. The God who so loved the world he gave, is the God who now gives. To reflect theologically, therefore, is to deal with what is now happening rather than simply to add footnotes to the past.

This kind of epistomology has revolutionary implications not only for traditional approaches to truth but for the way in which we deal with prevailing standards. It has led black Americans to question what Andrew Billingsley refers to as the Anglo-conformity doctrine, the grand illusion which infests the American value system.[2] An example of this collective deception is to be found in the illusions concerning morality.

This centers around the adoption of standards of morality based on white European cultural norms. When I was in Ghana, I was appalled to learn that many white missionaries were more interested in the form of marriage than the content of the marital relationship. Long-standing cultural practices were denounced as immoral while Western standards were lifted up as divinely ordained. Black Americans are now joining other non-whites in rejecting anglo-illusions about what is good, true, and beautiful. In so doing, they are demythologizing European addenda and going back to the oppressed community which gave birth to Christianity.

It should not be assumed, however, that the adoption of a process epistomology means that black people applaud the increasing tendency to seek eternity in the instant and the contingent. The electronic age with its instantaneous experiences has led to a triumph of contemporaneity, but while white youth alternate between a rejection and a celebration of the present, black youth are in search of a past. The black revolution has called our attention to the relationship between self-identity and historical consciousness. We now know that the severance of a man from his past is a threat to his sense of self. We now know that the easiest way to avoid treating a man as a human being is to refuse to report his accomplishments and, instead, foster images which denigrate his self-esteem. For this is precisely the crime of the Western historian. Not only has the black American been left out of history, but a larger body of American historical writing was written with an anti-black bias.

Yet it is not only black history which has been distorted. When black Americans call into question traditional views of history, they are seeking a new historiography which emancipates all Americans from their enslavement to cultural mythology. The new black theology, therefore, must begin with a theology of history.

The Past as a Present Memory

Present day black theology proponents have brought to public consciousness a style of theology and a socio-political vision that appears on the surface to be radically new, but which on closer examination has deep roots in the Christian tradition and in the black experience. It is only as we come to understand the roots of this new theology that we are able to put the present discussion in perspective.

From its infancy black theology has been related both to black consciousness and black liberation. While it is not religious nationalism, it is religion seeking to respond to a mood of political and social nationalism. It is an affirmation of the relevance of Christianity to the black condition.

The Christianity first encountered by black slaves was a form of religious nationalism which supported the values held by the white slave masters. The prevailing theology held that the slave did not become either free or more of a man by the acceptance of faith and baptism. He was not only regarded as different in status but different in kind—belonging to a lesser order of being. Therefore, it was considered the duty of a slave's master to give him Christian instruction as long as it was simply aimed at salvation from Satan and not redemption from servitude. Many missionaries went so far as to argue that slaves well-instructed in the Christian faith were less likely to develop revolutionary inclinations.

This religious nationalism, which has many of the elements of what has come to be known as cultural racism, has always had three basic characteristics: 1) a disparagement of all non-whites and all of the components of their culture; 2) an affirmation of the anglo-conformity doctrine which holds that values held to be normal in the white community are to be highly valued and any deviation from this norm is to be highly disvalued; 3) a celebration of only those cultural symbols identified with Anglo-Saxon achievements. In response to the religious nationalism among white slave masters, the slaves at a very early stage began to appropriate and adapt the white man's religion to their own psychological and sociological needs. In discarding its racist elements and re-appropriating Christianity to speak to their own condition, they were the first to develop a black theology. It was at first a theology without theologians, for the early slaves neither preached their religion nor articulated their theology. They continued the practice of the African tradition and danced it instead.

The second phase of black theology as response to the religious nationalism of the white slave master can be seen in the way in which Christianity was appropriated by the insurrectionists. A few examples will suffice to establish this point.

Reference has already been made to the way in which Nat Turner used both his personal charisma and his instruction in Christianity to organize his followers for rebellion. But even before the Nat Turner revolt, a slave known as Gabriel sought to convince blacks that they were the new Israel called upon to rise up and restore their manhood. He not only used the Bible as his authority, but his position of influence among slaves was a direct result of his religious leadership as a kind of lay preacher.

Denmark Vesey also used Christian teaching as the basis for the recruitment of followers for the Charleston, South Carolina, revolt in 1822. He argued that God's word made plain to his people in Israel was the same word addressed to the slaves. He pointed out that the virtues of equality, justice, and freedom were at the heart of the Christian message. It was, therefore, the Christian duty of the slaves to overturn the master-slave relationship through whatever means necessary.

This radical appropriation of Christian theology to serve the cause of black liberation was followed after the Civil War by an equally radical accommodation to an American theology which emphasized patience and conciliation. In reaction to the black churches' unwillingness to deal with either liberation or positive black consciousness, there developed a series of splinter movements aimed at creating a religious nationalism to cement the black community into a new cultural bond.

In 1913, Timothy Drew founded the Moorish Science Temple in Newark, New Jersey, which began to reject the symbolism of the white churches and to forge a religion based on eastern philosophy, black cultural pride and the Holy Koran. Teaching that wholeness for blacks was possible only through the rediscovery of their original identity, the Moorish Science Temple Movement spread throughout the major urban areas.

Black churchmen seeking to respond to the rejection of Christianity as the white man's religion began to aggressively affirm the relevance of Christianity to the black condition. This new phase of black theology led to the publication of a book on *The Black Christ*.[3] The same historical cycle continued into the nineteen-fifties and -sixties. Building upon the foundation laid by Marcus Garvey, the Black Muslims developed their own brand of religious nationalism. Maulana Ron Karenga argued for cultural nationalism. Black Power became the new slogan of black consciousness. In response to the mood in the black community, black apologists began to speak of a black theology.

What now becomes clear is that throughout history black theology has always been both an act of affirmation and a concrete response: an affirmation of the relevance of Christianity to black people, and a response to the rejection of Christianity among black people. It is from this perspective that one must see the present discussion.

The Ethics of Reparation

The most significant contribution of the black theology debate in the nineteen-sixties was its exposure of the American churches as basically oriented toward the maintenance of power by the powerful at a time when black Americans were in need of a theology oriented toward the acquisition of power by the powerless.

It may be that the most important contribution now being made by black churches and black churchmen centers around the discussion of the Black Manifesto and the demands for reparation. Ironically, the Christian church which has so long had a monopoly on rhetoric seems paralyzed by the development of a counter-rhetoric. From the beginning the Christian churches have taught that restitution is an essential part of penitence; but when an actual demand is made in contemporary form, it is denounced as contemptuous and treated as alien. Most Americans have been too concerned with retribution to entertain any thoughts of reparation. They want a God of vengeance against black people rather than a God of justice for black people. But it may be that the God who comes to us in the present is neither the domesticated deity of nationalism nor the dead God of the suburban church, but the word become flesh in the community of the oppressed.

If Jesus was an oppressed Jew when he walked among men in the flesh, it may be that in the twentieth century he is where oppression is most acute. In the words of James Cone, Christian theology is a theology of liberation.[4] The understanding of the covenant community of Israel is inseparable from an understanding of the Exodus as the liberating incident *par excellence*. An acceptance of the claims of Christianity is the acceptance of the good news that liberates, and not of the distortions that have been used to enslave.

I am suggesting, therefore, that the theology which is normative in developing an ethic of reparation is clearly what some in our time are choosing to call black theology. To denounce it as heresy is unrealistic, for it simply draws from the historical contextualism of biblical theology. Christian theology is never abstract. It is always the theology of a community. It evolves out of and speaks to the condition of the community. Naturally, for black men it speaks to the condition of the black community. So when the Black Manifesto issued the demands for reparation, the discussion of moral responsibility was taken off the dusty shelves of theological abstraction and placed in the sanctuaries of existential reality. What many have failed to realize is that the subsequent discussion has called into question the whole of the moral tradition which now defines the ethics of giving. The tone of the demands clearly indicates that this is not a call for traditional charity, but a call for a new sense of responsibility based on moral duty rather than moral feeling.

The Christian church is fond of pointing out that the essence of the moral duty is summed up in the commandment to love thy neighbor; yet the age-old question of "how" remains the subject of constant theological debate and the source of continuing moral reflection. One way of putting the problem is to suggest that man as moral being lives in constant tension between the *good* ab-

stractly conceived and the *good* concretely defined, between im-
personalized love and personalized justice.

There has developed a heretical tradition within the Christian
church which assumes that the distribution of love to one's neighbor is based on liking one's neighbor. It assumes that giving,
the sharing of resources, is based on the self-serving luxury of
charity. And since most blacks are beginning to say "to hell with
your love, we want justice," many whites are alienated and consequently feel no moral responsibility to work for a more equita-
ble distribution of the goods of society.

What black theology proponents must now point out is that
the Christian community is being called upon to transform its
love ethic into a social policy based not on the interest of those
who give but in the interest of those who receive. Secondly,
serious ethical reflection must avoid the tendency to sentimental-
ize love and define justice in such a way as to limit our standards
of equity by the distinctions between the friend-neighbor and the
enemy-neighbor. Christians are called upon, therefore, to share
their resources not in order that other men may become like them,
but to enable other men to live more fully human lives.

Until recently, the black community was preoccupied with
those people identified as enemies. Now the concern has shifted
to those people who have identified themselves as friends. It is,
therefore, no coincidence that the Black Manifesto was addressed
to the church. Throughout the civil rights struggle, the representatives of the institutional church were always present; not
only suffering with us in Alabama and Mississippi, but also
doing some of the dying. The religious institutions responded
during that period with what those of us who were bailed out of
jail or provided with legal aid considered relatively impressive
commitments.

A decade later, most of the major denominations agreed to
make available funds to upgrade life in the city. American Bap-
tists even elected a black president. The United Church of Christ
appointed a Secretary of Black Ministry. For those blacks who
remembered when churches made available their facilities to
circumvent desegregation, this new trend seemed impressive. But
to those who have not been blinded by personal acts of goodwill,

this is pale when compared to the amount that the churches spend annually for new construction and other items of lower priority.

The demands are directed to the churches, however, not simply because they have failed to rearrange their priorities, but because reparation is also a very substantive theological idea. The concept is consistent with both the legal and theological traditions of the Western world. It has roots in both our Judaeo-Christian and Greco-Roman heritages. The word "restitution" is at the heart of Western theology, while the concept of redress dominates Western legal tradition.

When the early Hebrew communities sought to establish standards of equity for those who had been exploited, they developed a system requiring symbolic acts of restitution as well as substantive acts of redress. Exploitation and robbery were considered offenses not only against the immediate victim, but against the whole of society. The guilty were required not only to restore what had been stolen but to participate in an elaborate ritual of reparation, involving what the biblical literature refers to as trespass or guilt offerings.

In the book of Leviticus, we are told that:

> The Lord said to Moses, "If anyone sins and commits a breach of faith against the Lord by deceiving his neighbor in a matter of deposit or security, or through robbery, or if he has oppressed or wronged his neighbor then . . . . he shall restore it in full, and shall add a fifth to it, and give it to whom it belongs, on the day of the guilt offering."[5]

Many people who would agree that on the basis of biblical theology and New Testament ethics reparations appear to be morally justified, would argue, however, that there are no precedents for claiming such group reparations. They are likely also to contend that the idea has no political merit because of its emotional rhetoric. They forget, however, that the "freedom budget" was a carefully reasoned, well-documented statement of the immediate needs of the black community, but it got very little support. They also forget that there are precedents for repayment to racial or ethnic groups by the government.

Even though the attempts have been sporadic and insufficient, attempts have been made to pay American Indians for the damages inflicted on Indian nations. Attempts have been made to repay Americans of Japanese ancestry for the financial losses they incurred during their enforced relocation during World War II. In both cases the repayments were ludicrously inadequate, but even those inadequate payments are more than anything ever offered Americans of African ancestry. We could go on to cite subsidies given to farmers, the GI bill, subsidies to the Merchant Marines, and many other examples that are analogous to reparations, but I think the point is clear. There are legal precedents as well as legal traditions for reparation.

But my concern is not to present legal arguments for reparation. I am simply suggesting that the demands of the manifesto are perfectly consistent with both our legal and technological heritage. Furthermore, it is the role of the black church to point this out.

But the trouble is that black religious institutions have too often mounted the barricades in the wrong direction, fighting the wrong enemies. Instead of being concerned about its function, it has been far too concerned about its form. It has been far too concerned with free love and not enough concerned with free hate. The new mood in the black community, however, is giving the black church an opportunity not only to *do* something different but to *be* something different.

What is now happening among younger black churchmen must be seen not simply as a new reformation, but as something much deeper than that. The Reformation is a bad parallel because it happened suddenly. Our situation is more like the renaissance in this regard. It is less an event and more a mood. But the mood has roots as far back as the tribes of Israel. Theologically, it is as old as the oldest of the Israelite tribes. Intellectually, it is as wise as the wisest of the Israelites.

The Future as a Present Expectation

We are now led to the question about the future of belief and the future shape of institutional religion in the black community.

The first thing that must be said is that the black church of the future must minimize concern with God while maximizing concern with man. While black men will still have very definite metaphysical questions, they will be less concerned about the nature of God and more concerned with the duty of man. The futuristic theology which was onced based upon fulfillment through otherworldly speculation must now concern itself with building the kingdom of God in and through the black community.

A second aspect of the black religious consciousness will be the development of a new vocabulary. In the Middle Ages, when traditional religious thought came into contact with Greek thought, it was greatly stimulated by Greek philosophy. As a result, a complete new vocabulary had to be created in order to deal with these new themes. But abstract Greek concepts as they have been appropriated by Europeans really do not express the heart of the reality the black community experiences. As in no previous historical moment, black men are intent on seeing the world through their own symbols and using their own language to explain reality. They want a religion with soul.

While some theologians are likely to regard any emphasis on religion with soul as pop theology at its worst, it is now clear that American theology at its best is no longer relevant to a black community seeking to accelerate the process of change. To re-interpret Christianity is not to ignore the earlier credal formulations but it is to step outside of the traditional categories now being used by many who talk about black theology. It is to make it clear that religion, especially Christianity, is always about freedom. To simply blacken the church and its theology in order to affirm its relevance to the black condition is to miss the point.

There will continue to be Sunday morning gatherings with group psychotherapy and soul music, but a religion which expresses the soul of a people must also seek to fulfill the aspiration of a people. Those whites who have accepted black theology believing that their white Jesus will simply now have a black face misunderstand what is now going on in the black community. The rhetoric of reparation represented the first phase of both the substance of a new ethic and the symbolism of a new reality.

To understand what it means to speak of reparation as a symbol of a new reality, it is necessary to understand the role of symbols and slogans in the life of a people. It is no mere coincidence that reparation in the life of Israel involved both symbolic rituals as well as actual restitution. Symbols are often the means by which a group affirms its identity and develops unity and cohesion allowing the group to move from a non-people to a people.

In the turbulence of the present we are beginning to recognize the importance of group identity in the affirmation of individual identity. The individual's sense of selfhood is influenced and largely determined by his sense of peoplehood. Yet this is not a recent, radical, or reactionary discovery. From the time when man first blossomed into self-consciousness, he has resorted to symbolic rituals to affirm his understanding of divine reality as well as his personal sense of being, sometimes as a member of his tribe, sometimes as a member of his race, and sometimes as a citizen of a national community. One day in our history as a nation, words and music were put together and a song created to regularly re-enact a common commitment to a common past. And so the national anthem became a symbol of American peoplehood. One day stars and stripes were painted on a piece of cloth and a symbol was created to portray a sense of nationhood.

But ironically, the same people who find symbols so important in their own identity find it difficult either to appreciate or to understand the symbolism of a John Carlos or a Thomas Smith in a moment of pride in victory at the Olympic Games. It is ironic that those people who have made Jesus Christ into a blue-eyed Anglo-Saxon are unable to relate to the symbolism which pictures him with kinky hair and dark skin. For while this sort of symbolism can sometimes reflect superficial gimmicks rather than substantive meaning, a black Jesus is an affirmation of the Christian claim that God comes to man where he is. Albert Cleage, who wrote *The Black Messiah*, may be accused of errors in his treatment of history but he must be credited with taking Christian theology seriously.[6]

Towards a new theology

Looking at the church historically, examining how it served as a home base for protest, and analyzing the present mood among black churchmen provide a necessary insight into the potential of the black church in the seventies. But while it is important to understand the chronology of black religion—how it developed during slavery and continues even now—the really significant contribution in the seventies may come from the new exponents of black values, not the seminary trained nor the traditionally credentialed preachers, but the people like Lou Smith of Operation Bootstrap in Los Angeles who are proclaiming the good news of the black experience. These are the men who are developing the new black theology. They are the new breed who have broken away from traditional religion, but who may force the black church to liberate itself from American theology.

The traditional black clergyman must now get himself together and decide who he is: agent of white Christianity or servant of black people. If he develops a new religious consciousness, the black church has an opportunity to become both a school of ethics—raising questions of how, why, and what—and the central agent of liberation. This does not mean, however, that it should follow the style or function of its American counterpart. Black theology must have a different emphasis. Law must be emphasized as secondary to love. For love is the fulfillment of the law rather than the perversion which sees law as the fulfillment of love.

But it is not simply the concept of love which must be liberated. The same is true of the concept of justice. The new emphasis must be on the justice of distribution rather than the justice of retribution. Distributive justice emphasizes equality of opportunity while retributive justice emphasizes equality of punishment. Religious authority must also be re-interpreted. The authority for theological reflection in the black community is the black experience. Black theology must continue to be addressed to black people. Whites may be allowed to eavesdrop on the discussion but white theologians cannot expect to dictate the terms or call the shots.

Finally, the new theology will greatly affect the institutional form of the black church. The present congregation model may be obsolete in another decade. The proposal made by black Methodist clergy in the Chicago area for a community centered ministry which takes shape around a Neighborhood Center rather than a Sunday chapel may be a forecast of things to come. If one argues that religion has to do with any part of man, he must also argue that it has to do with the whole of man. Black religious institutions must be made to reflect this wholeness. Those who worship a God who is always in the process of re-creating the social order, who is concerned about the poor and the powerless, must be concerned about the acquisition and exercise of power. Form will undoubtedly follow function. As the function of the black church changes, its form will change.

Some may call these observations radical. Others may call them conservative. But I believe that the black church will survive. What is emerging out of the present discontent may appear to the older generation to be radically new, but it is both classical and contemporary. It is both a re-Judaized Christianity and a religion with soul.

NOTES

1.   Rosemary Ruether, "Black Theology and the Black Church," *America* (June 14, 1969), pp. 61ff.
2.   Andrew Billingsley, *Black Families in White America* (Englewood, N.J., Prentice Hall, Inc., 1968).
3.   Countee Cullen, *The Black Christ* (New York & London, Harpers, 1929).
4.   James Cone, *Black Power and Black Theology* (New York, The Seabury Press, 1969).
5.   Leviticus, Holy Bible (Revised Standard Version).
6.   Albert Cleage, *The Black Messiah* (New York, Sheed and Ward, 1965).

We now turn to a Black Arts Festival where music and poetry embrace to define and delight their audience. Black art must inspire black people to see ourselves as the vanguard of our destinies and the architects of a new nation.

EUGENE PERKINS, *the editor-publisher of the Free Black Press, was educated in the public schools of Chicago. He received his B.S. and M.S. degrees from George Williams College, Chicago, Illinois. He has done extensive work as lecturer and consultant on Afro-American culture and literature, and has taught creative writing at Malcolm X. College in Chicago. Perkins is a board member of the Museum of Afro-American History and the South Side Community Art Center, both in his native city. He is the author of three volumes of poetry, including* An Apology to My African Brother. *His work has appeared in* Freedomways, Black World, *and* Liberator Magazine.

Eugene Perkins

The Black Arts Movement: Its Challenge and Responsibility

It was a typical bleak December evening and the throng of black people milling outside had to conceal their dashikis and wrap-around robes under heavy winter coats. But once inside the converted movie house, they could remove their outer garments and display the various bright hues and intricate designs of their African-styled clothing. Then, after being seated, a group of black musicians walked on a wide stage and began playing Afro-American rhythms which stimulated the audience to clap hands and pound their feet to complement the polyphonic sounds of the band. Later, the tempo changed as the spiritual voices of a quartet resounded with soulful modulations which recapitulated a legacy of West African chants, Charleston Street Cries, and the Memphis Street Blues. Upon their completion, a tall black curvaceous woman led her dancers through a series of precision maneuvers that exemplified the elegance of ancient African cultures. To culminate the festive evening, a group of black poets began reading poems which electrified some, delighted others, and even sent a few scurrying out. But black poetry is that type of poetry: a new voice, vibrant and timely.

The scene was the Afro-Arts Theatre in Chicago and the event a Black Arts Festival. It is not an unusual scene. The picture which I've delineated is becoming a common one. Common because the Black Arts Movement is beginning to show a significant impact on the lives of black people. Once again the seeds for a Black Esthetic are being planted. However, the search for such a movement is not peculiar only to this generation. Black artists over the years have grappled seriously with this same problem. The "New Negro" of the twenties, about whom Alaine Locke wrote, had sought, in many respects, a similar type of expression to articulate his identity and cultural heritage. But the Harlem Renaissance eventually succumbed, like dry autumn leaves, and again black artists were left in confusion as to the direction their art should take. Cultural dualism has always presented a dilemma to black artists; an ambivalence which has seen them vacillate as often as a chameleon changes colors. But now this conflict is being confronted from a different perspective, for the new Black Art sees itself as fostering a national entity, and not merely re-affirming a sub-culture that seeks approval of white America. On the contrary, its philosophical reference is the antithesis of the Anglo-Saxon Protestant tradition.

But the movement has not been limited to Black Arts Festivals. It encompasses much more . . . its dimensions broader . . . its energy more penetrating. Art for people's sake has taken on a functional meaning . . . becomes part of the natural environment . . . a tangible feeling; functional in the sense that art becomes a true reflection of the community, like a camera which photographs the empirical fabric of life instead of merely dramatizing its abstractions. In some black communities, the movement is symbolized by beautifully painted murals, usually etched on tenements, that celebrate and give recognition to black heroes. The Wall of Respect in Chicago was the first of these picturesque art forms and has influenced similar murals in other cities. One can also discern other developments which are helping to perpetuate this neophyte renaissance, such as the emergence of a new school of black writers, the creation of community theaters, new black publication companies, the trend toward black studies, and a general overall feeling of exuberance and pride within the black community. Amidst the social holocaust that is casting its tremendous shadow over every hamlet and city in America, a cultural movement is being born.

However, there is an inherent danger to any cultural movement which arises during a period of social crisis that is bordering on revolution. Unless the esthetics of the movement support and reinforce the struggle, then they have no real social or political significance, and become only sterile fads that are destined to be buried before their fruition, and rightfully so. The Black Arts Movement cannot afford to isolate itself from the Black Revolution. It should be as Larry Neal says, "the aesthetic and spiritual sister of the Black Power concept." For like the Black Revolution, the Black Arts Movement must seek to liberate black people from what Neal calls "the Euro-Western sensibility" that has enslaved, oppressed, and niggerized black people since the merciless slave ships first began shanghaiing our ancestors from Africa to America. There can be no dichotomy between the two. Both have to be interrelated and supportive of each other if true liberation is ever to be realized. So long as white America was successful in suppressing the culture of black people, it was able to impose its own decadence and thereby deny us our cultural heritage. Frantz Fanon makes this point quite explicit when he describes the rationale used by France in its colonization of the Algerians:

> Every colonized people—in other words, every people in whose soul an inferiority complex has been created by the death and burial of its local cultural originality—finds itself face to face with the language of the civilizing nation; that is, with the culture of the mother country. The colonized is elevated above his jungle status in proportion to his adoption of the mother country's cultural standards. He becomes whiter as he renounces his blackness. . . .[1]

The American slave institution attempted to do just this: destroy the originality of black people and make them solely dependent upon the culture of the oppressor for survival. Historically white America has done everything humanly possible to make the black man's original culture extinct and force him to assimilate into the so-called dominant culture; thus negating his own fundamental existence. And for years, black Americans have consciously or subconsciously strived to mesmerize their psyches into a state of whiteness. Black people have attempted to emulate every ethnic group but their own—we celebrate St. Patrick's day, dress like English squires, learn French or German, idolize white racist heroes, take vacations to Canada and Europe, adopt values of other cultures, fight other people's wars . . . and worship a god which is not even our own color. This obsession and adoration for whiteness has only negated black culture and, as a result, propagandized a subservient image of black Americans. However, today there appears to be a radical departure from this tradition. Many black people are repudiating the "Euro-Western sensibility" and are seeking to express an awareness and appreciation of their own blackness. And much of this new hope is being generated by the Black Arts Movement. This, then, places a grave responsibility on the movement. It must, in fact, be prepared to perpetuate this awakening and also give it counsel to provide it with an everlasting vitality, the kind of vitality that can help enable black people to emerge from the depths of oppression and rise to self-determination, control of their destiny, and, finally, complete liberation.

In assuming this challenge, the Black Arts Movement must be fully cognizant of its responsibilities and be prepared to enter the revolutionary arena and confront those forces which inevitably oppose any movement that deviates from white controlled norms. A strong cultural base is essential to revolution. People evolve from culture . . . gain from it common values . . . a sense of national unity . . . essential ingredients for revolution.

If the goal of the Black Arts Movement is, as I have suggested, to help liberate black people from the oppressive chains of white America and to create a functional esthetic that expresses the total black experience, then, it must continuously be subjected to an introspective analysis of these objectives. Black artists cannot allow themselves to be nurtured by slogans and pragmatic assumptions that lead them astray from their basic responsibility. If the Black Arts Movement is to be a movement for people, it must consciously and critically make every effort to assure that the people are participants, and not just observers being led by a few self-styled spokesmen. We are not seeking a vogue . . . the movement must have permanency . . . a sense of the future . . . a facsimile of order. There is no place for non-revolutionary art during a period of revolution. The art must, as Leon Trotsky indicates, "either deal with themes which reflect the revolution or [be] colored by the new consciousness arising out of the revolution."

Because the poets are generally seen as being among the vanguard of the Black Arts Movement, they have a major responsibility for maintaining its integrity and functionality. Whereas poetry cannot be a panacea, curing all the ills of black people arising from the wretchedness of white America, it can be a strong psychological and spiritual force. Black Poets should be concerned with creating authentic images of black people and dealing with the realities of black life as they actually exist, and not as some distraught illusion. They must be committed to describing the total feelings/emotions/attitudes and values of black people so that black people can better understand themselves and then be able to define/redefine themselves within a black frame of reference. But more important, Black Poets must write *real* poems. I mean *real* in the sense that one can *almost feel, hear, smell, and see* that which the poem is attempting to illustrate. By *real*, I mean poems that can stimulate people like Ray Charles singing/poems that make people do things/react to things/be things/create things/and change things. Black Poetry must deal with language that people can understand, and not allow itself to be prostituted by archaic semantics which are non-representative of the people. Black Poets should write expressively to black people and not as an esthetic exercise to masturbate their egos.

Though poetry can be an inspirational and educational force, it is not an entity unto itself. Art has many modes of expression and cannot be fully appreciated unless each mode interacts with the other to present a unified image. When we speak of a Black Esthetic it is implied that there is an interaction between the various art forms which embodies a secular philosophical reference. This means that these art forms must search for common themes and work toward common goals. If, for example, the poets are going one way and the artists and musicians embarking in another direction, then the esthetic becomes only a conglomeration of unrelated constructs. Black artists should exchange viewpoints and seek ways to polarize their ideas so that each art form reflects the central elements that distinguish one type of esthetic from another. If we are to claim a Black Esthetic, then we must also define the qualities which make it so. Our art cannot be defined by simply calling it black. It has to be articulated in a more concrete context for it to have meaningful substance.

It seems to me that the totality of Black Art can best be defined through the theatre. A functional theatre consists of many art forms, each interacting with the other to project a collage of expressions—music, dance, arts, prose, and poetry. This combination of art is paramount if we are to mirror all aspects of the Black Experience. However, the Black Theatre has yet to reach the masses of black people. Unfortunately it still must compete with the movies and television, which continue to be the most influential media. Nevertheless, the Black Theatre must make every effort to negate this resistive influence. Black theatre groups must use every possible means to involve the community. Community involvement is the life of the theatre. To facilitate community involvement may mean reaching out to black clubs, churches, civic and social groups, and other *status quo* organizations which do not generally see themselves as part of the struggle. Although the Black Theatre, like Black Poetry, must be revolutionary, it cannot be so politically oriented that it turns off certain groups. Instead, it must try to gain their confidence first before it can, in fact, begin to sensitize these groups to acknowledge their roles in the revolution. It must be able to project identifiable themes that blend with the day-to-day life struggle black people face. Most black people, at this time, are not revolutionaries; and if we want this majority's support, and we definitely need it, then our theatre must capture those daily experiences and tribulations which are living documents of their very existence. The brother on the corner must be exposed to a theatre which interprets his natural environment in such a manner that the stage itself becomes synonymous with that environment. He must be made to see himself in an image that is transferable to his own "turf."

The Black Theatre must encompass the magnitude of expressions which are peculiar to black Americans. We are in need of a theatre that is able to make all black people feel they are involved in every phase of its creation. Our theatre must reach the brothers in the taverns and pool halls, and touch the lives of junkies and prostitutes. It must have a message for the mother on ADC, and for the frustrated husband who comes home from work each day to realize that survival in the ghetto is only an amplification of his own misery and grief. The Black Theatre should endeavor to incorporate every aspect of the Black Experience, and, in so doing, develop humanistic/realistic themes that grow out of the day-to-day struggles which confront black people, and then use these themes as energizers to help destroy the plantation mentality that tends to strangle our lives. It must depict the *total/ complete/absolute/full* expression of ourselves.

This does not mean the Black Theatre needs to violate its revolutionary posture. On the contrary, its underlying goal must be one of education, to move people from a "daily survival" kind of existence to a more aggressive type of self-control and direction. But education is a gradual process and cannot be fully internalized by having an accelerated program that attempts to circumvent its systematic progression.

While the western theatre continues to degrade itself with abstract absurdities (a là *LuV*), sick melodramas (a là *Boys in the Band*), and animalistic musicals (a là *Hair*) that claims to liberate people from the provinciality of American imperialism, the Black Theatre must not fall prey to this "honkie" type of cultural revolution. The western theatre is dying because it has failed to communicate truth, and, in its frantic search for survival, it must depend upon illusions and psychedelic themes that allow people to "cop out" from reality. On the contrary, the Black Theatre must face the oppressive force of this country with a realism that it can *see/hear/feel* and use whatever means necessary to expose the hypocrisy that keeps America bleeding from her ass and being the world's most dangerous carrier of VD. We must call a spade a spade and deal with tangibles that will enable black people to cope with reality, not avoid it. Our theatre must be aggressive and armed with plays that will inspire black people to see themselves as the vanguard of their destinies and the architects of a New Nation.

If America is ever to develop a conscience or morality, then it will have to come from the impulse of black writers. For it is only out of our experiences that America will ever see herself as she actually is: a whore dressed in bourgeois clothing. The experience of black Americans is the only authentic expression that can reveal to the world the deep rooted injustices which are manifest in this country. America has been able to mask its sickness to some extent by perpetuating a mythology that gives people false hopes and altruistic visions of a new society, while its present society endures a masochistic fate. But the Black Theatre cannot be a foil to America's conspiracy to keep its people floundering in a maze of ignorance and fairyland exposés. The legend of Superman and John Wayne ridicules our intelligence, and the conventionality of the TV industry and commercial movies insults our sensibility to distinguish myth from fact. Much work has to be done before the Black Theatre will be seen as a permanent institution of the black community. As an appendage of the Black Arts Movement, it has a large responsibility. It must provide the gravitation the movement needs to synthesize our music, dance, poetry, literature, and art, and make these forms into spiritual forces that come from the peoples' energy. It should be the voice that articulates every expression of the community, its soul/heart and unyielding vitality.

While the Black Arts Movement has, to a large extent, been successful in its appeal to young adults, especially students, I do have concern for its failure to develop functional programs for black children. The seeds of a viable esthetic must be planted during the formative years of a child's development, if the movement is to effectively serve future generations. Too many of our black children are still being subjected to white-oriented programs, such as Head Start, and then fed into school systems that are insensitive to their culture and which, instead, advocate institutional racism. Even though there is a discernable emergence of black awareness, many black children continue to suffer from inferior attitudes, stereotypic images, negative concepts, and the lack of appreciation/understanding of their historical and cultural origin.

The Black Arts Movement must begin to infiltrate the programs and curriculums of racist institutions and provide constructive alternatives which can move black children toward an early acceptance of their blackness. When this is not possible, which will be most of the time, we must create parallel structures to achieve this task. Baptism into the Black Arts should not be a latent reaction to white America's indoctrination, but a spontaneous orientation which starts when a child is first beginning to develop his sense of identity and scale of values. The revolution at this stage is primarily a psychological one. Being a war of the psyches, it behooves all black artists to begin transforming their art to this younger generation so that our children can begin to see black culture as a total ongoing process and not just as a fragmented vision. Our black children need to be exposed to a new set of models and purged of white-oriented models. Black artists must bury snow white/cinderella/mother goose/little red riding hood and yankee doodle dandy. They must, as James T. Stewart states, ". . . construct models which correspond to their reality." These new models should provide the child with a better understanding of himself, his community, family, and world. Our models must not only be shaped by the mythology and legacies of heroes, but also represent the daily deeds of "non-heroic" people. But equally important, we must begin to show our black youth their relationships with other black people throughout the world. For "blackness" is not confined to Black Americans, and until a youth is able to appreciate his blackness from a world perspective, then, I'm afraid, he will always have a limited appreciation of his culture. We have to do more than tell a youth that "Black Is Beautiful." We have to show him why . . . enable him to internalize its deepest meaning . . . see it in his everyday experiences.

I have attempted to list below some of the goals which I feel the Black Arts Movement must achieve if it is to be functional to the masses of black people. Of course, there are others for, as I've attempted to illustrate, the challenge that confronts the movement in the seventies demands that it accepts many responsibilities.

1. Establish multi-functional cultural institutions, whereby there can be cross-communication between artists, writers, photographers, dancers, and musicians.
2. Create cultural programs that are designed to raise the level of black awareness among our children.
3. Organize black movie companies that will produce films

which are representative of the black experience.

4. Encourage community groups to sponsor cultural activities such as writers' workshops, art fairs, festivals, community theatres, etc.
5. Establish our own (black) awards for achievement in the different fields of art.
6. Use the Black Arts in fund raising events to solicit funds for black organizations and political prisoners.
7. Develop a central communications center for the collection and distribution of information.
8. Create a major black publication company that can publish quantities of black literature and distribute them throughout the world.
9. Support the Black Studies movement by assuring black students that the resources they seek are available to them.
10. Build repertory theatres which can produce plays at a nominal fee which can be made accessible to the black community.
11. Publish an annual Cultural Directory that will reflect the movement on a national level.

The wave of black consciousness spreading throughout America is indeed gratifying to see. There can be seen in this revolutionary tide a profound sense of pride that is giving black people a positive image of themselves. But more important is the new-found strength that the pride is engendering. Again, I must reiterate the necessity for the movement to consciously support the revolutionary struggle. The art can remain legitimate only to the extent that it is relevant in helping liberate black people. Once it ceases to support this fight, the art becomes irrelevant and, therefore, subject to destruction. It requires a stern discipline on the artist's part to make his art functional to people . . . be real to real things . . . serve visible needs. He must, for his own survival, strip his psyche from personal idiosyncrasies which create the private man, and envision himself as an integral member of a family unit with common interests and goals. Black artists should be missionaries who are dedicated to helping black people move from a negative state of existence to a positive state of survival. Our art must embrace all dimensions of blackness, resurrecting those forms which have withered, and creating new modes of expression to withstand the future. The movement cannot be one to escalate the status of the artist but, instead, must transcend the lives of the people to free themselves from the bondage of white-imposed values.

In some cities Black Art is being viewed as a popular commodity and, as is true with American economics, one has to guard against the disease of capitalism contaminating our culture. Many white businesses have already begun to produce items, publish literature, and finance groups that purport to represent the movement. This exploitation of our art cannot continue. Black Art must be controlled by black people. Period. Unless we have complete authority over it, our art will always be vulnerable to commercial imitators and parasitic gluttons. The movement has to be sustained through our own energies, and not allowed to be manipulated by paternal-minded white "liberals" or pacifist government-funded programs. We need to be sophisticated enough to distinguish between those who may use the movement for personal gain and those whose involvement clearly shows an interest in the liberation of black people. We cannot, and should not, look to our oppressor (white America) to provide us with the resources that may, in the final analysis, be turned against him. White Americans may have masochistic tendencies, but I sharply question whether they have suicidal inclinations, too.

Our art can be kept relatively sovereign from subversion if we keep in mind its relationship to the Black Power Concept. For fundamental to this philosophy is the underlying strategy for closing ranks and making the maximum use of our own resources and power. This examination of omnipotence takes into consideration the political, social, and economic potential of our community to ascertain its multilateral ability to achieve self-control. As yet, this painstaking examination has not been fully undertaken and consequently our barometer for measuring total strength is, at best, speculative and pragmatic. However, until we tap these potential areas of strength, I'm afraid that it would be fatuous on our part to even think of coalescing with other groups. Our culture should be sacred to us and, as with anything inviolable, it must be protected as if our very lives depended upon it. Above all things, *the Black Arts Movement must be controlled by black people.* To allow any compromise would be to say that it really doesn't exist.

In his classic essay, "The New Negro," Alaine Locke speaks of the "new mentality" that many blacks personified during the turn of the century. He saw in this "Zionism" the dawn of an era where black people would begin to reaffirm their cultural heritage and escape the seemingly irrevocable world which, as W. E. Du Bois stated, "yields him no true self-consciousness." Locke's "New Negro" never quite achieved this realization of self. Instead, the black man continued to be a stepchild of white America, wandering through a hostile society that refused to accept the black experience as being able to nourish a viable esthetic. But our experience and esthetics are one, and it has been due to our failure to recognize this correlation that we have failed to accept ourselves. The new Black Arts must understand this relationship and be able to synthesize the art with our experience, thereby making the art a true reflection of our life.

The Black Arts Movement cannot be expected to remedy all of the problems confronting black people. It cannot fill the stomach of a starving child nor comfort the pain of a brother whose head has been battered by a policeman's club. However, it can help to provide us with a meaningful cultural foundation that can, hopefully, harmonize the differences which exist among black people. The sharing of a common culture invariably helps to make groups aware of certain kinship bonds which can take priority over their variance of ideology. And if the Black Arts Movement is capable of meeting this challenge, it will have helped us to overcome a major obstacle that impedes unity. For if there is ever to be a "fighting revolution," one can be absolutely sure that the energy of every black person will be sorely needed. The movement must help to prepare the people psychologically for this confrontation. Unless it can do this, it has no real purpose for existing, other than to prepare black people to accept death with a false sense of pride and dignity.

NOTE

1.   In his book *Black Skin White Masks* Frantz Fanon describes the psychological strategy employed by the French colonial army to indoctrinate the "Negro of the Antilles" with the culture/language of the oppressors, thereby making the culture of the Antilles the subordinate means of achieving success. Likewise, black Americans have adopted the culture espoused by white Americans to achieve greater economic and social mobility.

The black seventies demand a national black political party that will help mold the future of all black people struggling against oppressive forces. This party will make black people identify with the whole Pan-African world, not only culturally, but politically.

S. E. ANDERSON *was born in the Bedford-Stuyvesant district of Brooklyn, New York. He is co-editor of* Black Dialogue, New African, *and* Mojo, *and is on the advisory board of Drum and Spear Press. His work has appeared in various anthologies, among them* Black World, Black Fire, *and the* Journal of Black Poetry. *Presently a teacher of mathematics, Anderson plans to co-author a black mathematics teacher's manual for use at all educational levels. Also planned are film versions of two of his short stories.*

S. E. Anderson

Revolutionary Black Nationalism and the Pan-African Idea

Fear not the number and education of our enemies, against whom we shall have to contend for our lawful right . . . let no man of us budge one step, and let slave-holders come to beat us from our country. America is more our country, than it is the whites—we have enriched it with our blood and tears.   Bro. David Walker, 1829

Ever since the first slaves were forced upon the American shores the Black Liberation Movement has embraced at least six different goals. In the past, the styles and rhetoric have been noticeably different for each goal. Today there are dangerous similarities in style and rhetoric between those who seek incorrect goals (accommodationists-withdrawers) and those who seek the correct one (revolutionary).

At this pre-revolutionary juncture, as we commence the seventies it is vitally imperative for black people to be informed about our fragmented and stagnant Movement. What is attempted here is: 1) a contribution to black critical analysis of the five major factions within the Black Liberation Movement; and 2) a contribution to Revolutionary Black Nationalism as a struggle toward Pan-Africanism.

1. The Integrationist   Historically the Integrationist has incorrectly viewed the American institutions as racist by exception rather than by rule. The Integrationist believes in the deception of the American governmental structure as having provisions for black redress of grievances. He also believes that he can actually participate in the decision-making processes of "his" country, but for a few racist and economic barriers black people have been denied their full "first-class" share of the capitalistic goodies. The Integrationist sincerely believes that we have "progressed" through moral suasion via civil rights legislation. In most cases he accepts black culture as a somewhat lesser tributary culture of the perverse white American cultural mainstream.

Most Integrationists do not see America as a powerful but degenerating world imperialist. And those Integrationists who do perceive America as such feel that injecting blackfolk into the existing American framework will cool out the degeneracy. It is clear that Integrationists do not fathom the fact that when power corrupts it corrupts absolutely. The Integrationist believes in the minority-concept: America is at once a melting-pot and a pluralistic society. This belief hides the most rampant and fundamental problem: racism.

It is extremely important to take note of the Integrationist's religious acceptance of capitalism being the best (most humanistic) politico-economic form. To them, all capitalism needs to fulfill the American Dream is some black reform.

In the final analysis, the Integrationist suicidally depends upon white analysis and white assertions to determine black people's destiny. He views self-determination as solving the bourgeois desires of materialism and immoralism: to have the money to choose an El Dorado over a Continental; to be able to determine without guilt which white bitch should have her racial myths fulfilled. Because the Integrationist mimics white America to the "T" his interests are selfish, corrupt, and diametrically opposed to the liberation of blackfolk.

2. The City-Statesman There are similarities between the Integrationist and the City-Statesman with regard to their reactionary attitude to every white American assertion. One segment of the City-Statesman group envisions the American politico-economic structure as legitimate and thus seek to enter it by initially withdrawing and building the blackening cities into politically and economically powerful quasi-autonomous city-states destined to vie for influence and "control" of white America's capital and resources. The other segment believes that black cities can be simultaneously autonomous of the American politico-economic structure and exist within it as communal (non-capitalistic) city-states.

What City-Statesmen cannot or refuse to believe is that white America will allow a pluralistic society only on *its* terms with respect to how the white society will be benefited. Yes, white America will "give up" her cities to blacks—and move all of its important institutions (industry, communications, banks, airports, etc.) into the suburbs. The black city-states would be surrounded by white police and military, forever on the edge of their triggers. Most of the city-state's capital would be funnelled in through federal aid. This would mean that the U.S. Government would have the first and last say about how and when to spend; who should work and should not. Dig it: just like they do now.

Many City-Statesmen believe that these neo-colonial islands of black people surrounded by the hostile sea of white America physically constitute a black nation. They fail to realize that to have a nation is to have land and control of human and natural resources, to have a defense system, and to have a culture defined and common among the people. The "nationalism" of the City-Statesman serves merely as an aid for white America to maintain black people as colonial subjects. More precisely, colonies have the façade of being independent if the colonized bourgeoisie are the administrators and civil servants. The immediate authority is loyalist black, and the ultimate authority is the white colonizer. We need only to witness the struggle for community control of schools in the black community. The Government will allow community control—as long as it determines the framework, philosophy, hiring policies, and finances.

Currently, there are two major political proposals being discussed among the City-Statesmen. One is to deal politically through the Democratic and Republican parties as militant black blocs; the other is to form a third political party: some say all black and others say a black/radical white coalition party, viz. the Peace and Freedom Party. The basic premise of these parties is that America's discriminatory policies can be changed through voting, that by casting millions of black votes for black and/or white liberal candidates blackfolk will have "equality" with white people. The blacks who seek changes through these two proposals fail to understand the following: a) one of the fundamental reasons why political parties become viable parties within the American context is that they are founded upon racist assumptions; and b) the limitations of black political parties within this context because of a lack of an alliance with the military-industrial complex. For it is primarily because the Democratic and Republican parties are *institutional* extensions of the military-industrial complex that they are existing. A black political party cannot align with any type of white military or economic institution, unless it is a political party of suicidal blacks. We must never forget that it is the nature of every white institution—be it radical, liberal, or conservative—to be racist and therefore exploitative to blackfolk.

3. The Black Panther Party   To many brothers and sisters the idea of placing the white radical in the same bag with a Nixon, Wallace, or a Mayor Daley appears to be in itself paranoid *and* racist. But if we look at the history of white radicalism in America, Europe, Russia, and elsewhere, the concept of white radicals-as-racists becomes the correct concept of caution and fervor for self-determination. When Brother James Forman says: ". . . that white people in this country must be willing to accept black leadership, for that is the only protection that black people have to protect ourselves from racism rising . . . in this country . . . ,"[1] he is not coming out of a racist or paranoid bag. He is basing our present and future positions upon the actions and attitudes of white radicals down through history. Brother Jim knows of white radical racism from experiencing the agonies and frustrations of whites in SNCC. He has read about and spoken to many brothers and sisters who were deep into the Communist Party thing (with all of its factional offshoots). If we are serious about Black Liberation and Black Revolution, then the writings about the struggles with white radicals in the Communist Movement by George Padmore *(Pan-Africanism or Communism?)*, W. E. B.

Du Bois, Richard Wright, and Harold Cruse are writings of historical and political necessity. The brothers revealed the insidious and racist arrogance of radical whites in the constant and often fanatical attacks upon the strong nationalist urges within many blacks of the nineteenth and twentieth centuries. We may find many of our anti-Communist Party brothers' nationalist ideology contradictory, but fundamental in all was (and is) the desire for Black Self-Determination; for blackfolk to create their own culture and to experience their own achievements and mistakes.

And if we still have doubts about the history of racism in the White radical movement we can go back to the early days of Frederick Douglass, Gabriel Prosser, David Walker, or Monroe Trotter and witness the stifling actions of the nineteenth century white radical/liberal abolitionists. They only wanted the brothers to be entertainingly descriptive about the horrors of the slave experience. Despite their desire to be political, each "free slave" was told to remain entertaining, "exotic contraband" niggers if they wanted the company and assistance of these "dedicated and determined" white abolitionists. Hence, brothers and sisters broke away and attempted to determine their own political and anti-slavery destiny. Or we could go back to the late eighteenth century and witness the mealy-mouthed quibbling of the French "radicals" and their paternalistic and exploitive attitude toward Toussaint L'Ouverture and the Haitian Revolution.[2] It is through the reading of the history of white radicalism and, whenever possible, through a brother's or a sister's personal struggle-relationship with ofay radicals, that one can confidently conclude that because of the many pyscho-social complexities of white racism the white radical, for the most part, has asserted himself as being superior to the black man. (See *White Racism: A Psychohistory*, by J. Kovel [Pantheon Books, 1970]. It is an excellent psychohistorical account of the development, personification, and institutionalization of white racism.)

The bombings that are occurring against some of the major racist-imperialist companies have been initiated by the anarchistic "Weatherman" faction of SDS—or some such similar white desperately radical group. The bombings are not only premature, they are in fact arrogantly racist. The white radicals who are performing these acts of revolution-for-the-hell-of-it have not politicized the black and Puerto Rican worker (who are usually the night custodians) prior to the bombings about *why* these buildings symbolize racism and imperalism. Moreover, it is paternalistic to act *in advance* of the most oppressed because it directly reinforces some black militants' dependency upon whites defining our struggle. White liberal/radicals have historically taken this position because their culture deems racist paternalism to be their role and hence their nature in white American society.

On another level, it was a racist act for SDS (Students for a Democratic Society)—a white radical organization—to announce to the world that *they* have chosen and sanctioned the Black Panther Party as *the correct* organization for black people. For what has resulted is a most detrimental contribution to our Black Liberation struggle. Because the Panthers lack a black ideology having its foundation firmly implanted in the fertile soil of the history of Black Nationalism, the evolution of a creative Black Culture, and the comprehension of the racist ramifications of the ofay left, right and middle, and because of the Panther Party's religious dependence upon a white analysis (1935 Marxism-Leninism Yippyized) we discover that a part of American history is repeating itself *for the benefit of whites.* Once again we see the pale, deaf, and blind head of that old and decrepit Communist Party of the 1920's, 30's and 40's. It perceived blackfolk as mere tools/weapons against the evil machine of U.S. Capitalism and Imperialism. We were the hammer and the sickle striking blows for the liberation of the (white racist) workers, peasant, farmers, lumpen-proletariat, reaping the Harvest of Marxism-Leninism! Such splendid rhetoric . . . such racist deeds. This time, the Communist Party returns to haunt and mislead Black America through the *potentially* most vital and progressive black organization since the days of Garvey: the Black Panther Party. The legitimization of Georgi Dimitriov (a Polish dude famous for his anti-Nazi coalition structure at the August 1935 Commitern) emanates from the Panther's white lawyer, Charles Garry, Bro. Eldridge Cleaver, and an old Afro-American Communist, William Patterson.

The Black Panther Party as formed in San Francisco is primarily activist oriented. There was, and still is, much conflict between the Panthers, "cultural nationalists," and many black intellectuals. In order to understand this most important but extremely misdirected black organization, it is necessary to trace briefly the history of the Black Panther Party.

In the fall of 1965 SNCC was struggling with certain nationalist ideas: a) becoming an all black organization, b) instituting black cultural concepts within the Southern movement, c) setting up all black co-operatives, and d) forming an all black political party. Thus, SNCC began to pull away from a purely activist-integrationist and white-analysis-bound position and move in the direction of becoming an activist-intellectual organization whose tendencies were toward Revolutionary Black Nationalism. The formation of the Lowndes County Freedom Organization (Alabama) became one of the most crucial moments in the current history of the Black Liberation Struggle. For it was in Lowndes County, Alabama that we saw the political power and psychological encouragement that black people are able to create. By the Summer of 1966 SNCC had successfully registered more blackfolk in Lowndes county than ever before. Their diligent and courageous work impressed and inspired some nationalist followers of Brother Malcolm X to start forming more Black Panther Parties (the Black Panther was the symbol of the Lowndes County Freedom Organization). Harlem was the base of the second Black Panther Party during the summer and fall of 1966. Its very active and inspirational life was short-lived, primarily because of agents provocateur and the lack of funds.

In the latter part of the same summer, a few west coast brothers began corresponding with the Lowndes County Black Panther Party and the Harlem Black Panther Party. What resulted was the Northern California Black Panther Party. Inside and outside this organization were two warring groups generally broken down into "street brothers" and "college or intellectual brothers." At the same time, Oakland, California had its Community Alert Patrol which followed the police to check out jive arrests and brutality. Some of the "street brothers" and C.A.P. brothers bogarted the Northern California Panther Party out of existence, and Huey Newton, Bobby Seale, Bobby Hutton, etc. formed the Black Panther Party for Self-Defense. The group's style and militancy

attracted many brothers and sisters in the Bay area. The Party began publishing *The Black Panther*, the party paper. In it they
published their total community control and anti-draft program.
The Party gained national prominence when they stormed Sacra-
mento's "sacred" political halls bearing arms in an attempt to support the "Right To Bear Arms" Law.

Ever since then police harassment has increased a million-fold!
A significant turning point was when Bro. Huey Newton had the
alleged shoot-out with some Bay Area cops. He was thrown in
jail and the cry went out for money. For a multitude of reasons,
good and bad, many non-Panther nationalist brothers did not
respond as enthusiastically and with as much money as the SDS-
types and the Communist Party did. "Free Huey" was psychologically easier for whites to say than "Black Power!" And with
Eldridge Cleaver being influential within the Party, the atmosphere became more and more receptive to white radical "aid."
This was 1967-68 and *Soul On Ice* (which exposed Bro. Cleaver's
inconsistencies about white women and white radicals) was a
skyrocketing best-seller. Hence, the floodgates opened and a
myriad of weird radical/liberals gave "assistance" to the Panthers, "assistance" in the form of money-linked-with-white-ide-
ology The Panthers began to say: We're looking for *people* who
are willing to work. So they declared the non-Panther nationalists
"porkchop" nationalists, "cultural" nationalists, and racists and,
to top it off, were incapable of getting themselves "together."
The so-called "mother country radical" became more important
than the conversion of a cultural or porkchop nationalist. As more
and more blacks began to read the Panther newspaper jingoistic
dialogue blossomed between the Panther brothers and SDS-types.
Thus, *The Black Panther* became merely an extension of SDS's
Movement newspaper and *Ramparts* magazine, and the Communist Party's ancient and nonfunctional line. Therefore, the
Panther Party no longer catered to the Black Community. The
Breakfast for Children Program and free medical service implemented in a number of black communities were the only attempts
at establishing a black base of support through political and social
work. Because there has been no other major community organizing by the Black Panther Party, its leadership can be cut

down and its only retaliatory acts can be rhetorical cries of constitutional rights and fascism.

More specifically, to push the anti-fascist line of the 1935 Commitern only exposes the Panther's reliance upon the old Communist babblings of William Patterson, Charles Garry, etc. It is a fact that White America acts in a fascist manner towards black people. American-style fascism is a manifestation of American-style racism: the larger, more dangerous aspect of the American Reality. It is that part of the American Reality that is beyond the traditional Marxist-Leninist analysis of social change. That is to say, neither Marx nor Lenin adequately knew or utilized the fact that Europeans and Americans had racist attitudes toward Black and Bandung (Third World) peoples (even *before* they went to Africa and Asia for slaves and exploitation! [3]). Thus, to completely transpose the 1935 anti-fascist statement of Georgi Dimitriov is to:

a. believe that White America's oppression of Blacks is the same as Nazi Germany's oppression of the Jews;

b. assume that Black people lack the ability to develop an analysis from their own unique experience, i.e. assumption that a white analysis is better than a black analysis;

c. believe that blackfolk are going to accept the sterile cultural style of a "scientific" and "objective" Marxist-Leninist;

d. believe that white radicals are at this time capable of overcoming their complex racial, social and psycho-sexual hangups.

The Man is unrelentingly clamping down on the Panther brothers across America. Whites see the revolutionary potential of a black political organization like the Black Panther Party. But they also see its small black community support. For the FBI and various local police departments have been briefed to the fact that the most opportune time to suppress a black political organization is when the majority of black people either oppose it, feel indifferent about it or feel too helpless to support it. And the scatterbrainism of the white radicals will only accelerate the tragic death of the Panthers. What is more important is that the concept of a Black Political party will not die.

4. Back to Africa-ism This sect splits itself into two general factions: 1) the brothers and sisters who want only to return to Africa physically and 2) the brothers and sisters who want only to return to Africa spiritually, culturally, and socially. From a superficial standpoint the two ideas sound good. But upon a deeper analysis we discover that they are not good ideas; rather, they are symptoms of withdrawal.

The Afro-American who wishes for a permanent mass migration of blackfolk, or even a permanent migration of intellectuals and technicians to Africa is one who consciously or unconsciously affirms the myth of the invincible white man. In most cases it is the intellectual rationalization of a brother's or a sister's inability to struggle on a day-to-day basis against the oppressive forces. Hence, some suggest that we return to Africa and *lead* Africa toward a colonial-free destiny. How does the repatriatist know that our African brothers want us to lead them anywhere? Our African brothers are having enough hard times struggling against their internal and neo-colonial contradictions to cope with the psycho-cultural hangups of Afro-Americans. This is to say that we *do not* abandon our communication, our military, economic, and cultural exchange. Rather it is to accentuate *at this stage* the necessity for a two-way exchange of individuals rather than a one-way mass migration.

We cannot escape the racism and colonialism of America by "running" to Africa because America's racism and colonialism is institutionalized everywhere. Moreover, if most of our revolutionary forces were in Africa we would be committing a cardinal sin: withdrawing one's forces from the belly and brain of the enemy. It should be made very clear that this does not mean brothers should go over and join the African Liberation Armies. It means those chosen Afro-American brothers who do go should not only be highly skilled in guerrilla warfare, but also skilled in some field relevant to the social and economic needs of the African country for which they are fighting.

On the other side of the Back-to-Africa mask we are confronted with the apolitical cultural nationalists. They stress that if black people just dig on the natural fact that black is beautiful and ancient then they will be liberated. The apolitical cultural nationalists fail to check out the neo-colonies of Africa: Nigeria, Ghana, Senegal, Niger, Liberia, Malawi, etc. In these countries blackfolk, by and large, still see blackness as beautiful (and this too is rapidly disintergrating), but it has not liberated them. They do not control their resources, their capital, or their politics. Witness all the military coups, Americo-European industries and military aid. Despite the arrogant imposition of white culture, African culture is shakily intact and sporadically creative, but without a *political* framework African culture is not a liberatory force . . . and it too will die. The root of the matter is that Afro-American apolitical cultural nationalists perceive blackness as a necessary *and* sufficient liberating factor; when, in reality, blackness is a necessary factor but not a sufficient one.

On the psycho-cultural level, apolitical cultural nationalism is a reaction and a withdrawal rather than an assertion. Once again we see that it is a negative spiral inward because of the belief in the myth of the white man's invincibility. It is also a desire to prove to one's ego and to the white man that a black man is, in fact, creative. Out of this frustration of contradictions sprout black cults and mysticism: i.e., withdrawal symptoms. The Black Artist becomes more of a nihilist than a creative person. He perceives blackfolk as his burden instead of his inspiration. The center of the universe becomes an overglorification of his ego, African History, and, paradoxically, the black masses. Through constructive criticism (which is sorely lacking in the Black Cultural realm) within the existence of a correct ideology, many of the straight-up-and-down cultural brothers and sisters will be able to redirect their creativity and become functional people embraced by a revolutionary political structure.

5. Black Nation Concept   Imbedded in the rationale of most blacks seeking a New Black Nation are withdrawal symptoms resembling those of the Back-To-Africa brothers and sisters. The Black Nation Concept does not and cannot deal with the fact that black people built America with their enchained sweat, blood, and brains. America is ours for the Take. Withdrawing from America does not weaken or eradicate its global, racist-capitalist stranglehold. To the contrary, America is strengthened and offered an almost perfect political and military framework for black genocide. White America would view the New Black Nation, be it Islamic or otherwise, as a black communist threat. More concretely, the brothers and sisters who believe in the New Black Nation concept feel that it is impossible to liberate black people within the awesomely powerful confines of white America.

One of the most blatant contradictions is that of white people being willing to pay for the birth of a Black Nation at their doorstep. On the one hand the New Nation Separatists vividly describe America as being (by nature) a racist country that has systematically excluded blacks from all its institutional processes. Indeed this is true. Then by what twist of fate would white racist America wish to *aid* in the development of a Black nation? . . . unless exploitation and genocide was in thought.

Many of the New Nation Separatists suggest that scattered black-controlled areas constitute a nation. This contradiction was discussed above. A Federation of cities as a nation is stressed rather than the evolutionary development of Revolutionary Nationalism among black people. Many discuss the idea of getting electoral control of the cities and the Black Belt, then inviting the United Nations as world observer while white America, because of international law, allows five or six southern states to secede from the union.

History has exposed the United Nations as anything but humanistic and neutral. History has shown the United Nations and its international laws as mere tools of America and its Western allies for the maintenance of their imperialistic machine. Witness the U.S.'s breach of the Geneva Convention's decision concerning Vietnam. Witness the Arab-Israeli conflict. Witness the U.S.'s instantaneous intervention into the Dominican Republic in 1965. Witness the Congo intervention by the UN and U.S., but only U.S. capitalistic aid to South Africa. It is crystal clear that the United Nation's international laws deal with nonwhites exactly in the same manner as do America's constitutional laws: as colonial subjects.

The Republic of New Africa appoints Brother Robert F. Williams as President. Bro. Williams is a romantic revolutionary partially of his own making and partially because he has not been continuously on the American scene, having been a brother in exile for eight years. One should take note of the other governments-in-exile such as the tiny anti-Communist island of Formosa (Taiwan) and the counter-revolutionary CIA-guided "Revolutionary Angolan Government In Exile." When the so-called leaders or groups are not physically and spiritually in touch with their people, they fall prey to romanticism and co-optation.

When the New Nation Concept fails to understand the relationship between military strategy and geography we witness a pathetic and self-defeating contradiction. The Republic of New Africa is to be created from the southern states east of Texas and north of Florida! Strategically, Florida would become an ideal American military base of operations. The New Republic of Africa would have to spread its military forces to defend three land borders and two sea borders.

Even more important is that the New Black Nation concept fails to realize that white America can economically do without black people. Its world-wide racist-imperialist control would not be weakened. In fact, no matter how many blackfolk separate, our jobs—meager as they may be—could be taken over by unemployed whites and/or automation. And the global exploitation could proceed more efficiently; meaning that the colored peoples (including the separate Black Nation) would have to fight against a more efficient and technologically advanced Beast.

In brief, the New Nation Concept is the pipedream of black nationalists frustratedly overwhelmed because of their simplistic analysis of white racism and colonialism.

Revolutionary Black Nationalism and The Pan-African Idea

Brother Bill Strickland (a faculty member of the Institute of the Black World, Atlanta, Ga.) constantly reiterates that in the twentieth century there has been no critique of the American Society vis-à-vis the Black Reality. As seen above in the five fragments of the Afro-American Movement, there have only been *reactions* to the racist-capitalist system and not a development of a counter-system. Why? Because black intellectuals and activists, for the most part, accept white analysis and assumptions as the correct analysis and assumptions. Throughout history this has resulted in black people taking on the ways of assimilationists and withdrawers rather than resisters. This is not to deny the historical fact of daily slave rebellions or the current urban uprisings. It is merely to emphasize that our rebellious acts have been apolitical and often vacuous because of a lack of a black critique of the American scene.

A further negative consequence of blacks' dependency upon white analysis is the *legitimacy of corruptness* within the Black Movement. Because whites are corrupt and immoral, their "liberal/radical" analysis and actions are corrupt and immoral. The Movement's corruption is just the symptom, the flame. One of the root causes or fuels is the absence of a well-defined Black Ideology. Serious black terminology is loosely thrown around by integrationists, separatists, and psuedo-revolutionaries (the black fascists) alike. A do-your-own-thing (individualism) atmosphere surrounding the Movement makes it valid for accommodationists like Whitney Young and his Urban League Colleagues to support "Black Power." It makes it valid for an opportunist such as Roy Innis to "negotiate" with the colonial powers for the sake of "black self-determination" and black "economic (capitalistic) power." The rootlessness of the terminology invites a myriad of weird and immoral people and agent provocateurs to satisfy their twisted and often anti-black lusts.

In essence, if we are truly about the business of liberating Black People throughout the Pan-African world, then we must seek the correct path toward Revolution, that is, the path of Revolutionary Nationalism and Pan-Africanism. More precisely, we must seek change; change in institutions, change of who is in charge, change in values. Then we must be able to implement and enforce these changes. *In other words, America as it exists today must be completely destroyed and then rebuilt in terms of the New Black Man, for whites have rendered themselves incapable of humanistic creativity.* Hence, black people must struggle for total control of America. The methodology that will follow calls for Revolutionary Black Nationalism to be comprised of reformist stages, dialogues aimed to change negroes into blacks, education, developing and institutionalizing our culture, life-long commitment and consistent criticism of self and ideology, and, most important, winning the confidence of black people.

It will be shown that through Revolutionary Black Nationalism a tightly defined terminology of Black Ideology and Morality will develop. Its existence would transpose every act, including the sexual act, into an ethical *and* political act. Revolutionary Black Nationalism will not be entrenched in rigidity. It will *naturally* mean the coexistence of firmness and flexibility as is exemplified in the revolutionary struggles of the Vietnamese, Guinea-Bissau, and Angolan brothers and sisters.

Some Aspects of Revolutionary Black Nationalism

One of the most fundamental assertions of Revolutionary Black Nationalism is that white people and their institutions are *irreversibly incapable* of fulfilling the needs of black people specifically and Bandung (Third World) people in general. This situation exists due to an almost hereditary racist-imperialistic mentality plaguing the white race. Hence, Revolutionary Black Nationalism asserts that Black America should have no political, economic, cultural, or psychological allegiance to White America. Rather, Black America should move to control America, not from a minority standpoint but from being an important strategical component of the anti-racist/imperialistic global struggle.

As a political alternative, blackfolk should develop physical, economic, psychological, and cultural allegiance to: 1) Black America, 2) the Pan-African World, and 3) the Bandung Peoples. Clearly not a blind allegiance, but an allegiance along progressive, anti-capitalist, anti-racist, and humanistic lines. Moreover, for this allegiance to materialize black people must have a thorough understanding of the psychological profundity of white racism within us. Before we can control a country as vast and complex as America, we must be capable of controlling our communities. And indeed, before we can control our communities we must be able to control our families *and* ourselves: the segment of our existence where we are most vulnerable to the bestiality of white racism.

It is of major importance with Revolutionary Black Nationalism for black people to realize that it was, more than anyone else, our African forefathers who built the Americas into what they are today. If it was not for the millions of Africans slaving for over 350 years white Americans today would just be reaching the Rockies—if the "Indians" hadn't dealt with them first! It is clear that we have moral and spiritual obligations to our enslaved African forefathers and to our genocidally depleted "Indian" brothers. Both courageously and consistently resisted the European's technologically superior military and racist onslaughts.

Thus, Revolutionary Black Nationalism views Afro-Americans as needing to begin to institutionalize our cultural and therefore political similarities with the rest of the Pan-African world so that the brother or sister on the streets of Bahia, Brazil, or Ponce, Puerto Rico is able to identify not only culturally with the brother or sister from the streets of Harlem or Nairobi, Kenya, but also to identify *politically*.

What facilitates the inception of institutionalized and internationalized politico-cultural relationships is black people being aware of the need to develop an anti-capitalistic/anti-materialist Spirit. More precisely, it is initially through restructuring the family and community control struggles around all things necessary for our survival (urban and rural) by which we can instill the cooperative and communal Spirit.

Let us not forget that history has shown that generations build a people's revolutionary movement. Because our movement is no different in this regard and because Black Americans have to struggle against the highest form of white racism and capitalism, *our struggle will not be an instantaneous phenomenon.* Perhaps it will be our children's children who will see the fruits of *our* revolutionary seeds. Further, in order to insure a generation-to-generation consistency, and, therefore, a day-to-day commitment to the Revolution, it is necessary to build from a united front of progressive black forces a national black political party. In the beginning, the party would be organized around such reformist goals as community control of the schools and police, black mayors in predominantly black cities, building independent black educational and economic cooperatives, etc. Clearly, the essential thrust of the political party would be to mold the tradition of black people striving for humanistic control of America.

Inseparable from this is the Revolutionary Black Nationalist's need for *limited* use of Negro and white colleges' facilities in a manner similar to the Vietnamese or Angolan's use of the French or American universities: 1) to gather useful political, technical, and military information about the enemy; 2) to make contact with brothers from other liberation struggles; and 3) to gain those technical and military skills of the oppressor that are applicable to our struggle.

It is understood by the Revolutionary Black Nationalist that forming a national black political organization, building politico-cultural and physical bonds in the Pan-African World, and creating independent black institutions that actually meet the needs of blackfolk are, in the eyes of white America, violent and seditious acts. Naturally, white America would try to find ways of destroying our liberation struggle on all levels. We must, therefore, not only be on the defensive, we must take to the offensive whenever the time is strategically, politically, and psychologically ripe. And it will be at this crucial juncture that one could conceivably suggest:

> . . . For the purposes of a black revolutionary strategy, the political subdivisions of California, Alabama, Mississippi, Midwest, and Southwest have no meaning. We must define areas and institutions according to the amount of control that we exercise over them. The new division would be into three areas: liberated areas, areas totally under enemy control, and contested areas.
>
> *Liberated Areas* are areas which we control. These areas constitute our experimental social laboratories in which we would produce politically conscious and socially responsible human beings. These liberated areas would also form the base from which continued struggle would be launched.
>
> *Areas totally under enemy control* are areas in which the land and all institutions would be controlled by the enemy (the United States government and its lackeys).

Contested Areas are areas in which we would carry on a reasonably high-level struggle, for example, the educational system.[4]

Innovative strategies and tactics of revolutionary violence would also be needed. More specifically, the sophisticated uses of violence would include terrorism and other forms of psychological, and possibly bio-chemical, warfare wedded with urban and rural guerrilla actions *primarily* developed through our struggle and secondarily through our thorough analysis of similar struggles. Whenever the Black Liberation Movement needs to rely upon revolutionary violence, we must always be consciously aware that: *revolutionary violence may be a necessary means but not a sufficient one.*

The Vietnam war is providing the Black Liberation struggle with more than 100,000 potential revolutionaries. In Vietnam, blacks confront the daily racism and physical affronts of the True American White and come away with more black allegiance and understanding of the whiteman than ever before (see "Black Veterans Return," by James Fendrich and Michael Pearson in *Transaction* magazine, Vol. 7, No. 5 [March, 1970], pp. 32-37). Combine this basic nationalist sentiment with their combative and technical skills of contemporary warfare, and we immediately can see these returning brothers (and sisters) as one of our most cohesive, vital, and powerful forces. What is needed in the initial stages is an organization that not only secures jobs and/or educational opportunities (as the National Urban League is attempting) but also educates politically. In the initial stages it might be necessary to call for a Black Veterans' conference to discuss their needs and the mechanics of how to institutionalize and politicize the Black Vets' experiences and skills. At a later stage some veterans might aid in the training and fighting in the liberation struggles in African and the Caribbean (and Black America, too!). These warriors will understand that the politics of our struggle and the allegiance to black people must at all times govern the military strategies and tactics. It must be constantly stressed that to be a warrior is not only to be for the life of your people, but to be for Life itself; and that violence is used against the enemy only when the political and psychological need calls for it.

In its attempt to be a comprehensive and provisional governmental concept Revolutionary Black Nationalism calls for, in the twentieth and twenty-first centuries, advanced forms of communications. Brothers and sisters will find it expedient to have expertise in long and shortwave radio technology, scramble-phones, television, cinematic and laser communications, the printed media and, yes, even telekinetics and telepathy.[5] One can readily see that it is extremely important to constantly emphasize to our youth the need to enter the scientific and technical fields. Due to America's ecological crisis it is also vital that we have black scientists. Because of the waste and greed of a technologically advanced capitalist society, Nature suffers. And, therefore, so does Man. When America will truly become a Black Nation, we do not want to give our children's children a nation whose earth, air, and animals are poisoned with the Frankenstein byproducts of an advanced anti-human and capitalist structure. Indeed, *we have to create a tradition of Revolutionary Black scientists and technicians with the same spirit and vigor in which we create a tradition of Revolutionary Black Warriors.*

Another aspect of Revolutionary Black Nationalism is the establishment of a New Morality or Ethics and, hence, a *New Black Man.* Brother Danny Aldridge clearly and accurately defines the New Black Man:

> . . . First of all, the new man is completely devoid of all vestiges of selfishness, individuality, egotism, and "me-firstness."
> Second, he is a man with every possibility of individual development whose energy and work lead him to tasks for the benefit of the collective.
> Third, the struggle against injustice constitutes the basis of his morality. The basis of the new man's morality is his willingness and aggressiveness to struggle against injustice no matter where he finds it. His human sensibilities have been developed to the point where he can deal efficiently with everyday problems. His social sensibilities have been

developed to the point where he is willing to struggle against the exploitation of man by man and the division of society into classes.

Fourth, the new man is a fighter. The two aspects of his emerging personality that make him a fighter are:

(a) The will and determination to struggle. The new man is not the kind of faggot-like, gutless wonder who runs around talking about what he is going to do. He is ready to mobilize and to organize. He builds himself up daily both intellectually and physically to prepare to struggle. He understands what struggle is and he is not afraid.

(b) The development of a human conscience and intelligence. The new man is willing to fight to the the death and never gives up in the daily political struggle. He is willing to work every single day to make each day a revolutionary work-day.

Fifth, the new man is a rebellious, heroic, and studious creature. He studies and studies and is continuously analyzing problems and seeking their solutions. He is highly disciplined and socially responsible. He understands that the revolution has all rights: the right to exist; the right to advance; the right to triumph. He understands also that for him there are no rights other than those of the revolution.[6]

Further, let us not forget that sisters are also intricately a part of the struggle on *all* levels. Sisters should be respected for what they can intellectually and physically offer to the Black Revolution—not *solely* for what they can offer a brother in bed or in the kitchen. History has shown us that a sister can indeed be physically part of a struggle and still retain her femininity and motherly ways. Witness Harriet Tubman, Gabriel's woman, Mozambique, Zimbabwe, Algeria, Vietnam. . . .

There have been a number of territories that have been genocidally seized by whites which should rightfully be returned to their original settlers. Revolutionary Black Nationalism calls for the support of and alliance with the revolutionary "Indians," Puerto Ricans, and Mexicans who are struggling to gain control over *their* land once again.

Finally, if there exist revolutionary whites, their revolutionary qualities will be defined by the political struggle they wage within the white masses. And it must only be on this basis that we can consider them our allies, being guided by *our* dictates.

The Origins of the Pan-African Idea

For us to perceive clearly how Revolutionary Black Nationalism directly ties in with the Pan-African Idea we need to understand that both of these concepts are not products of the 1960's, or even the 1860's. The roots of Revolutionary Afro-American Nationalism and Pan-Africanism run deep. They run back to the first shackled African pushed onto a European slaveship. They run back to the millions of brothers and sisters who decided that *Freedom* was a salty death of the Middle Passage. They run back to the eighteenth and nineteenth centuries when Toussaint L'Ouverture and Dessaline seized Haiti from the French; back to David Walker and his inciteful words: ". . . America is more our country than it is the whites; we have enriched it with our *blood and tears"*; back to the Nats and Gabriels and Veseys; the John S. Rocks and Henry Highland Garnetts and Paul Cuffees. . . . Yes. We must study more of our history of how our African forefathers refused/resisted contributing to the development of white America and Europe.

Bro. Martin R. Delaney looked for the colonization of blacks in Canada, the Caribbean, and South America. Ultimately (in 1860) he decided upon the motherland. Bro. Delaney's goal was to establish a strategic base from which blackfolk could launch a counter-offensive against the white slave traders.

Edward Blyden went to Africa in the latter part of the nineteenth century, initially to bring the philosophy and culture of Western "civilization," only to later discover that much of what Western "civilization" was about was a bastardized form of African Civilizations and their achievements. He was going to christianize the "savage heathens" but instead discovered that Christianity was heathenized. Bro. Blyden consequently saw Islam as a religion and a way of life more functional to the Black Man. Bro. Blyden was instrumental in the development of Black Pride and African National solidarity.

Initially in heated opposition to each other, Marcus Garvey and W. E. B. Du Bois in the early part of the twentieth century grew closer together in their ideological beliefs vis-à-vis Africa and Afro-Americans. Garvey fostered a type of "cultural" nationalism along with a form of Black Capitalism (more as a reaction to the racism of the Communist Party). In the 1920's Garvey had no faith in the American system, whereas Du Bois had some faith in it. In the 1920's Garvey saw Africa as the world's most potential empire with Afro-Americans as its main strategists and technicians. Du Bois saw potential political power in Africa, but did not view it as a black empire being primarily controlled by Black Americans. From the 1940's onward Du Bois spent the rest of his life struggling to make balkanized neo-colonial Africa into a unified Africa for Africans, a concept that Bro. Garvey called forth in the 1920's.

Another brother who significantly contributed to the development of the Pan-African Idea was a man who spent several years within the Central Committee of the Russian Communist government. At that time (the 1930's) Bro. George Padmore sincerely believed in Russia's spiel that it was the true color-blind socialist state. As Padmore gained more political consciousness and came into contact with African and Asian progressive brothers, the façade of Russia's "color-blindness" rapidly pulverized. As colonialism gave way to neo-colonialism, Bro. Padmore became more sensitive to the needs of Africa from a nonviolent Pan-Africanist position. He clearly saw that the ideological struggle which was occurring in Africa was (and still is) a struggle to create communal unity of African nations.

Brother Padmore raised many theoretical questions and created a number of ideological assertions which Kwame Nkrumah began to answer, extend, and implement. Nkrumah, like Amilcar Cabral, Frantz Fanon and Sekou Touré, sees the necessity to include revolutionary violence within the Pan-African Idea. Without it, white Imperialism can strengthen its stranglehold upon *all* African nations. Nkrumah also added another analytical dimension to help in the African anti-imperialist struggle. Bro. Nkrumah checked out African history, the philosophy of Garvey, Du Bois, and Padmore, and has proceeded to build a viable humanistic system around Revolutionary Pan-Africanism: that no African or African nation is free until *all* Africans are free. And *that* freedom can only come through struggle.

And there is one brother who has constantly reiterated revolutionary struggle as a necessary political and therapuetic force for the re-humanization of the world: Bro. Frantz Fanon. He has offered his life to seeing that we minimize our psycho-political hangups and maximize our commitment to revolutionary struggle. Fanon's book, *The Wretched of the Earth*, is an indispensable and inspirational monument to the understanding of the human need and human essence of *Revolutionary Black Nationalism for the sake of Pan-Africanism for the sake of Bandungism.*

These microscopic synopses are included merely to create a sense of historical continuity concerning the Pan-African Idea. Indeed, some revolutionary-minded brothers and sisters should have to study the life and works of these and other dedicated Blacks who have contributed to the creation of a black ideology.

Revolutionary Black Nationalism For Pan-Africanism

We must begin to perceive Revolutionary Black Nationalism as an interlocking stage in the worldwide (Bandung) struggle against Racism, Imperialism, and Capitalism. More precisely, Afro-Americans must institutionalize Revolutionary Black Nationalism *not* as a narrow and chauvinistic way of life, but rather a way of life that affirms its belief in and faith in the Pan-African Liberation Movement and a way of life that is flexible in the day-to-day growth of the domestic and international aspects of the struggle. In short, Revolutionary Black Nationalism implies Pan-Africanism which in turn implies Bandungism.

Just as Revolutionary Black Nationalism had to develop into a more complex and comprehensive idea than what Bros. David Walker and John S. Rock conceived in the nineteenth century, so has Pan-Africanism expanded its complexities and inclusions. No longer can black people in America or Jamaica act as isolated struggles with only incidental relationships to each other and Africa. No longer can black people define Pan-Africanism as that human drive which only moves to unite Africa into a communal bond. Out of its unrelenting ruthlessness, white racist-imperialism has forced us to expand our perception of Black Existence as the bearers of and warriors for humanity and nature. There is no room for egocentric or tribalcentric "nationalism." Nor is there room for premature and sensational alliances with white radicals and Zionism.

African nations must realize that the Black Liberation struggles in the Americas are *inextricably* a part of their struggle for national independence, and the struggle for the unification of Africa into a powerful anti-racist, anti-imperialist force. Simultaneously, African people in the Americas must realize that the African Independence struggles are *inextricably* a part of their liberation from white racism and capitalism. Clearly then, the Pan-African Idea of today is a much more political and international ideology than it was in the late 1940's and '50's. It is a political idea that has placed less and less reliance upon moral suasion, appealing to the white conscience and other nonviolent means. Revolutionary violence and psychological warfare have proven to be most effective mechanisms against Euro-American racism and imperialism.

In the final analysis, the political and moral thrust of Revolutionary Black Nationalism and the Pan-Africanism Idea can be summed up in Bro. Fanon's immortal words:

> . . . So, Comrades, let us not pay tribute to Europe by creating states, institutions, and societies which draw their inspiration from her.
>
> Humanity is waiting for something other from us than such an imitation, which would be almost obscene caricature.
>
> If we want to turn Africa into a new Europe and America into a new Europe, then let us leave the destiny of *our* countries to Europeans. They will know how to do it better than the most gifted among us.
>
> But if we want humanity to advance a step further, if we want to bring it up to a different level than that which Europe has shown it, then we must invent and we must make discoveries.[7]

Can we let the trinkets of Capitalism and the brothels of Imperialism entice us for those moments of selfish and seditious pleasures? Can we continue to let white racism erode our peoples' racial essence?

In answer, we must act out an emphatic NO!

We must assert that Black Ideology and Black Morality possess a vitality with which the Aesthetical becomes the Ethical, and vice versa. With it a brother or sister sees himself or herself as a Revolutionary Man or Woman.

More than that, it is the Brother or Sister who asserts that to be a Revolutionary, indeed to be a Pan-Africanist, is to be for Life.

Through our future years of struggle it will be shown that wherever we are, we must take up the Banner, the Spirit, and the Arms of Revolutionary Black Nationalism and Pan-Africanism for the sake of defeating white bestiality so as bring forth the New Man.

NOTES

1. From the introduction to the *Black Manifesto* (Detroit, April 26, 1969), p. 5.

2. For an excellent account of the Haitian Revolution, see C. L. R. James' *Black Jacobins* (New York, Vintage Press, 1968).

3. See *White Over Black* by W. D. Jordan (New York, Dover Publications, 1968); an excellent account of pre-colonial and colonial white racism.

4. Bro. Danny Aldridge, "Politics in Command of Economics," *Monthly Review*, Vol. 21, No. 6 (November, 1969).

5. Telekinetics: moving objects through the use of mental energies; telepathy: the ability to mentally communicate, to control another person's mind, to "read" another person's mind. White folks have put many years of research in these two fields. Judging from various scientific reports, it appears that they have either accomplished or are close to accomplishing a major breakthrough in these fields.

6. Aldridge, *op. cit.*, pp. 23-24.

7. Frantz Fanon, *The Wretched of the Earth* (New York, Grove Press, 1965), p. 255.

BIBLIOGRAPHY

Because the preceeding essay is but a mere sketch of the larger and more complex mosaic of Black Political History, what is extremely important is a compilation of books that deal with the various types of Black Nationalism and the Pan-African development. There are numerous excellent essays on Black Nationalism and Pan-Africanism hidden in large and small academic journals; in many revolutionary journals and magazines. There are also essays and books written in other languages that have never been translated — for whites know they would be of great educational value. Hence, this bibliography may be perceived as a primer or foundation to inspire us to dig deeper and analyze more politically and scientifically for the sake of Black Liberation.

Historical

Edward W. Blyden, *African Life and Customs*. London, African Publications Society Reprint, 1969.

————, *Christianity, Islam & the Negro Race*. Chicago, Edinburgh University Press Reprint, 1967.

John Bracy *et al*, *Black Nationalism in America*. Indianapolis, Ind., Bobbs-Merrill, 1970.

Martin R. Delany and R. Campbell, *Search For A Place*. Ann Arbor, University of Michigan reprint, 1969.

Martin R. Delany, *The Condition, Elevation, Emigration & Destiny of the Colored People*. New York, Arno Books, reprint, 1968.

Frederick Douglass, *The Life & Times of Frederick Douglass: The Complete Autobiography*. New York, Collier, 1962.

Thomas F. Gossett, *Race: The History of an Idea in America* (rev. ed.). New York, Schoeken Books, 1965.

Cyril L. R. James, *Black Jacobins: Toussaint L'Ouverture & the San Domingo Revolution*. New York, Random House (Vintage Books, 1963.

Winthrop D. Jordan, *White Over Black*. Baltimore, Penguin Paperbacks, 1969.

J. Kovel, *White Racism: A Psychohistory*. New York, Pantheon Books, 1970.

Hollis Lynch, *Edward Wilmot Blyden: Pan-Negro Patriot 1832-1912*. New York, Oxford University Press, 1967.

William McAdoo, *Pre Civil War Black Nationalism*. Progressive Labor Party Pamphlet. (Very hard to find. Try Liberation Book Store, 421 Lenox Ave., Harlem, N.Y. 10037).

Edwin S. Redkey, *Black Exodus: Black Nationalist & Back-To-African Movements, 1890-1910*. New Haven, Conn., Yale University Press, 1969.

V. Bakpetu Thompson, *Africa and Unity: The Evolution of Pan-Africanism*. London, Humanities Press.

C. M. Wiltse (ed.), *David Walker's Appeal*. New York, Hill & Wang, 1965.

Julius Nyerere, *Freedom & Socialism*. New York, Oxford University Press, 1969.

——, *Freedom & Unity: A Selection from Writings and Speeches 1952-1965*. Dar Es Salaam, Oxford University Press, 1967.

George Padmore, *Pan-Africanism or Communism?* London, Dennis Dobson, 1956. (This is hard to find, and has not as yet been reprinted.)

Walter Rodney, *Groundings for my Brothers*, London, Bogle-L'Ouverture Publications.

Black Political Thought and Action

Willie E. Abraham, *The Mind of Africa*. Chicago, University of Chicago Press, 1963.

The African Communist (London-based periodical). Issues 1-40.

Danny Aldrich, "Politics in Command of Economics," in *Monthly Review*, Vol. 21, No. 6 (November, 1969).

Robert Allen, *Black Awakening in Capitalist America*. New York, Doubleday, 1969.

James Boggs, *Race & Class Struggle*. New York, Monthly Review Press, 1970.

James and Grace Boggs, *Manifesto for a Black Revolutionary Party*. Philadelphia, Penna., Pacesetters Publishing House.

Amilcar Cabral, "Guinea: The Power of Arms," in *Tricontinental Magazine* (Havana, Cuba), No. 12 (May-June, 1969).

John Henrick Clarke (ed.), *Malcolm X: The Man & His Time*. New York, Macmillan, 1969.

Harold Cruse, *The Crisis of the Negro Intellectual.* New York, William Morrow, 1967. Apollo Editions paperback, 1968.

———, *Rebellion or Revolution.* New York, William Morrow, 1968. Apollo Editions paperback published in 1969.

Basil Davidson, *The Liberation of Guinea.* Baltimore, Md., Penguin Paperback, 1969. (This includes an excellent introductory essay by Amilcar Cabral, leader of the revolutionary movement of Guinea-Bisseau.)

Frantz Fanon, *The Wretched of the Earth.* New York, Grove Press, 1965.

———, *Studies in a Dying Colonialism,* New York, Grove Press, 1967.

———, *Toward the African Revolution.* New York, Grove Press, 1968.

———, *Black Skin, White Mask.* New York, Grove Press, 1967.

James Forman, *The Political Thought of James Forman.* Detroit, Michigan, Black Star Publishers, 1970.

Amy Jacques (ed.), *The Philosophy and Opinions of Marcus Garvey,* New York, Arno Publishers, 1968. Paperback edition by Atheneum Publishers, 1969.

C. L. R. James, *A History of Pan-African Revolt.* Washington, D.C., Drum and Spear Press, 1970.

Robert July, *The Origins of Modern African Thought.* New York, Praeger Publishers, 1968.

Robert S. Lecky and Elliot H. Wright (eds.), *Black Manifesto,* New York, Sheed and Ward, 1969.

Eduardo Mondlane, *The Struggle for Mozambique.* Baltimore, Md., Penguin Paperback, 1969.

Agostinho Neto, "Angola: People in Revolution," in *Tricontinental Magazine* (Havana, Cuba), No. 12 (May-June, 1969).

Kwame Nkrumah, *The Challenge of the Congo.* New York, International Publishers, 1967. (Paperback edition published in 1969 as *Challenge of the Congo: A Case Study of Foreign Pressures in an Independent State.*)

———, *Neo-Colonialism: The Last Stage of Imperialism.* New York, International Publishers, 1969.

———, *Revolutionary Warfare.* New York, International Publishers, 1969.

II
Inward

Black artists often capture the flame of a time and, like Prometheus, carry that flame to all people. We open this section with a study of black artists; their present and future.

MARGARET G. BURROUGHS, *who is a teacher of art in Chicago, was born in St. Rose Parish, Louisiana. She received a B.A.E. from Chicago Teachers' College in 1937, and an M.A.E. from the Art Institute of Chicago in 1948. She has done advanced work at Teachers' College of Columbia University and Esmerelda Institute of Art in Mexico City. Her articles have appeared in* Chicago Schools Journal, Black World, Elementary English Journal, *and* Child Life. *She has published several books for young people, including* Jaycee the Drummin' Boy, Did You Feed My Cow? *and* Whip Me Whop Me Pudding. *She is the founder of the DuSable Museum of African American History in Chicago.*

Margaret G. Burroughs

To Make A Painter Black

Yet do I marvel at this curious thing:
To make a poet black, and bid him sing!

Thus wrote our black bard, Countee Cullen, some years ago in a poem which gently questions the wisdom of the Almighty when He created black poets and did not consider the vicissitudes of racism. In this essay, I shall substitute artists for poets since they are cut from similar cloth. I marvel that in spite of the lack of fulfillment that comes to the black artist, we continue to create. As truly creative human beings, we can do nothing else. Yet, it is obvious to all who are sensitive that racism permeates all fields of American life. It certainly has not taken a holiday in the area of the arts. Racism operates more subtly, but its spectre is there none the less!

Racism has not, however, stopped our creativity, for it is conceded that without the creativity of blacks, American culture would indeed be greatly deprived. Racism has, however, been a discouraging factor to hundreds of us who have chosen art as a lifework and thousands more who would be potential artists. Until quite recently, fine black artists have not been able to look forward to the normal rewards which are taken for granted by even the most mediocre white artists. For the most part, black artists in this country have been overlooked, if not downright ignored. It is only in very recent years that galleries and critics have been shocked into realizing that there are black artists, too.

Until recently, few major museums have shown the works of black artists. Even fewer top commercial art galleries handled the works of black artists. (Well, it just wasn't done.)

Occasionally the art establishment has singled out those it deemed to be our "great" artists by placing the white "stamp of approval" on them. In this way, a small number of our artists have been rewarded with crumbs, while numerous other superb black artists have been left out in the cold.

Nor has the black artist been able to look to the black art patron for support; generally, the black art patron does not exist. There are some among the black bourgeoisie who could be potential patrons for black artists, but they have yet to arrive at the art patron stage. Unfortunately, our black bourgeoisie often tend to ape the pattern of the establishment in all respects except one: the buying, collecting, and acquiring of art.

A painting that you have chosen because you like the color or the subject, or which gives you a respite from the rush of everyday life when you look at it, grows on you, possesses you, dominates your room. I have a piece of African sculpture, a mother and child, which I paid seventy-five dollars for (five dollars down, five dollars a week.) I loaned her out to be photographed for the movie "Cry of Jazz." The movie-makers were slow in getting her back. After living with her for several years, the room didn't seem the same without her. I finally called and told them that if they couldn't bring her back immediately I would come and get her. She had become so much a part of us that nothing went right unless we could look up and see her presiding serenely over our everyday lives. That is what a work of art can do for you.

W.E.B. Du Bois summed up the responsibility of the black patron in Chicago, 1958:

> We should encourage Negro Art and literature and buy Negro books and products. They must be good art and books worth reading, and if they are, we must buy them, and each Negro family should be ashamed which has not bought at least ten books by Negro authors each year or ten works of art. How else can the story and dreams of Negroes be told and preserved? Certainly we cannot de-

pend on what whites folks buy of us when we do not buy our own. Our churches, for instance, waste their funds publishing Sunday school lessons when they should be publishing the lost lives of the great leaders of the past. This race-loyalty need never become hatred of other people or envy of their success, but rather an unending and self-sacrificing effort to be our own very best selves.

Accordingly, the success of a black artist has been based on how many "white" shows he has made or how many awards he has received or how many paintings or sculptures the white world has purchased from him; not by the acclamation of our own people.

It was the white man who approved or disapproved of our subject matter or technique. If the white man said it was good, it was thought so and accepted by us as good. If the white man didn't recognize the work of a black artist, blacks considered the work to be of no significance. We are not yet quite free of this brainwashing. How can we be? The white man has the money, Honey, and he who pays the piper calls the tune. Furthermore, this approach has sown disunity and mistrust among our artists, one for the other. Each has been a "loner," trying to make it on his own. If he happens to make it, he slams the door shut on others who are struggling upward.

Now, some of our artists mistakenly operate from the view that success is a broad plateau with plenty of room at the top. They soon find this is a fallacy. There is generally room for only one black artist at the top, if there is room at all. Many black artists have felt that they can make it by being as non-black as possible. They are not black artists. They are not African-American artists. They do not handle "black" subject matter. They do not even paint or sculpt black people or anything of an ethnic nature. They are one hundred per cent American artists and their works are no different from the mainstream of white American art or non-art. They have become masters of the non-humanist techniques. In some cases they have sur-passed their white counterparts and painted themselves into a corner away from their black soul people. They have carried this meaningless non-objectivism to a fine point and often are touted and lauded by the "establishment" for this nonsense. Unfortunately, they have influenced many younger artists who follow their model, not because it is what their soul dictates but because of the material rewards to be gained from doing so.

Happily this is not the case in general. There are black artists all over the country, many more unknown than known, who have not "copped out," who realize that to be a black artist is to be one who is close to and deeply involved with life and humanity, and who express themselves creatively within this framework.

In considering racism's effect on the economy of the black artist, we find that racism has consistently deprived the black artist of an opportunity to make a living from his art. There are a few exceptions in recent years, due, we suspect, to the current demand for instant black Exhibit A.

Yet, despite the problems of the black artist caused by the hostility of a racist society, there is today a lively ferment. All over the country, black artists, young and old, are painting and sculpting as never before. They are seeking to reaffirm themselves and their black culture, to rescue American culture from an artistic decadence void of human emotions and full of junk-yard sculpture, paintings shot from pistols and flung from step-ladders. Again the creativity of the blacks arises to save and revitalize American culture.

This is not a new phenomenon. It was so when the European traders went into the African continent seeking a way to the spices and riches of the East and discovered the gold of Ashanti, the bronzes of Benin, and the fabulous terra cottas of Ife.

It was so at the turn of the century when young French modernists declared the art of their society decadent and started a new school of art which is with us today. This new school was inspired by *highly sophisticated* African carvings, masks, and figurines, made by so-called "primitive" peoples!

It was so when rhythms brought from Africa took root in the Caribbean and South America and gave America its only original music, folksongs, spirituals, folk-language, and folk-lore.

It was so when at the end of World War I, the lost generation — those who were disillusioned with the unfulfilled promises to make a world safe for democracy and the garish, phony character of the Victorian era of their parents' generation — sought something real, honest, and sincere. Where did they go to find it? They went to the black American, the haunts and habitats of a poor, despised, and deprived people. They went to places like Harlem in New York and the southside of Chicago and Beale Street in Memphis and Rampart Street in New Orleans. Here they got a reviving shot in their cultural arms, and out of this intense period of creativity came the Negro Renaissance of the twenties which gave soul to the culture of the day.

And so it is today. Black artists once again exert their creative influence over a decadent culture. A group of young black Chicago artists decided that art should be brought to the people. They combined their talents to depict black heroes and heroines on the wall of a tenement in the heart of their community. They called it the "Wall of Pride and Respect." The idea has spread to black artists in other urban communities, and has inspired many other exciting black art movements.

The desire to make significant contributions to the "movement" and rights "revolution" has highlighted the expression of black subject matter. Demonstrations, roits, and confrontation are depicted often with more passion than technique. Lively dialogue has precipitated the search to define black art and the black esthetic. There are as many points of view on the subject as there are schools of artists. I have had the opportunity to discuss the matter informally with several artists. A few comments selected at random from those I respect can serve to bring my paper into contemporary focus.

Lois Pierre Noel of Howard University, Washington, D. C., expressed a dilemma which is perhaps confronting many teachers of art, black and white. She stated at a recent National Conference of Artists meeting:

> There's really black art going on at Howard. The students
> are very strong. They have identified themselves as artists.
> Many of their subjects have to do with social change,
> movements, the riots, Africa. When I give my criticism

based in my training, what do I get? "Well, I like it like that; I don't agree with you!"

There is a growth of independence of spirit on the part of the students. How can I carry them on to the point where they will do good art? The question is, yes, this is black art but is it good to train them to be good artists in all they do, or do we just let them paint black art, the expression of subjects, emotions and colors, and set that up — this black esthetic — as the best?

Artist Eugene O. White of Los Angeles favored a black esthetic. He stated:

I traveled a lot and I didn't see exactly what I wanted to see, so I decided to do what I see in the way I felt. The way I felt would link into the Revolution. Yes, there is a difference between a work done by a black hand and a white hand. I feel you have to be black to do the work I am doing. According to the feeling I get, you have to be part of what you are involved in.

Selma Burke has been active on the art scene more years than many of today's "New Breed" black artists are old. When asked about this question, she said:

There is no such thing as black art. My work is done by a black artist. I paint a leaf. It is green. It is not black art. My influence of geometric forms, etc., was inspired from African sculpture that my uncle brought over from Africa. There are black artists and black subject matter.

By the same token, there is no such thing as white art. Much bad art is being passed off as "black" art. Is there a black esthetic? Yes. But in this sense: take, for example, the dance. It is what the Negro puts into it, his heritage. I am not denying whatever school he chooses to express himself in. Our contribution must ultimately be the rejection of racism. Art in Africa is not a thing apart, but a way of life. Africans created things of beauty which had meaning and significance to them.

There is a black esthetic in the sense that black folk are the true creative forces in America. So much of what is creative in western culture comes straight from us, black folk.

Ernest Crichlow of New York told me:

> Yes, there is a black esthetic. However, not every black intellectual has to adhere to it. The black artist or intellectual has a dual personality. This may not be so noticeable among all blacks. We are taught the technique and history of our craft from the viewpoint of the white establishment (white, western, Anglo-Saxon European) culture. The purpose of this is to ignore, deny, to wipe out any positive aspects of black culture — to deny its validity and to force the black to accept the established form of esthetic, of culture, or ways of doing things.
>
> The black intellectual or artist in his training period goes off into that realm of white-oriented western esthetic for a time or perhaps during the whole of his schooling. He is on the other side of the tracks, as it were, but he has to come home sooner or later, if only to sleep or to get his battery recharged. When he comes back home, he is forced to deal with his own personal esthetics, even if he is determinedly non-black in all aspects and paints abstract expressionism in white-on-white!
>
> The black artist therefore develops a *dual* personality and *dual* ability to express both esthetics, white and black. He may work in the white, but he cannot avoid the black experience. It is the nature of American society to try and hide what you are. A black painter cannot hide it. He may paint white, he may disassociate himself from any recognizable, identifiable subject matter totally, but deep down inside himself, he hears a small voice telling him, and he knows, that he is a black artist.
>
> Some have tried to ignore and stifle this voice, but it still persists, and in some black artists, if ignored over a period of time, the personality of the artist can be affected. Yet, a black artist has a right to express himself as he sees fit. If

he sees the world as cold and mechanistic, it is his prerogative to paint the world that way. That is the way he sees
it. However, the black artist must realize that his is not the
only and the most important expression of what he is. It is
only a part of the expression of what he is.

Romare Bearden takes abstraction and makes it serve him
meaningfully as a black artist. He incorporates African sculpture and familiar symbols into his work which his black audience
is able to note and appreciate.

While speaking with Charles White, I asked whether he
felt "content" alone was enough to legitimize black art. His comments are well worth passing on to the young, aspiring black
artist:

> Anything you do, if you don't do it well, it is not going
> to have the impact. It's kind of lost. Take Miles Davis or
> Cannonball Adderly or Max Roach; just name it in terms of
> music. None of them would be the great artist he is if he
> hadn't studied and mastered his instrument and gone
> through all the academic problems dealing with his music.
> The same thing applies to dance and to literature. A book
> that is badly written, no matter what the intent of its
> author — if the form is bad, if it doesn't have too much
> sophistication of style, if the structure is bad, who in hell
> is going to read it?

> The same thing applies to art. If you don't take the time to
> master your craft, your statement is going to be lost and
> the impact is going to be lost. It's as simple as that.

Evangeline Montgomery of Oakland said:

> In dealing with the whole universal humanity, I feel that
> black people are leading the way and that one of the
> causes for alienation among many of the young white
> artists in this country is because they do not want to be
> identified with the major society as they know it. This has
> resulted in a kind of alienation which has been reflected in

their paintings of non-art for material aggrandizement. The black artist through his art may even be leading America toward a more human world.

The debate may go deep into the seventies; the black artist, young and old, will continue to create.

For it is the artists who have ushered us into the era of a new black renaissance. All that they are doing may not be excellent, but much of what they are doing is honest. They have again given American culture that needed shot in the arm. And just think, all of this comes from a people who are called culturally deprived, who have been cordoned off into compounds and denied their basic human rights.

I like to imagine what American art and culture would be like if black folk were granted all the rights and privileges of citizens of this country. How the art and culture would flourish in such a free society! What a great, rich culture would be ours! But this cannot happen under a system infected with racism. Cannot and will not.

There is much talk of black publishing ventures and often not much knowledge about those black publishers who have been on the line for some time. This article is in itself an example of a black and growing concern.

DUDLEY RANDALL *was born in Washington, D.C. He received his B.A. in English from Wayne University in 1949 and his master's degree in library science from the University of Michigan in 1951. He is a prominent Detroit poet who has published numerous poems, short stories, and articles. In 1962 he won a Tompkins Award for fiction and poetry, and in 1966, a Tompkins Award for poetry. From 1962 to 1964 he worked with Margaret Danner and other black poets in the Boone House cultural center in Detroit. He lives with his family in Detroit, where he is a reference librarian in the Wayne County (Michigan) Federated Library System. He is currently working on a novel and a book of poems.*

Dudley Randall

Broadside Press:
A Personal Chronicle

Broadside Press did not grow from a blueprint. I did not, like Joe Goncalves when he planned the *Journal of Black Poetry*, save money in advance to finance the press. Broadside Press began without capital, from the twelve dollars I took out of my paycheck to pay for the first Broadside, and has grown by hunches, intuitions, trial and error.

Our first publication was the Broadside "Ballad of Birmingham." Folk singer Jerry Moore of New York had it set to music, and I wanted to protect the rights to the poem by getting it copyrighted. Learning that leaflet could be copyrighted, I published it as a Broadside in 1965. Jerry Moore also set the ballad "Dressed All in Pink" to music, and in order to copyright it I printed this poem also as a Broadside. Being a librarian, accustomed to organizing and classifying material, I grouped the two poems into a *Broadside Series*, and called them Broadsides number one and number two. Since Broadsides, at that time, were the company's sole product, I gave it the name Broadside Press.

In May 1966 I attended the first Writers' Conference at Fisk University, and obtained permission from Robert Hayden, Melvin B. Tolson, and Margaret Walker, who were there, to use their poems in the *Broadside Series*. I wrote to Gwendolyn Brooks and obtained her permission to use "We Real Cool." This first group of six Broadsides, called "Poems of the Negro Revolt," is, I think, one of the most distinguished groups in the *Broadside Series*, containing outstanding poems by some of our finest poets.

At that time my intention was to publish famous familiar poems in an attractive format so that people could buy their favorite poems in a form worth treasuring. A reviewer in *Small Press Review*, however, suggested that I could serve contemporary poetry better by publishing previously unpublished poems. Beginning with Broadside twenty-five, I have attempted to do this. I try to make the format of the Broadside harmonize with the poem in paper, color, and typography, and often employ artists to design or illustrate the Broadsides. Some Broadsides outstanding for their appearance are number four ("The Sea Turtle and the Shark," by Melvin B. Tolson), designed in blue by sculptor-painter Cledie Taylor; number six ("We Real Cool,' by Gwendolyn Brooks), lettered white on black by Cledie Taylor to simulate scrawls on a blackboard; and number eighteen ("Black Madonna," by Harold Lawrence), gold on white with an illustration by painter Leroy Foster.

The first book planned (but not the first published) by Broadside Press was *For Malcolm: Poems on the Life and the Death of Malcolm X*. This book had its genesis at the first Fisk University Writers' Conference. As I was walking to one of the sessions, I saw Margaret Walker, the poet, and Margaret Burroughs, the painter, sitting in front of their dormitory. Mrs. Burroughs was sketching, and Miss Walker was rehearsing her reading, for she was to read her poems that afternoon. I sat down to watch and to listen, and when Miss Walker read a poem on Malcolm X, I said, "Everybody's writing about Malcolm X. I know several people who've written poems about him."

"That's right," Margaret Burroughs said. "Why don't you collect the poems and put out a book on Malcolm?"

I thought it over for a few seconds, snapped my fingers, and said, "I'll do it. And you can be my co-editor."

Thus the anthology *For Malcolm* was born.

Most conferences have much talk, but little action. Mrs. Burroughs and I decided to inject some action into this conference by announcing our book at the final session, and offering the writers there a concrete vehicle for their poems. David Llorens promised to announce it in *Negro Digest* (now *Black World*) and in a few days I received the first poem. This anthology is notable not only for the many fine poems it includes, but also because it brings maturer poets such as Robert Hayden, Margaret Walker, and Gwendolyn Brooks together with younger poets such as LeRoi Jones, Larry Neal, Bobb Hamilton, Sonia Sanchez, Julia Fields, Etheridge Knight, David Llorens, and others. My editorship of the book acquainted me with many of the younger poets and with the periodicals *Soulbook* and *Black Dialogue,* and led to rewarding friendships with some of the poets.

Although this anthology was the first book planned by Broadside Press, it was not the first one published. Because of printer's delays, it was not published until June 1967. In the meantime, *Poem Counterpoem,* by Margaret Danner and myself, was published in December 1966; it is the first book published by Broadside Press. It has a unique format, as its title suggests. The poems are arranged in pairs, a poem by each author on facing pages, and each pair of poems is on the same or a similar subject. The most obvious example of this pairing is the last pair of poems, each of which bears the title "Belle Isle."

The first edition, limited to five hundred numbered, autographed copies, had a four-by-five inch format like that of the Russian poetry series "The Young Guard," which sold for ten or twelve kopeks (eight or ten cents), and which favorably impressed me when I visited Russia in 1966. The American public, however, buys books like cabbages, by weight not by content, and it did not sell well in this format. The second printing was enlarged to the regular book size of eight by five inches, and although it contained the same poems and the same number of pages, it sold better. The book is now in its second, revised edition and its third printing. I suppose a few copies of the original printing are still available at a few bookstores.

The next book to be published by Broadside Press was one of our best selling books, *Black Pride,* by the popular young poet, Don L. Lee. I had met Mr. Lee when the copies of *For Malcolm* arrived at Mrs. Burroughs' Museum of African American History. Don Lee, at that time an assistant at the Museum, whose quiet manner belied the fires underneath, helped us as we autographed and mailed authors' copies. Later, he sent me some poems for comments, and then sent me a copy of his first book, *Think*

Black, which he had had privately printed in an edition of 700, which sold out in one week. I wrote him a note thanking him for his book and commented on it.

When his second book, *Black Pride,* was ready, he asked that Broadside Press publish it, and that I write the introduction. We published *Black Pride* in 1968, and took over *Think Black.* In 1969, we published his *Don't Cry, Scream,* in both paperbound and cloth editions. The cloth edition of *Don't Cry, Scream* was a first with Broadside Press, but shortly afterward we put out our second hardcover book, the second edition of *For Malcolm.*

At this writing, *Think Black* has had twelve printings, and there are twenty-five thousand copies in print. *Black Pride* is in its seventh printing, and *Don't Cry, Scream,* just out in March 1969, had its third printing (5000 copies) the following September. It is only lack of money which prevents these printings from being 10,000 instead of 5000, as they sell rapidly and it it hard to keep bookstores in supply. All together, there are about 55,000 copies of Don Lee's books in print at this time. This has occurred without book reviews in the mass media. The only reviews of Lee's books have appeared in small black and underground magazines. In March 1969 there was an article on Lee by David Llorens in *Ebony,* a widely circulated black magazine, but the article appeared after, not before, Lee had attained his popularity.

Another poet who has been warmly praised is Etheridge Knight. He contributed three poems to *For Malcolm,* and I corresponded with him in Indiana State Prison. I asked him to do a book for Broadside Press, and we published his *Poems from Prison* in 1968, which is now in its third printing. Mr. Knight is now living in Indianapolis, and is working on his second book of poetry.

James Emanuel's first book of poetry, *The Treehouse and Other Poems* was also published in 1968, as was my second book of verse, *Cities Burning.* The same year we became distributors for Nikki Giovanni's second book, *Black Judgment,* and published Margaret Danner's *Impressions of African Art Forms.* This book, which is a facsimile of the original edition privately printed in 1960, has the distinction of being the only volume of poetry completely devoted to the vivid, varied, sophisticated arts of Black Africa. In 1969, books by Jon Eckels, Beatrice Murphy and Nancy

Arnez, Sonia Sanchez, Marvin X, Keorapetse Kgositsile, and Stephany were published.

Our list has expanded considerably from the two Broadsides with which we began in 1965. Now, in 1970, we have sixteen books and thirty-two Broadsides. Scheduled to be published are books by Lance Jeffers, Doughtry Long, and John Raven. Among books promised to us are two by Pulitzer Prize-winner Gwendolyn Brooks and Margaret Walker, winner of the Yale University Younger Poets Award.

In 1969 we published our second anthology, *Black Poetry: A Supplement to Anthologies Which Exclude Black Poets.* Robert Hayden and I, both of whom have taught at the University of Michigan, were asked by the chairman of the Department of English to compile a small collection of black poetry, as students had pointed out that the anthologies used in the introduction-to-poetry courses contained no black poets. Because of pressures of time in moving to different teaching posts, Mr. Hayden had to withdraw from the project, but I completed it, and the new anthology can be used both by students and by the general reader. We are also distributing an anthology of poetry and prose, *Black Arts: An Anthology of Black Creations,* edited by Ahmed Alhamisi and Harun Kofi Wangara, and published in 1969 by Alhamisi's Black Arts Publications.

In a different dimension is *Broadside Voices,* which is a series of poets reading their own books on tape. So far, James Emanuel, Dudley Randall, Etheridge Knight, Sonia Sanchez, Jon Eckels, Beatrice Murphy and Nancy Arnez, Marvin X, Willie Kgositsile, Don Lee, and Stephany have taped their books. James Emanuel was the first to complete a tape, and he read so well that Etheridge Knight, to whom I sent Emanuel's tape as a model, said that Emanuel gave him an inferiority complex in regard to his own reading. Knight made four tapes before he produced one which was satisfactory.

There are interesting sound effects in some of the tapes. An explosive sound which occurs at a dramatic moment in Emanuel's tape near the end of "A View from the White Helmet" is the sound of an automobile backfiring. The percussive sounds at the beginning of Sonia Sanchez's tape, which she recorded in my home, are the tapping of her shoes as she walked back and forth while reading. When I played back the first few poems, I detected the noise, and asked her to pull off her shoes.

In 1968 Broadside Press began United States distribution of Paul Breman's *Heritage Series,* imported from England, which includes Conrad Kent Rivers' posthumous *The Still Voice of Harlem* and Russell Atkin's *Heretofore.* Eventually the series will include books by Lloyd Addison, Ray Durem, Owen Dodson, Audrey Lorde, Dudley Randall, Ishmael Reed, and other poets.

Up to now, Broadside Press has published poetry only. A new departure will be the series *Broadside Critics,* which will be pamphlets of criticism of black poetry by black critics. James Emanuel has consented to be editor of the series. Pamphlets for which tentative commitments have been made are: Don L. Lee on poets emerging during the 1960's, Arna Bontemps on Jean Toomer, Robert Hayden on Countee Cullen, James Emanuel on Langston Hughes, and Dudley Randall on Gwendolyn Brooks. It is hoped that these pamphlets will be enlightening and influential.

I have not locked myself in any rigid ideology in managing Broadside Press, but I suppose certain inclinations or directions appear in my actual activities. As clearly as I can see by looking at myself (which is not very clearly, because of the closeness) I restrict the publications to poetry (which I think I understand and can judge not too badly). An exception is the new *Broadside Critics,* which, even though prose, will be concerned with poetry. I reserve the press for black poets (except in *For Malcolm*), as I think the vigor and beauty of our black poets should be better known and should have an outlet. I try to publish a wide variety of poetry, including all viewpoints and styles (viewpoints as opposed as Marvin's X's and Beatrice Murphy's, styles as diverse as James Emanuel's and Don L. Lee's). I deplore incestuous little cliques where poets of a narrow school or ideology band together, cry themselves up, and deride all others. I believe that in the house of poetry there are many mansions, and that we can enjoy different poets for the variety and uniqueness of their poetry, not because they are all of a sameness.

Broadside Press has not been subsidized or funded by any individual, organization, foundation, or government agency. It is, has been, and always will be, free and independent. It is a free, black institution. Support for the Press has come from the grassroots, from poets who donated their poems to the anthology *For Malcolm*, in honor of Malcolm; from the poets in the first group of the *Broadside Series*, who steadfastly refused payment for their poems; from the many persons who subscribed in advance for the *Broadside Series* and the anthologies, so that they could be printed; and from others who donated sums above their subscriptions. It is the poets and the people who have supported Broadside Press.

I've declined partnerships, mergers, and incorporations, as I want freedom and flexibility of action; want to devote the press to poetry; and am afraid that stockholders in a corporation would demand profits and would lower quality or go into prose in order to obtain profits. Income from the press goes into publishing new books in an attractive and inexpensive format. I pay royalties to other poets, but royalties on my own books go back into the press. I'm not against royalties for myself, or profits for the company, if they ever come, but I'm more interested in publishing good poetry.

Once Gwendolyn Brooks asked me what title to call me by. I replied that since I, in my spare time and in my spare bedroom, do all the work, from sweeping floors, washing windows, licking stamps and envelopes, and packing books, to reading manuscripts, writing ads, and planning and designing books, that she just say that Dudley Randall equals Broadside Press.

In a broader sense, though, Broadside Press is, in embryo, one of the institutions that black people are creating by trial and error and out of necessity in our reaching for self-determination and independence. I don't think it's necessary to belabor the importance of poetry. Poetry has always been with us. It has always been a sustenance, a teacher, an inspiration, and a joy. In the present circumstances it helps in the search for black identity, reinforces black pride and black unity, and is helping to create the soul, the consciousness, and the conscience of black folk.

Instead of trying to justify poetry and the necessity of our own presses such as Broadside and the others like it—Don L. Lee's Third World Press, Tom Dent's Free Southern Theatre, Eugene

Perkins' Free Black Press, LeRoi Jones' Jihad Productions, Ed Spriggs' and Nikki Giovanni's Black Dialogue Press, Joe Goncalves' Journal of Black Poetry Press, Casper Jordan's and Russell Atkins' Free Lance Press, and Norman Jordan's new Vibration Press— it would be more fruitful to look toward the future and plan how to turn these small beginnings into viable and permanent institutions. One must recognize, however, their lack of capital in a capitalistic society where a large proportion of small businesses fail every year.

I admit that I am not well qualified to operate in a capitalistic society. I came of age during the Great Depression, and my attitude toward business is one of dislike and suspicion. Writers who send me manuscripts and speak of "making a buck" turn me off.

Capitalistic writers praise the profit motive as a powerful incentive. I think they're liars. I have to confess that I seldom think of profits. My strongest motivations have been to get good black poets published, to produce beautiful books, help create and define the soul of black folk, and to know the joy of discovering new poets. I guess you could call it production for use instead of for profit.

Nevertheless, I think we should remember the lesson of the Negro Renaissance, and try to stay solvent in this jungle society. Negro writers who were a fad during the twenties were dropped by white publishers and readers when the Depression came in the thirties. Black publishers should try to build a stable base in their own communities. It is the black bookstores which are most genuinely interested in their books. In my own home town, Detroit, neither of the large department stores (in a black neighborhood, incidentally) and almost none of the white book stores stock Broadside books. Vaughn's Book Store (black) alone carries all of them. There is an interdependence between black booksellers and black publishers. One Chicago bookseller, who had just opened a store, told me, "Only Broadside and Free Black Press would give me credit. The white companies wouldn't do it."

Publishers should foster the closest and most helpful relations with these small bookstores, should visit them, furnish them with advertisement and information, and help them with ordering.

They should encourage their authors to give readings in the bookstores and to meet their readers. They should encourage sound
business practices among them by such means as giving extra
discounts for early payment. Black book jobbers should be developed, as the white book jobbers are singularly uninterested in
the small black publisher. Baker & Taylor, Campbell and Hall,
and other large white jobbers, for instance, do not stock Broadside Press books, but only order single copies when they receive
an order. We need black distributors who'll buy large quantities
of books from black publishers and furnish them promptly to the
trade.

We need more small publishers who will specialize in other
genres besides poetry. We have always had good actors, but we
have not had black playwrights to furnish them material. Today,
however, we have a flowering of dramatists in LeRoi Jones, James
Baldwin, Ed Bullins, Douglas Turner Ward, Owen Dodson, Sonia
Sanchez, Marvin X, and others. Black publishers, like the French
and the Baker Companies, could publish their plays in inexpensive pamphlets like poetry, and could supply mimeographed
copies of parts to the many schools, colleges, churches, and grassroots theatres springing up over the country which are clamoring
for meaningful material.

We have produced many fine essayists, of eloquence and moral
urgency, from Frederick Douglass through Du Bois, Wright, Ellison, Baldwin, and Jones to Addison Gayle and Larry Neal. Essays,
like poetry and the drama, are another genre which could be
published in inexpensive pamphlets, singly or in collections.

Reference librarians, like myself, have often been frustrated
by the gaps in reference materials on the Negro. Ira Aldridge,
for instance, one of the greatest Shakespearean actors, has only
in the last few years been included in biographical or theatrical
reference works. Teachers, librarians, professors, and scholars
could compile bibliographies, handbooks, directories, indexes,
and biographical works to supplement inadequate reference
works like *Who's Who in America, Encyclopedia Americana,
Contemporary Authors,* and others. These would find a ready
market in libraries, schools, colleges, businesses, and homes.
A forthcoming example of such a work is Charles Evans' *Index*

to Black Anthologies, which will index anthologies likely to be left out of *Grainger's Index to Poetry.* Another example, although not a reference work, is my own *Black Poetry: A Supplement to Anthologies Which Exclude Black Poets,* the title of which is self-explanatory.

Large works such as novels, biographies, and non-fiction books, which are more costly to produce and market, will have to be left to more affluent publishers, like the Johnson Publishing Company, which has already published several novels and non-fiction books.

There is a growing market for black books, not only among the young black high school and college students, but also among older, less educated persons. A neighbor told me that he saw a worker on the production line of an automobile factory with a copy of the anthology *For Malcolm* in his hip pocket. I often get orders for poetry books which are scrawled and misspelled on paper torn from notebooks, and once received an order scrawled on part of a brown paper bag. I am more pleased to receive such individual orders than to receive a large order from a bookstore or a jobber, for they show that black people are reading poetry and are finding it a meaningful, not an esoteric, art.

We are a nation of twenty-two million souls, larger than Athens in the Age of Pericles or England in the Age of Elizabeth. There is no reason why we should not create and support a literature which will be to our own nation, and to the world, what those literatures were to theirs.

Soul *can be the ability to move from the heart.*
Mrs. Ruelas relates a personal experience which
forced her to define "soul" in her own way.

YVONNE RUELAS *was born and raised in New-*
port News, Virginia, where she attended public
school. She lived for a while in New York City,
and in 1955 moved to Massachusetts. She began
writing about five years ago, when she felt the need
to look deeply into her life and into herself. Since
then, she has written numerous stories and **poems:**
"Poetry becomes difficult to explain at times, simply
because it is a thing to see, read and feel within
oneself. Its main purpose is to see yourself and,
above all, to see the real you." Her poetry appeared
in the anthology Fire Exit, *published by the New*
Poets' Theatre of Cambridge, Massachusetts. Mrs.
Ruelas has worked as an instructor in creative writ-
ing at the Store-Front Learning Center, located close
to where she and her children make their home in
Roxbury, Massachusetts.

Yvonne Ruelas

Mr. White Liberal

It was evening, the sun had gone down behind the trees, and night was soon to appear. A knock came to the door and I went to answer. There stood before me a young white girl I had never seen before. I spoke a hello and she smiled, may I come in? With this I opened the door a wider gap and she then entered. I noticed about her a somewhat shy mannerism, and somewhat quick smile, a feeling of uneasiness came over her. I then thought maybe it's because she's on the other side of town, in which I somehow could see she did not belong, for about her now stood a poor woman and dirty street's broken glass and dim-looking houses. She was now in one, though clean.

Would you like to come and sit in the kitchen, I asked. Oh that would be fine, she said. Make yourself comfortable, now pulling out a chair for her to sit upon. Would you like a cup of tea? To that she answered and said no. What I really come to talk about, now giving me a smile, is your poems. She had learned about me through a person named Agnes, who also came along, whom I had known for a short time. Though the both of them were white, Agnes and I had more in common, for the two of us were poor and subsisting on charity.

I suppose the young white girl wanted to know how one would feel to live and be from day to day at the hands of someone else. Of course I said that I would try my best to give her my feelings, knowing deep down inside that I would make her the villain, for I felt in most ways whites were responsible for my condition, and why should I give them the satisfaction of hearing me cry a sad song? I must admit I played a good role in saying that I was indeed satisfied the way I was, for I felt that time brings about a great change. At this she seemed somewhat surprised that I felt that way.

Agnes spoke and said, sitting opposite of me, I wish I could feel that way. Then she went into her thing of how sad she felt and how badly her husband treated her and of her black eyes she often or more than often received; of how she longed for so many material things, and at one point felt like killing herself. Though I felt proud of not admitting to all these things she talked about, yet I felt sorry for her. So the evening went to Agnes. The two parties went away knowing no more than before, for I did have some pride left and why should I let myself go to a total stranger, whom I felt in the first place knew nothing of what I would like to have said, and if so spoken to her, would not have understood.

During the evening the young girl asked if she could see any of the poems she had heard about. At her question, I brought out some poems and she began to read. The best ones to her were "The Nude Lady" and "Dreams Journal." She asked if she could re-copy the two and I said yes. Before going, she neatly tucked the poems in a black briefcase. I have a natural habit of giving to one a warm embrace, which I did to her at our saying good-bye.

I usually think of the persons I meet, but for some reason I did not think of her, for in the business world, you see them and then you don't. Though she had not mentioned her affair as being business-like, I knew there must be some connection, or why would she be so eager in seeing me?

A month or more passed and I received a letter in the mailbox. I slowly opened it. To my surprise it was from her. It was in the early evening and all seemed to stand still. The children had not awakened to give their cries to the isolated city, or either they felt what to hell! I suppose they were becoming tired of trying to doll the empty city with joyful glees and felt to stay inside for a while longer, for heaven knows, one would have to have a lot of guts and courage to try to overcome the glance of shabby dwellings and broken glass. It would take a lot of singing and shouting to erase the nightmares one can easily get from lack of everything that goes from day to day. I entered back into the apartment and began to read the letter:

. . . Agnes and I talked with you late last summer about welfare, for a book I have been writing with Carl Andrews, who is associated with Community Concerns. Well, we are just about finished. We have a publisher who has suggested that the book would be stronger if we were to give autobiographical profiles of some of the women we interviewed. In this way the readers can get a picture of the face behind the voice.

I won't be here this summer but Carl would like to see and talk with you when you can spare the time. He was very impressed with your poems and we would like to use them if we may.

Carl will probably ask you about that too. He wants very much to meet you and will be writing you soon. Hope things have gone well with you . . .

I wasn't surprised to hear from her, but I was surprised to learn of her friend and the book bit, which she had not mentioned the time I met her. The letter slipped my mind.

Then one day that summer I decided to go into my front parlor and look out the window. People were going about, but as I kept looking, one person was pacing from one end of the street to the other, looking from one address to another. His face was not familiar, but I knew he couldn't be looking for me and tried to let it pass. Then I heard him asking a lady did she know where I lived. She said yes, pointing up to my window. I started to go down but felt whoever he was would come up. A few minutes later, footsteps came upon the steps. Then a knock upon the door. I went into the hallway to answer. I opened the door and there stood the tall man I had been watching for some time.

Hello, his soft but masculine voice spoke. He still hadn't entered, for I was not certain who he was. I was supposed to write to you, I am Carl. With that, memories came back to me. Oh I do remember, would you come in, as he let his feet cross the threshold, coat draped over his shoulder. I asked if he would like to come and sit in the kitchen or in the parlor. The parlor will do, he said. The two of us took a seat with our backs to the window. He first talked about the hot sun and of the hard time in finding me.

He said he was just about to give up until he met the lady next door and she gave him the address.

I told him I was sorry that he had such a hard time in finding me. He talked with the children a while and they to him. He was very friendly, which made me notice him all the more. While he was at talk, I noticed his well-made blue suit and shrewd-looking shoes placed upon his feet. My eyes went from his shoes to his neatly placed tie, to his brown briefcase. Though he didn't say, I knew he didn't live around here.

After his conversation with the children, we began to talk about the works he had heard about from his friend. May I see some of your poems? With that, I went out and fetched the poetry, now returning to sit close to him as to explain some of the misspelled words if need be. But he managed without my help. After he had glanced over all of them, he looked up and said, the one I like best is "Nude Lady":

Nude Man — Nude Lady
Man holds out hands swiftly they walk
Love
Silence
Cries
Screams
Sweat
Pain
Joy
Baby
Window glass see himself thoughts wife tenderness
home watch baby
grow
Love again
School
College
Complete collegian
grown up
Nude Man — Nude Lady swiftly they walk holding hands
Clouds
Beautiful blue clouds

I have read it a thousand times, he said, I have it in my house. Though I began to think, I spoke no words, but gave a smile. We talked for about two hours. At the end of his visit he asked if I would write a story for him. I said yes I would, how soon, I asked. As soon as possible he said. Since it was near the end of the week I told him Monday would be a fine day to start. That's fine with me. Do you have a typewriter? With this question I brought out my old and out-dated typewriter. Does it work? Yes, I spoke. He placed it in front of him and began to type. His fingers told me that he was not accustomed to the old-style of typewriters. At first I felt proud for I had saved up enough money as to purchase the typewriter, but somehow I began to feel ashamed and the smile left my face, seeing him trying not to let on that he was used to better.

I have a used typewriter in the office I will bring you, now looking up at me somewhat sad. You can use it if you like. That will be fine, I spoke. I can bring it over to you Monday, he said.

The following Monday he brought over the typewriter at the said hour. This time we sat in the kitchen and I asked if he would like a cup of tea. He shook his head with a pleasant smile of no upon his face. I would like very much to talk about the story I would like for you to write, he said. I was eager to listen. When he mentioned welfare I was not shocked but I felt that I could not write what he really wanted to hear. About the system, about how it makes you feel, about how it feels to be on welfare. Yet I told him I would, for in the back of my mind he was, it seemed, meaning to be real about the book he was working on and really wanted to know the effects welfare took on one. It wasn't the fact that I was ashamed of being poor, but I could somehow see that this person was well in means of good living and life owed him nothing. I had also learned from the deep South the way the white man picks our brains—be it out of bona fideness or destructiveness.

I will pay you well, he said, which sounded good to my ears, though I would not let him know. There were four corners to my table but he sat next to me. I could see him give me a glance, but the whole time I was thinking as how I could write this story without making it personal. Of my life and of my children's. After he went over all the details of how he wanted me to write the story, he bade me good-bye with a kind smile.

All that night I thought of the story in which I was to write, and how I would write it. The next day I sat at the electric typewriter he had brought me, thinking and watching the hours. Carl paid me by the hour. I thought of the time when the apartment we lived in was too small for three people. So I began to look from one end of localities to the other end until I came upon a larger place. A sign was in the window but yet I felt reluctant to ask. For some seven years there had been only white tenants, but felt, what the hell? Being born in the South I had become used to being denied, though I never accepted it and looked upon it as being barbaric. Being in the North made it no better, for one cannot shade his skin and I feel it's equally hard to shade one's ideas. I stepped across the street and asked the home-owner about his sign in the window. He did not say no, but said I should come back, for he wasn't certain of the children. With this I felt not to ask any more, but then something inside said why not, for I had a right to a better place. His decision took about four of my visits. The next week I moved in. It was nicely painted and large enough for the three of us. Being on the third floor, I purchased a large amount of screen to keep the young ones from falling off the high height of the back porch. Sometimes we would take long walks and sometimes go to the zoo. We would retreat to the back porch, it became our private life. There we talked in secret and enjoyed eating light sandwiches. We played games and listened to records. One of our favorites was Cinderella. I say ours because once you are around children, you become them and learn to laugh and sing.

I began to write. The title of the story was *I Believe.* I told about how I loved my offspring. How I watched them grow through the long years. How we shared conversations as they passed from infancy to talkative childhood. How I managed to buy them books from the small salary I received from charity. Of how they grew strong from the cheap foods I more than often had to buy. Of how God creates in one the strength if he only believes.

I talked in my story of how I prayed that God would help them to see that I loved them dearly no matter how they came. If I had the best wedding bestowed upon me, I could not have loved them more.

I sat down and re-read the story carefully, and tears came to my eyes. All the truth that was in me was now on paper, live and walking about, it seemed. The telephone rang, it was Carl on the other end asking how the story was going. Fine, I said. I will be over to see it; I can't come tomorrow but I will come the next day. That will be fine with me, I said.

On Wednesday Carl came. Again we sat in the kitchen, striking up a conversation before we began to look over the story. He asked how had I been and I told him fine. You look okay, he said. With that, I gave a smile. In a somewhat shy way, this time his knees met mine as we talked. A piece of lint fell upon my dress and he brushed it off, smiling in a boyish way. Would you like to see the story, I asked. That would be nice, he said. He sat close by and began to read.

I sat there waiting for his answers. He placed the story on the table and then picked it up again. He began to read it over, a sad look came to his face. He looked from the story to me and then back to the story. At the end of it, he did not speak for a while. He sat with his hands folded under his chin, looking up to the ceiling. That's a good story you wrote. Thank you, I said. You have strong and powerful feelings. At this I did not speak. I can't use it, he said. Oh, I said, as if I didn't know. However, I will pay you for the time you put into it and you can keep the typewriter.

I cannot say that I was not happy over this, for I was. Thank you, I said, now looking him face to face. He gave me a smile and took my hands, placing his soft white lips upon each of them, lifting up his head to my deep dark lips, working his knees between my legs. I now placed my hands upon his face giving him a soft kiss. Can I be your friend? Yes, I spoke. We then had a long conversation and he said he would call me soon.

It was about two weeks later before I heard from him. The summer was heading towards early fall. I had gone next door for a few minutes, to return and find him sitting among the children. As I entered he gave a broad smile and said hi. I smiled back and said hello. Are you glad to see me? Yes, I spoke. I was away on a business trip. To this I did not answer for it held no meaning to me. We walked to the kitchen, for it was cooler there. Again we sat at the shabby table, talking of his trip. He did not mention what the trip consisted of but said he had been out to California.

He smiled and said, he had noticed some posters I had placed upon the walls. Would I mind if he brought over more? I told him I wouldn't mind. The following week he brought to me three large posters which I hung and admired. A month passed and he mentioned no more my writing for him, but at his every trip he would leave forty and sometimes fifty dollars. I accepted gladly and felt I used the money wisely. Though he did not speak, I knew he was after more than writing, but *what* I could not figure out, as I looked upon his well-made suits and nice ties. I kept thinking of all the trips he would talk about. I knew in some way this person was not in need of a second home, or was he? Though I began to enjoy his visits, things began to race through my mind. What did he want? For it was certain, charity could not afford me mink coats and fine homes and the what-have-you the other half of the world owns.

At the end of the month I asked him how he could find time to come over and was so busy. He told me to let him do the worrying about that, he would make time. I asked him about his wife. He said to me, she is not my boss. With that, he gave me his office number and home number and told me to feel free to call any time I wished. Which I did over a period of two years. I am not a good liar and must admit it didn't faze me in the least. I had begun to like him, yet I was puzzled.

Out of nowhere he came one day and knocked upon my door; a month had passed now. He asked would I like to go and get in bed. Without answering him, I took him by the hand and he, me. We both stood tall and erect looking each other face to face. His hands half-way down the lower part of my body, now placing a kiss upon my lips. We entered into the front part of the apartment towards the bedroom. I looked to see him shedding his clothing, standing before me nude, and I, with my long slim dark body, shedding my garments. He gently walked over with his medium sized private standing stiff. Again he took me by the hands. With the words flowing from his lips, he said, Nude Man and Nude

Lady. We lay upon the twin bed talking to each other, he touching me about the body from head to legs and back again at the breast. He kissed each breast and then my belly. I returned his kiss at the navel.

Love has a way of talking for itself. I lay back, he took his right hand and placed it mid-way between my legs, opening them so as he could place his organ and let it rest. After love-play, I asked did he enjoy himself. He smiled and said, I knew you were a person so full of love, and, yes, I did enjoy myself. That's what we were made for, isn't it? Don't forget I have read your poem a thousand times and could see in it things I have never seen before. So he didn't really want me to write for him, but I spoke nothing.

I purchased him a lovely card of sweet sentiments. He kept it in his pocket and would bring it over for me to see, each visit. He would call promptly and leave money each time, saying it was in case of an emergency. After a while he would send money through the mail. I used it to buy clothes for the children and felt proud to be able to send my mother some, for I knew she had a difficult life.

It was now nearing the eleventh month, close to Christmastime. Carl called and said, about three weeks before Christmas, we had to go away, and would I like to stop-off and see my family which lived out of state. He asked had I ever flown by plane. I told him no. Would you like to? With this, I answered him, Yes. Well, don't worry, for I will pay your way. All was set.

I had intended to take the children along but things didn't work out, so I got someone to keep them. His next call I told him I would not be able to take the children and asked if he preferred my not going. He asked what plans I made. I told him. That's fine, he said. There's one thing, his voice now low, my wife will have to take us to the airport. Why, I asked. Because I am not coming back for three weeks. With this I did not feel too pleasant and made it known. He told me it would be all right and not to worry. I will come over if that will help you to feel better. Please do, I said, for I did not want to see her.

The next day he came and we talked about my feelings of not wanting her to take us to the airport. But I am telling you, he said, things will be all right. Can't you see, he said with a disgusted look upon his face, I don't think more of her than I do of you? Now will you please listen to reason, would you prefer to go to the airport first and then I come along? No, I said, that would look even worse. Then stop worrying, you are making me tear-assed! I said no more of who would come to take us, but mentioned the fact that I did need money to buy a suit of clothing, which he handed over gladly. Does she know how much money you are giving me? No, he said, I told her I was giving you a small amount. Has she suspected anything? He said she asked him could he become involved with me. And what did you tell her, I asked. I told her no, he said with a smile. What else did she ask, I questioned him. She asked how could I find so much extra time in coming over here, the poorer side of town, when I was so busy. And what was your answer to that? I did not answer, he said; I will see you around noon on the 14th. With this, I said, yes, I will be ready.

I purchased a lovely suit and coat with the money he had given me. His wife knew I was a charity case so I had to do my thing. I had about me a pixie hair-do, a lovely pair of bone color shoes and olive-green suit with blouse to match, and bone-china coat with bag to match.

At twelve noon I heard his footsteps nearing the door. He gave a knock and I opened it to see him give a smile and say, my, you look lovely. Are you ready? Yes, I spoke in a soft voice. The two of us walked down the steps. He opened the car door; I took the backseat. He gave to his wife my name and hers to me. I spoke a soft hello. How are you, she said. I am fine, thank you. She wanted to talk but somehow found it difficult. As we drove along, she would now and then give me a glance in the car mirror; she was driving. About half-way to the airport she became nervous and came close to an accident. What's wrong with you, he said to her. I don't know, I am just nervous. I guess mid-way of traffic she came close to another accident. He then gave her a look not so pleasant, after which she composed herself and began to drive again.

He went into details of asking did she take care of all the chores. Yes, I did, she spoke. Are you certain? Yes, Carl, I am certain.

When we arrived at the airport, he took the suitcases out of the car and had them checked, leaving her to go and park the car. The two of us went inside, whereupon he led me to a chair, and there I seated myself until he purchased the tickets.

At the counter stood before him a pot of long-stemmed flowers. He would peek from behind them and every now and then give me a smile and a wave of the hand. I would smile back.

It took his wife about thirty minutes to find a parking space, at which time she entered and found a seat beside me. He got a chair and sat in front of us. She again tried to talk and I would answer no more than what was asked. Carl told me about the story you are writing. That's fine, I said. Have you ever been on a plane? No, I spoke. My mother doesn't like planes, she said. Oh, I answered her. At this point his masculine voice came in and said, I think I mentioned the fact that Yvonne was a shy person and didn't care to talk much. I am sorry, she said. He then looked at me and asked me if I would like a magazine. Thank you, I told him. He departed bringing back a *McCall's*.

The plane had readied itself for the passengers. We are ready to go now, and he turned to give her a quick kiss of good-bye. She had a sad look upon her face. However, I spoke nothing. The two of us walked towards the plane, not looking back. We took a seat and comforted ourselves. The plane was about twenty minutes in the air when he reached down and took his briefcase upon his lap. What would that be, I asked him. Just a lot of business papers. I took out the magazine. I had gotten about half-way when he asked would I care for a drink. I said I would love a drink of hot tea. He beckoned to the stewardess and ordered two small bottles for himself and hot tea for me.

He was sipping the second bottle when he side-glanced and said to me, you know, you have a good mind. We were in a conversation of rich and poor and how high society thinks it is always right about everything. I felt he had forgotten the fact that he was a rich white man talking to a black domestic woman. I thought of the brainwashing quacks that rich people attend merely to avoid reality and mainly to stay hidden in their make-believe world of fantasy. I thought life wouldn't be strange if they would stop sitting on the psychiatrist's couch at the sum of fifty dollars a half-hour so as to listen to what they wanted to hear and faced up to life at the sum of no dollars and lots of sense! However, I concealed my true feelings and said nothing.

We arrived at the airport. Together we walked into the waiting-room. I am going to rent a car, he said, and will be right back. I sat trying to read my magazine, but found the looks from whites more interesting. So I stared back. All heads turned in our direction as his white hands helped me from the chair. We walked out into the cold brisk night, seating ourselves in the front seat of the car.

We talked about his brother and I, of mine. We shared many things such as the times Carl would come on Saturday during the summer and take me shopping. If he was late I was to call him at his house, which I did. He would arrive smiling, the same as a school-boy. We would put the children in the back seat of the car and sometimes stop and buy them toys. Or fetch them hamburgers or hot dogs. Sometimes he would give me an unexpected smile which held nothing for me, and I would wonder what he was thinking of. Could he really be so free and what did he *really* want? He was very secretive most of the time. Though he was nice, there was something very mysterious about him.

Before we reached our destination, I looked to him and said, how do you want me to act? What do you mean, he asked. Would you care for me to remain close to you like before or would you rather for me to stand ten feet away? What brought this on, he asked, you know I am not ashamed of you. Oh, I said. I thought back over the first times we met, how willing he was to get in bed with me, yet telling me he couldn't let anyone see him in my house. At his words I told him I would place a large poster outside my house whenever he came and let people know that he did not care to be seen with me. What did you mean by that, he asked. I meant what you said. Well I didn't mean it that way, he said, and with just those words he gave me all the clues I needed.

Now we were pulling up to my mother's. We entered the apartment and sat down for the both of us were tired. She cooked us a nice meal and made him welcome. I knew he felt good for smiles were now placed broadly upon his face. After dinner was over, he took a seat in the front-room, relaxing in the chair, looking first to the ceiling and then at me. We had another stop to make, so we gathered our coats and kissed my mother good-bye. I told her I would see her soon.

We drove ten minutes until we came to a lovely section of town. The houses were beautifully surrounded by large trees and green grass; tall lamp-like lights were outside and you could easily see the address upon the door. I pressed my fingers upon the chimes. My brother and sister-in-law greeted us warmly. I gave his name and they shook hands. Do come in, was the reply of my relatives.

We entered the large living-room covered with white carpets. Lovely paintings were on the walls and a lovely cut-glass mirror. We passed a modern kitchen leading into the oak-lined den. Carl placed himself in the reclining chair and I, on the couch. If he had an uneasy feeling about being surrounded by my family, he did not show it. An hour passed and he was beginning to warm up. We talked far into the night, tea and coffee being served constantly. About one-thirty all decided it was time to tuck in. As Carl passed through the dining-room he would look from one room to the other. Though he didn't say, I could see that he was amazed not only at the house but at the hospitality. He was shown to a bedroom of lovely color with dim lights which made the sheets on the bed a prettier pink.

I remained for a while in the den. Before he left, he came and gave me a kiss. I changed into my night-gown, now heading towards the door of his bedroom. Would you like for me to sleep with you? Why not, he spoke, sure. I turned out the lights and lay next to him. He turned towards me, letting one of his arms rest against my stomach. I gave him a kiss. He told me to awake him early in the morning, for he wanted to get an early start.

In the morning I sat on the bed watching him sleep. I bent over and kissed him, then walked out into the dining-room, and into the den where I sat for a while. I went to the glass door and watched a squirrel eating the red and yellow corn my brother had placed there for him.

The time was passing so I went into the bedroom to awaken Carl but he wasn't ready to arise. Call me later. I bathed and donned my clothing, for breakfast was being served. We sat at an oval-shaped table with a lovely tablecloth and pretty silver-ware about and tinkling glasses. He came out and went into the bathroom and then back into the bedroom, now stepping out fully dressed. Conversation and meal were taking place.

It was a hearty breakfast of eggs and real southern sausage, cold milk and toast. He sat there staring, at which my brother said, Eat up. Wow, what do you people think I have, two stomachs? And he began to eat. Half-way through he paused, holding a fork in one hand and knife in the other. Looking somewhat sad, he spoke aloud. All I get at home, he said, is cold cereal. He did not finish his food. His words struck a low blow in me, for in such a statement there are many meanings.

We talked for an hour and time was saying our stay must come to an end. He thanked my family for making him feel so welcome and sent love to my mother. She had come by early that morning and he liked her very much. He asked to me and to himself as how she could be so happy. I told him it was easy to be happy. He gave me a puzzled look, now bending to get his briefcase. We walked out and got in the car for our journey.

He spoke no words for a long time as we drove along. Why so quiet, I asked. I am thinking of your family, how sweet they are, of your mother, of how your brother and sister-in-law enjoy their home, how happy she seems to do things for him. How happy your children are with the small gifts you give them, how they appreciate things. For a minute I could not speak. I suppose, I said, that's the enjoyment of being real. After I had spoken, I felt a pang. I began to realize that all the months he had known me he had not learned to really feel things. I wrote to him many letters which he read and appreciated. He said my letters were very important to him and were the only things that kept him going. But his new words made me think back over the days when he spoke and said: I am ashamed of being white, we have no soul.

I, now looking at him seriously, said, think of what you could do for me. He then took one hand off the steering wheel and gave my knee a pat. With a half-smile he said, Yvonne, I really want to do something to help the poor area but I can't think of anything, can you? Yes, I can, I heard myself say. What, he asked.

Why not start a foundation for the poor with no strings attached? Wow, he said, how did you ever think of that? Soul, I said.

Still seeming surprised he later said, that's a damn good idea. What made you think of it? I, now looking straight into his face said, I feel there's enough liberalism and love-foundations with strings attached. At this he said no more. We drove for an hour before words were spoken again.

We were almost to the airport. We began to talk about the trees and houses and how he found the houses in the southern state to be of great beauty as compared to his hometown. Of the harmony among the whites and blacks, though it was somewhat mean. I said, it's not the state one comes from but the state of mind one is in. I guess you are right, he said, I thought it would be different. Most people do, I said, cutting him off. We were now in front of the airport. He returned the car and walked with me to catch the plane. We had to wait for a few minutes. I will write you a card before I get back, he said, so take care. With that he departed.

The next week he was to write:

. . . I hope you and the children are having a fine holiday. Please thank your mother and brother for me. I enjoyed meeting them.

Happy New Year,

Carl

After I arrived and unpacked the suitcase, and the children had settled down, I thought of him and of the gifts. I sat down and took out a pair of scissors and plain paper and crayons. I cut the paper in the shape of a big round circle. I attached it together then painted it red, placing an airplane on the front cover. I sat for a few minutes thinking of what would I say in way of thanking him. Without another thought, words began to flow into the bright red circle:

> Now I know what it means whenever I hear
> Allegheny moon, now I know what it's like
> to see a city from a high, filled with
> bright lights and tiny automobiles

> But most of all I know what it's like to
> see you look from behind a pot of flowers
> and give to me your soft smile and wave of
> the hand, even though I was shy, my heart
> was filled with love. so may I say thanks
> to you. and to Eastern. and to
> Allegheny

I set it aside until he would return. Two weeks later I picked up the phone and dialed his number. A voice on the other end gave a cheerful Hi, how are you? Fine, I said, can you come over? I told him I was in need of funds. He said he would be over shortly. After I replaced the receiver, an uncertain feeling came over me.

He came dressed executive-style. He pulled out a chair and seated himself. He asked did I enjoy my trip, and did I like the plane-ride. Yes, I said. I placed in his hands the red circle. He opened it and began to read. He looked it over again and rested it upon the table. I like that he said. I am glad you do, giving him a kiss. He crossed one leg over the other, looking away from me. He sat in this position for a time. You always speak of love, he said, still not looking at me. Yes, I spoke, does that bother you? It always has, he said. Feeling shocked, I asked, why? I don't know what love is, he said. What do you mean you don't know what love is, I asked him. I just don't know, he said. You don't love your wife of these many years? No more than I do any other woman, he said; I love her like the lady I slept with next door. You are but a doll with a painted smile upon your face, I said. I guess I am, he spoke. He damned himself and his society. After he finished I said to him in a soft but strong voice, you used me even before you came to see me the first time, didn't you? Yes, he spoke, and left.

I knew something had taken place. I felt I could write on paper better than what I could say in words. The next day I sent him my feelings of the real him and of his last words:

> Life is strange, but I say it's the people in it that makes it so.
> It's the way we think and feel towards each other. I feel that
> most of us have a habit of wanting to be real. You know

what the word means. For at childhood either mommy or daddy will pick up a toy and try to identify the stuffed animal. And maybe give his arm a pat and say this is real. But I wonder how many persons have thought to pat their hearts for a nice measure and say, this is real?

We have lots of nice people in the world as you and I know. From both sides. With that, the world can go along on an even basis. We know what the militant thinks and feels. With that, we can still go along and try to pick up the 500 years that have gone.

There is more, but some things hurt. And then you keep moving along as time passes like sand in an hourglass. And you chance upon the so-called White Liberal. He takes your hands and turns your hourglass from tail's-end on head. Which is to say your time won't be long. He takes your hands and glides them slowly about his body until they come to the word Liberal. Then he begins to smile and nod his head in a somewhat yes form, not realizing your gracious eye of knowledge has not caught his bona fideness. But most important of all, his eye is so cast upon your hourglass he's forgotten about the meaning of good faith.

Some of them think one born in poverty or living in poverty is already deteriorating. Or you might plain out and say dead. However, I say being born in poverty is like living in a body of heavy waters. What it really *do* is simply teach you to keep your head above the water. You keep paddling. Sometimes you may sink but you never go down as not to come up. You shall forever paddle.

I don't feel you and many others like you can understand this. Money has always been your means. You have indeed travelled in a class to your sweet little selves too long.

You said you learned a lot from me on my side of town. I never told you I learned so a lot from you. Oh, you vowed many things. I would smile and you would ask why. I did care, I had to. It was I that was happy. I had no dreams to dwell upon. Now at the end, I am unhappy. I wanted to give you a part of my reality. But now I say love is not cold cereal. It's not a nickel. Or a dime. It's not fancy. It's not poor. Love is simply love.

—Yvonne

This decade we shall reach many new shores. The following letters depict the continuing quest to find what is true in oneself and in one's blackness.

HENRY MARTIN *was born in Philadelphia, Pennsylvania. In 1963, he graduated from Bowdoin College in Brunswick, Maine, and received his M.A. in English the following year from New York University. He remained in New York to teach in the public schools of Spanish Harlem, the Lower East Side, and Bedford Stuyvesant. In 1965 Martin left the United States to take up residence in Milan, Italy. There, he has been an assistant professor in English language and literature at Luigi Bocconi University. He has published art criticism in* Art International *in Europe and in* Art and Artists *and* Studio International *in England. His first book, a critical study of the French sculptor Arman, is to be published by Harry N. Abrams, New York. He is presently at work on a non-novel and a film.*

Henry Martin

Letters from Abroad

Summer 1969—Greece

Dear Floyd,

I'm on the island of Mykonos. Which is doing its best to be St. Tropez. I'm not doing that scene however, have been living in a room in a restaurant beside a deserted, nearly deserted beach. Can't though—brandy just arrived—get away from the fake hippies. Will be leaving tomorrow for Samos. No hippies, fake or otherwise, out there. Before Mykonos—it's ten days or so that I'm here now—I was on Poros.

Life, right now, for me is simply a matter of taking stock. I made the mistake of thinking that this was the summer for decisions, and was trying hard to make them. Big ones. Have discovered, though, that decisions take time. Was trying to decide about the immediate years to come and how to live them. But the discovery is that the years themselves are not what I have to decide about. These next two or three years will *be* the decision, at any rate will be decisive, I hope.

The problem of course, or at least in part, is the problem we have both always known about—always known about but talked about too little—which maybe goes for me but not for you. The problem—or perhaps the solution, of being black, which is of course no easy problem, and likewise, no easy solution.

We talked about that a bit, not enough though in New York. You mentioned that you were about to begin putting together another anthology—which I suppose is the main reason I'm writing to you now, even though there would surely be plenty enough reasons to write you even without that. You mentioned that you might be able to use something from me. I have not forgotten that. I need to think every thing through. And now I have the time to do it. I suppose I could think it all through in a letter, or just on paper, privately, for me. But the idea of its being for you, and in public, of letting it all hang out—well, that would make it more real, more binding, more honest. More, in short, of a decision, more of an event. I'm sure you know what I mean. Let me know.

It was good seeing you in New York last winter. Am only sorry that it didn't happen for longer or again. All of the new friends have been drained already. I need a rest from them, just as they need a rest from me, even though I love some of them very deeply. And when new friends have been drained, one of course turns to the old ones. That's what they're for. They will probably have become new in the meantime.

When we met in New York I guess we were both fairly up-tight. But, of course, we're both used to that—both from ourselves and from each other. Which naturally enough meant that we both fell back on our styles—the mutual style that we've established over the years for all of our meetings and encounters. Which is all o.k of course, since it's a fairly good style, I suppose. But I do remember most of what we had to say, especially what you had to say to me—about my thinking I had secrets to reveal. I guess that I'm still trying to figure that one out.

.   .   .

All I am interested in right now, quite simply, is life. But the problem is largely a matter of definitions. Heard Stokely Carmichael say once—in London, just before they threw him out—(feels as though I've written you this before) that the greatest power of the power structure is the power to define. And what they have been defining most of all is what it feels like to be alive. They had fooled Hemingway surely, and what I hope is that I will have the strength and energy to keep them from fooling me.

More brandy. The sun has moved. Less light. Less hardness. Less color. Ice Cream. Cigarette. Finger cramps, waving hands, rocking boats. Noise. Coca cola. Amstel beel. Vat 69, Scotland's finest. A lady with sideburns. A red roof. Breeze, Nescafé. Miniskirts and see-through shorts. Transparency. The police.

I met a black girl a couple of days ago. On the path to the nudist beach. Really beautiful, splendid, lithe. She looked at me and said, "Hello brother, how are you?" and I said, "Swinging baby, absolutely swinging." She was on her way back from the beach and I was going there. End of interview. She made me feel so fine, like I have hardly ever felt before. Lay naked in the sun and felt clean.

Was in a bar. Not really on the make, but attentive. The juke box began to play "soul brother." A black man, as beautiful in his own way as the girl had been, walked across the room and silently shook my hand. It felt like communication.

But the girl on the path kept on walking and the boy in the bar was less interested in talking than in getting back to the Swedish girl he had been dancing with in the first place. Reappeared later with a gracious nod. I put down my drink and waved back. I too can be gracious. But I don't really think I could stand it if blackness turned out to be just another style—another appearance of ease or dignity with just the same old shit beneath. Really couldn't stand it. My only aim in life is to have decent relationships with the men and women around me. No fear, no modesty, no reserve, no guilt, no hiding, no shit. Lots of joy. Freedom, paradise now. Lots of love. The possibility of friendship. Communication. Feeling my heart beat, feeling the heat of the sun. Rainbows and armpits. I want to be black in so much as being black is a part of me, is a part of my being a man, a human being—going into life and living it. I don't want to be duped again. I want a life that is free from games. A life with real emotions in it. If blackness is just another game—well, there will be no forgiveness then for anybody.

The light has changed again. Against the whiteness of the houses it glows pink. The hillside is a deeper, more golden brown. The sky more azure, less blue; the rocks go silver; the wind less strong. Peasants walk by dressed in mourning. The seagulls play in the air currents above the harbor. The cigarette burns slowly away, the glass of water is warm. Glasses click against serving trays. Carmela flashes through my mind. The water is a deeper blue, the brandy feels stronger. my head clearer. Tomorrow to Samos. See you in Senegal.

love,
Henry

September 20, 1969 — Milan

Dear Floyd,

Thank you immensely for your letter, for the one that you wrote before receiving mine. I am very much impressed that we were both thinking in the same terms at the same time. On receiving my letter you no doubt realized the immensity of what had happened.

Right now my life is almost entirely about apartment changing. You know what a mess that can be. And if it's a hassle in the states it's even worse in Italy. I write you from the corner of a table no longer placed where it ought to be, and thinking I should be sick from the smell of all this fresh paint in an apartment that used to be mine. The end of this closet tragedy, though, should-must-will go on stage within the next few days.

You say you want to get the book into production soon. I think about what I want to write quite a lot. But little has gotten onto paper, and I know that nothing will get onto paper until I have gotten myself into a place to live and think in. Which should be about the beginning of October. Whether or not I can think through 27 years of being black in just under or over 27 days is more than I can tell you right now.

One of the biggest problems I have to face is a problem of form. Nobody writes essays any more, nobody wants to. Essay means *to try*, and it's about time that we all got around to succeeding. In what I write for you, I want to get absolutely to the bone of things — the heart is still too close to the surface. Half of my reason for staying away from the states has to do with the way in which the states make me and everybody else so goddamn sloppy. When you get whatever you get from me, it's going to look and read as though it had been written with a scalpel.

You say you want this book not only to define what is black but to create it. I like that very much, even though I take issue with your choice of words. To define *is* to create. This is one of the things I intend to talk about.

You say that you want this book to be prophetic. I will have even more to say about that.

And there is still another enormous problem to solve—a more personal problem. I keep writing phrases, sentences, entire paragraphs in my head that ring of self-justification, which obliquely is about the problem not of "how black do you have to be?" but about the problem of "how black can you *allow* yourself to be?" — which in turn is about what is the definition of black anyhow and who the hell made it, and think twice before you accept it, since being black in any part of the world has nothing to do; *must* have nothing at all to do with any kind of a feeling of guilt. Clear? If not, it will be. And if it isn't I hope that the kind of confusion created will be an expression of collective confusion, not simply of my own.

November 23, 1969 — Milan

Dear Floyd,

I've been trying to get to the point of writing this letter for over a week, maybe ten days, maybe more, ever since it became clear to me that for the moment this letter is the only thing I can write to you. Which is more than an admission of failure, perhaps less, or simply other. In New York I remember, and I mentioned this before, I think when I wrote you from Greece, I remember your saying that my problem was that I thought I had to say something to somebody — that I had something *to* say to somebody and that in fact I don't. I don't remember what I went on to say when I wrote you from Mykonos, but I said maybe that you were wrong. But no, you're right, or almost. There are things I think that I have to say maybe to you or to anybody else I come face to face with, but that's about the biggest audience I can manage. Not for fear of declaring myself, since I've even gotten to be fairly good at that, but rather because I have no concept of to whom any public statement is really being made and no concept of the real purpose that making any public statement can serve.

For the last four years I've been writing about art, and the experience has taught me a lot. The art has taught me a lot. Art now is ever more about systems. The medium is the message and all that. The picture — let's pretend that people still make pictures — the picture doesn't stop at its frame but is also about the wall on which it is hung and the people who are looking at it. Or rather, the picture, the frame, the wall, the room and the people in it are all part of a situation that ought, perhaps, to be judged only as a whole, and at any rate it's clear that no one of the parts can be judged without taking all the rest into consideration. But no, I was right the first time, it's a situation that has to be judged as a whole. That sounds wrong since the example I used is a picture, but what I'm really talking about is more like a happening, since happenings grew out of pictures anyway because of the suspicion that pictures lie, that pictures refuse to be about the whole situation of which they are a part. Recently I ran across the statement that "one of the major illusions of the art system is that art resides in specific objects. Such artifacts are the material basis for the concept of the 'work of art.' But in essence, all institutions which process art data, thus making information, are components of the work of art. Without the support system, the object ceases to have definition." Which is by corollary to say that it is the support system that gives the object its definition, purpose, use, function, etc. — that, in short, the medium after all is the message, or at least determines the availability and function of the message; that the institution is bigger than its components and can function in ways, when things are going badly, that are contradictory or inimical with respect to the individual components and of which the components are not even aware. Which is why it's really a very serious matter when I say I have no concept of to whom any public statement is really being made and no concept of the real purpose that making any public statement can serve.

When I told a friend last New Years that I was thinking of beginning to work on a book before long, he said, "Write it fast. In New York right now a black man can publish anything." Now, I don't care if that's true or not, since even if it isn't he obviously had reasons for saying it, for thinking it, and he was never, as I remember, too strikingly original (since maybe nobody is), and if he was thinking it, other people are thinking it too, and a funny thing about any thought you've got in your head is that there's a good chance of your acting on it at some time or in some way; or better, a funny thing about any idea that is running around in a society is that there is probably somebody who, somewhere, is already acting on it. When you shift from an individual to a social dynamic, the various possibilities of the activation of an idea are distributed no longer in terms of time, but spatially. This is after all the space age. Whether or not this assessment of the state of U.S. publishing is the truth doesn't matter. It can't possibly avoid being at least the reflection of some similar truth. And by now it's easy to see that talking about blackness, talking about revolution, is rapidly being made legitimate. Who, precisely, my question is, does this serve?

Evergreen has been running, for instance, an ad that says "paperbacks anyone?" flown in black on a grey background above a beautiful black woman — Afro hair, penetrating gaze, dressed mainly in sex and sequins. The two choice offers are the two latest stridently-titled black books, but the other books in the ad are *I Am Curious (Yellow)*, *Billy and Betty*, *Mother's Three Daughters*, and *Joy*. Who, precisely, does this serve? *Life* last week ran an article on revolution and didn't even bother to be sarcastic. It seemed to think of itself as simply another part of Mao's revolution in a different place, with a different modality, and really it's all quite respectable. On the front cover they were practically going into the business of selling marijuana, the back pages were dedicated to the praise of the new hippy life-style, and revolution slipped in to fill out a trilogy fit to be buried on America's coffee tables. Precisely what all of this is about, I don't quite know, but I do have an intuition or two, and I don't think I like it. I can't get over the fact, to give another example, that the letters you write me from your office fly the banner of "Porter Sargent — *Publisher of the Handbook of Private Schools.*" Which of course doesn't prove anything — even though in my day, at least, Andover and Exeter had "quotas" — but it does give one pause. I'm sure it's already given you pause too. Now, of course one uses whatever means one has at one's disposal, but you've got to be certain of how those means are using you.

By now, it seems to me that I am nearly totally uncertain of nearly everything. I have given up working, and am very much trying to start writing, start thinking. And I do know that my uncertainty is not entirely my own. My mind, after all, is in good working order, better than the order — I'm not humble — in which most right now are to be found. A mind is like a workshop, it's fitted out with a whole series of tools that are designed to do a specific job. And they determine the range of operations you can perform. The tools: though you've bought them on the market, you didn't design them. The tools of which I am in possession were designed likewise by somebody else. Most of them bear the mark *made in America.* There are some jobs that they don't know how — are entirely unequipped — to do. They were designed perhaps to make the world safe for democracy. They were designed to force upon us a certain reading of reality. They are instruments for certain kinds of predictions; most of all they determine predictable alternatives. They were designed to create only certain kinds of understanding and to inhibit others.

And all we've got left besides these tools are feelings. Which of course it's difficult to rely on. And it will remain difficult to rely on them until such time as we have become able to turn our feeling structures into new instruments of thought with new possibilities of predictability. In the meantime the only ground rule I have is the knowledge — the *knowledge* — that the world is not mechanistic, not a matter of cause and effect; that it is organic, a field, a question of statistic, that there are inter-relationships no matter how arcane they may seem, no matter how hard it is for us to define their exact configurations. I know that the risk I run is even greater confusion; that the risk I run is immersing myself in total un-predictability; that the risk I run is total paranoia; that the risk I run is becoming animistic and primitive, a foot-note to *The Savage Mind.*

But to get back to the point, what is it that my paranoia tells me? What unexplainable but feelingly signicant juxtapositions, synchronisms, coincidences do I see? It's very simple. I see all of these printed words about blackness, about revolution, with Malcolm and Mao quoted in *Life,* articles in *Newsweek* about the Panthers; and at the same time the Panthers are shooting it out with Karenga, Eldridge Cleaver is in exile, Stokely Carmichael has been forced to reduce his public activities to being the manager for Miriam Makeeba — things, in short are falling apart. Moderation is back on the scene with us again. The summers are no longer either long or hot, the militant sixties are over and the seventies are beginning to look sauve. I once again see the spectre of the real integration of the black man into an *untransformed* America with black history courses at city college mixing with white history courses at city college and turning into grey history. I see the spectre of a whole generation of self-respecting black men subtly at the service of General Motors. I think I see a war going on between the action and the words. I see America literally talking us to death and imbecility. Look at what they did to the moratorium for Vietnam. They turned it into a national holiday; a kind of procession for the dead even before they got around to dying — to being slaughtered. . . .

Let me get back into focus. Getting down to specifics I have already changed the subject, perhaps for the better. The ground I stand on feels more solid. I've shifted I guess from talking about the whole image that America seems now to present me and have begun to talk about a different order of contradictions. There are so many of them. But I'm not so much interested at the moment in other people's problems as I am in mine. Mine at the moment are the only defects that I have a fighting chance of eliminating, and everybody else likewise is going to have to work things out for himself. Another way of putting this is to say that I remember that you said you wanted the book to be prophetic, critical, and creative. In the course of the last months I've discovered that my bent for prophecy is in fairly good shape; you yourself know, that as far as complaining goes, I'm in a reasonably good category. But prophecy and criticism, I become ever more convinced, boil largely down to the talk machine, the talk war, covertly and unconsciously doing in the troops they naively thought to help, spreading confusion in the ranks of the people's army and helping the war-lords keep the shop-keepers happy with the myth of democracy and freedom of information.

This is maybe just another way of saying that the only thing that anybody needs to say right now is *solutions*. I have none. When you discover that everything is going badly it is not your first duty to reveal it. Your first duty is to do something — *do* something — that will make it go better.

Everybody is doing the best he can, which is good enough. Which is simply all that for now is possible. The best that I can do is to leave them all alone and start trying to do my best. All I am fairly clear on now are certain directions in which research is possible, certain areas of thought and language to be explored that may reveal a few buried agates — at least that much — even if things go badly, and that, if things go well, may reveal a copper mine or a supersonic x-ray gun, or a thought capable of becoming a real and unequivocal action.

But my ideas about directions of research are useful only to me. Everybody else is already doing his best, as much as he can. So until I have specific things to say to them, to the ones who are already doing, specific things that not only say what it is in what they are doing that is wrong, but also how to do it better, until then I have nothing to say at all. There is no point in my telling you what you have done wrong in the past until I can tell you what to do right in the future. And it's clear of course that when I tell you what to do I have to be there to help you do it. It was Genet, I think in *Esquire* — how bizarre, Genet in *Esquire* — who said that he thought the time had come for writers to be a real and physical, bodily and no longer simply moral presence on the scenes of action and confrontation which they believe in and represent.

This time around, as I see it, the struggle is total. Has to be total. There are less than 15 years left before 1984 — the era of total control masked by the appearance of total freedom. We are new to political thinking, though. We are new to real political understanding of the realities that surround us. And let's face it, none of us really understands exactly what it is that makes the world we live in run. The great thing about Marx in his time was that he understood the world he lived in better than did the forces that actually controlled that world. There is nobody around like him now. And of course his analyses are no longer exact. The world and the systems of control that make it function are no longer so simple. Marx lived in a world that was essentially guided by questions of economics and class, which are, of course, the same thing. But America was founded on the basis of a mysticism, on the basis of impulses and drives that are much more intimate, much more psychological, much more confused and confusing. Economics does not explain slavery. Or if it explains slavery it doesn't explain most of what has come after it.

The world, I feel, is running rapidly out of control. Nixon doesn't run America. Not even General Motors or IBM runs America. It is necessary to go beyond cause and effect thinking because cause and effect is no longer the fundamental rule of the world itself. What *are* the rules of this brave new world? This, I think, is what we have to get around to understanding. In Europe it makes no sense to talk about arriving at an understanding of the basic systems of image and symbol that run the world. Europe is still very simple. But unless this kind of understanding takes root in America, the ballgame is already lost. This is where I'm at right now. Trying to write, trying to think, trying to find a language that *Life* and *Evergreen* can't turn into rhetoric. I've given round one pretty much up for lost. Trying desperately to get into shape to step into the ring for number two. The fight may not go to a full thirteen. All of this too is rhetoric, I know, and you can't imagine how much that saddens me.

You once wrote me that you so much liked receiving my letters because it gave you such joy to see your friend grow. I was shocked when you said it, or wrote it, I don't remember which. I hadn't been aware of growth, hadn't been aware of change. I hope now that the tables aren't turned, that this letter can still give you some of that same joy — that now when I feel as though I'm growing that I haven't, on the other hand, started to stand still. I say this, I suppose, because I feel that this letter, even if what I'm trying to say is clear (which I know it isn't) must come as something of a disappointment. You asked me for more than this;

I promised you more than this, I thought it possible to give you more than this. This is the first time in a long while that I have bitten off more than I can chew. It leaves a bitter taste. But it's a good thing, on the other hand, to know exacly what it is that is too much to chew.

In my last letter, or from Greece, I told you that I wanted to contribute to your book because I had realized that my own understanding of my blackness had to be the necessary prologue to my ever breaking out of the circle I have drawn about myself, and becoming whole. Coming to an understanding of my blackness means coming to an understanding of my mind. Without this understanding all of the relationships of which my life are made remain a mystery. My balances, though, is not something I can clear up before getting down to work; it is what I may have begun to understand at the end of my work, if it ever has an end. It is the subject matter, the theme, the problem, the solution, it is anything and everything but a preliminary.

Let me hear from you soon,

Love,
Henry

The black community is enriched by many and varying strains. In the seventies it is imperative that a new understanding and concern exist among all black people for all black people.

ORDE COOMBS: *"I think West Indians are probably God's chosen people. They have a kind of belief in themselves, a confidence that they can do anything." Coombs was born in St. Vincent, West Indies. His mother not only demanded that her children do well in school, but left the comfort provided by her husband's small estate and dry-goods store to pick up Coombs' brother and two sisters and take them to England to go to school. Coombs later went to Yale University and in 1966, after a fellowship year at Cambridge, moved to New York, where he is a senior editor of the McCall Publishing Company. He is the co-author of* Eastern Religions in the Electric Age *and the editor of* We Speak as Liberators: Young Black Poets.

Orde Coombs

On Being West Indian In New York

There are no accurate figures on the number of West Indians
in New York. I have heard that there are 200,000 of us here, but
this is guesswork. At any rate, I seem to hear the various island
accents more frequently now, and Jamaican, Trinidadian, or Barbadian voices seem to be all around me when I take the subway.
There are colonies of West Indians in Brooklyn, in Manhattan,
and the Bronx. Not too many live in Queens, and there is no more
than a thimbleful on Staten Island. Through social clubs, cricket
teams, fund raising parties, soccer matches, and boat rides, West
Indians get together to measure each other's progress, to boast
about their children, and to keep abreast of the gossip at home.
"Comess" or gossip is a staple of island life, and West Indians
see no reason why things should be any different in metropolitan
New York.

The West Indian, confronting the stranger, will talk about "we
West Indians," but when he is comfortable or drunk or among
his peers, the phrase changes to "we Bajans," "we Jamaicans,"
"we Trinidadians." The gossip, then, is really about specific island
politics (West Indians love to talk politics, but are hardly a political people), or about enemies and friends.

"Have you heard Dora Stephens died?" you are asked, and
although you are a decade removed from island life, you are supposed to register shock, regret, and despair. If you, honestly, state
that you can't remember Dora Stephens, everyone is outraged.

"Of course you know Dora Stephens," they chant. "Don't you

remember Helen Lizzy's aunt? Well, she was Dora Stephens' good friend, and all you were cousins. You never know when you will have to go back. You might get sick. You shouldn't forget people."

The implication is always clear. It doesn't matter how long you have been in America; it doesn't matter that you are now a citizen of "the most powerful country in the world"; it is of little importance that you have no intention of returning to the islands during your working life, *America is not your home*.

West Indians in New York do not, I think, have any great affection for this country. They are here because they cannot find employment at home. If they are educated and live at home, they find that their skills are either not in demand, or that they can make more money here. So they come as quickly as their visas will allow them. Then after years of scrimping, of working three jobs, of seeing one's children—at last—doctors or lawyers, many West Indians go home to die. Home to the islands, to the sun, to the poverty-ridden versions of Paradise. The West Indian feels, at bottom, a sense of accomplishment, but not much more than that. It is what is expected; it is what one's peers are doing, and that fantastic journey of deprivation, of backbreaking work is of little import. He has done what he had to do. He goes home to build a three-bedroom bungalow with hot and cold running water, with electric gadgets. He buys some land on which he will plant vegetables, and if he is strong enough, he will "mind" a cow and some goats. He has had a full life. His children will never have to massage the calluses on *their* hands.

Since the 1966 change of the American immigration laws, West Indians have been flocking to New York. North America has become more than just the "land of opportunity," since Britain effectively barred West Indian migration. It is now, quite simply, an above ground railroad to economic freedom. Many who have relatives in Canada are able to get into that country, but it is to America that most West Indians look, since they feel that once they get here, anything is possible and all their bourgeois dreams will take shape. The West Indian does not think of Africa because he is not concerned with nation building. He is on this earth to reaffirm the validity of middle-class values, and America represents the triumph of the middle-class.

The islander who arrives here and has to take a menial job is fond of saying that he is only doing whatever he is doing until he "gets straightened out." The assumption, of course, is that upward mobility is not only possible, but *possible very soon*. When he arrives here with the smell of hydrangeas still in his nose he may be intimidated by many things: the height of New York's buildings, the frantic pace of its citizens, its size and noise and garbage. But he knows that he will be protected, "shown the ropes" by the other West Indians until he, too, can chew gum as easily as a Brooklynite. He learns, too, that some black New Yorkers call black strangers "brothers"; that the rhetoric of black unity is everywhere, and if the reality seems to be some distance away, he can always hope.

Forty years ago he would have walked into a cauldron. Black Southerners were escaping their agrarian legacy and coming to New York when this earlier West Indian influx was going on. The competition to be somebody's janitor or busboy or elevator operator was so intense that both groups developed a bristling undercurrent of distaste for each other. The black immigrants were called "monkey chasers" by American blacks, and when the latter wanted to be particularly vicious, West Indians became "Black Jews." West Indians, for their part, imagined themselves superior to American blacks. They based this vaunted superiority on the black's lower class status and his supposed lack of militancy.

The times have changed, somewhat. The language of opprobium direcfed towards West Indians has all but disappeared. But the flexed responses remain and the cementing of black West Indian-black American unity remains, as far as I can see, very tenuous.

Since Birmingham and Watts and Newark, a strange kind of West Indian duplicity has set in. The militant black American is no longer seen as an obsequious nincompoop, but as a threat to the social order. Now, not all West Indians think this. The intellectuals go to great lengths to proclaim their militancy, but I have spoken to too many "average" West Indians and gotten the same response for this similarity to be coincidental. Even when the islander approves of the black American's militant action, he finds some way of proclaiming the latter's insufficiency.

"They could do 'more'."

"They could own their own houses. We came here penniless, and within five years we bought a house."

"They spend too much money in bars."

"Education is free in New York; they could get some."

New York blacks are fully aware of what West Indians feel, and they retaliate by speaking of the West Indian's pushiness, his braggadocio, his delusion of how pleasant life is in the West Indies: "If it is so good there, why are you here?"

At the core of all this friction is the West Indian's arrogance. But there are sound reasons for this hauteur. With the memory of his poverty still with him, the West Indian in New York tends to be wary of extravagance. He wants nothing to do with Eldorados, with "hogs," with "dog-hogs." He makes being "uptight" a state of grace. He prefers the company of other West Indians, because he can measure how quickly he is acquiring the respectability that his poverty denied him at home. And above all, he marshalls his energies to buy a home, to send his children to school. When he first arrives here, he confronts all the blazing signs that have been lit to proclaim his black inferiority. It doesn't really matter what he has read—and he has read of Little Rock and Ole Miss and Governor Wallace—he is not prepared to face the poverty of New York's blacks. Poverty? In New York? There is something startlingly incongruous about this. God knows *he* is poor, and many of the black people on his island know only debilitating poverty. In fact, one could search some villages and not come up with more than four regular wage earners. Everyone else exists on seasonal work, or a relative's pound notes from England, the odd tourist's dollar, or divine grace. But this is New York. What he is seeing must be a mirage. When he knows it is not, his arrogance becomes the safeguard of his sanity, and it is this and his inflated ego that enable him—peasant though he may be—to come to terms with a hostile, sophisticated, and violent society.

He must function in the maelstrom in which he finds himself, because he cannot return home as penniless as he left. He cannot "dropout" here, because his drive to attain middle-class status was what pushed him to leave home in the first place. He cannot sit still. He must progress, because his island peers know that he came to America to work or to study and they are waiting for word about him. Of all *my* peers, only one went away to college and flunked out. He was so ashamed that he never returned home until his father died. By then, he had married rather well, and money compensated for his lack of a degree.

It seems to me that West Indians in New York—given the enormity of racial antagonism and discrimination—have prospered. When I say West Indians, it must be understood that I am talking not only about the new immigrants but also the descendants of the old. West Indians, among themselves, refer to "one of us" or "one of them" and very often "one of us" has never seen the West Indies, and has no accent. What he or she does have is a West Indian grandmother, and that is sufficient.

I keep running into sons and daughters of those who came here in the thirties and who are now as full of self-importance as middle management bureaucrats. Whenever I am introduced, it is immediately apparent that I am an islander. (I have a West Indian cum-pseudo-British accent. I have tried to speak black slang but had to give that up, since in trying to hang loose, I ended up sounding constipated.) I am usually told by the person I have just met, that he or she is first or second generation West Indian, and I am asked if I like meat patties and ginger beer. I find these descendants everywhere in New York, and I have come to realize that they have worked out a rather cozy deal. They can be black and they can be West Indian, and if they are dishonest or short-sighted, they can exploit being both.

In fact, many do just this, and one finds this Trans-Caribbean man everywhere. He is active in whatever black participation there is in the political, cultural, and educational milieus of the city. West Indians point to just these "triumphs" of middle-class status to "prove" how worthy they are. They point out that Garvey was West Indian, that Malcolm X's mother was from Grenada, that one of LeRoi Jones' parents came from the islands, that Stokely was born in Trinidad, that Shirley Chisolm is West Indian and Judge Constance Baker Mottley is West Indian, that Sidney Poitier is from the Bahamas and Harry Belafonte was born in Jamaica. No attempt has yet been made to claim Eldridge Cleaver. All of this breastbeating is supposed to indicate the special energy endemic to all West Indians.

The islanders are fond of saying that they are "different" from American blacks. They insist on their differences by constantly speaking of "back home": "Back home, we don't eat all this madness," says the young secretary, confronting pepperoni for the first time. "Back home children know how to speak to their parents." The West Indian in New York tries to let all his co-workers know that he is not American, that he is, despite his 20 year sojourn, *in transit*. This is simply a way of setting himself apart from, and if possible, above the New York black. And white New Yorkers love to play this particular version of Divide and Conquer:

"Oh I'm not talking about your kind," says my cousin's co-worker. She is again denouncing "people who get something for nothing," and my cousin having slaved in this country to acquire a modicum of security is enraged, because she knows the woman is talking about black people. "You know you're *different*," this harridan allows, "you're West Indian."

But there is no more than normal perversity—and pragmatism —in what I have called West Indian arrogance. As strangers in a new country and a frightening city, West Indians try to identify with the power, the prestige of the ruling class. After all, they are immigrants trying to escape the stigma of poverty and degradation, and although there are no guarantees that identification with the white ruling class assures upward mobility, it is certain, they feel, that affiliation with the black underclass does not.

Any attempt to explain why the West Indian has done well in America must deal with one crucial factor. At the heart of his endeavors was his belief that education was everything. The mother, illiterate, could hope that her son could learn, and that his knowledge would release him from the sweat of the cane fields. That joy, that promise of "no more sweat" explains how West Indian parents, with no resources, could marshall hope from the alphabet, could continue to believe in the magic of books. If the West Indian could, at any price, obtain an education, he returned to his island a respected man. He was accorded more than "Mr.," he was even called "Boss." And social recognition came with the correct pronunciation of a polysyllabic word. It did not matter that he was born out of wedlock, or that his mother washed the governor's underwear. He could now be invited to dinner, at the governor's house, and, if this was his desire, dance with the governor's lady. He was made to feel part of the establishment, he was absorbed into the rotting core of colonial society.

It must be pointed out that most West Indians accepted this bargain rather gladly, and once having been adorned with spurious laurels, became staunch upholders of the realm. If the West Indian took time to think when he returned home, he realized that no one cared for his moral worth, that the British were again the conquerors, that their long and careful tradition of maintaining exclusiveness by specific osmosis had triumphed. But he did not think. He had played the game, he had worked hard, and his "success," such as it was, was his to enjoy.

West Indians for the most part are insidious Anglophiles. In his island home, anything the British proclaim as "good" the West Indian unhesitantly adopts. This posture is particularly stultifying since the petit bourgoisie, the civil servants, ministers, and school teachers are the chief offenders. The West Indian underclass, having only the mirror of these black Englishmen into which to gaze, assume that what is British is best. Many young West Indian intellectuals try to fight against such ingrained identity problems, but their struggle will be a long one because West Indians play such a superb game of self-deception:

"We are not Anglophiles," they insist.

"We only like order."

"How can you say we ape the British when we love calypso and carnival and limbo?"

All this is said with the utmost sincerity at four o'clock tea.

In New York, the Anglophilia is double-edged. The West Indian knows that New Yorkers are Anglophiles, and so he plays up his nebulous identification with the Queen; with his brother who shovels coal in Croydon, Surrey; with his sister-in-law who is studying nursing in Birmingham. "That's Birmingham, *England*," he adds gratuitously. I returned home to St. Vincent after my graduation from college in the United States. This visit was

to be a short one, and I felt I should see everyone. I went to see
the local Anglican minister—a black man, fortyish, educated in
the West Indies, and the essence of pomposity. "Where did you
go to school?" he asked me. I told him. "Mr. Coombs," he said,
"I'm sorry you went there. We Barbadians, you know, have an
abhorrence of American education." It is not easy to change ingrained prejudices. I, too, you see, remember the Sunday school
and church picnics, cricket and soccer and afternoon teas, that
brought us black popinjays into the realm of English grace. Our
British affectations, 4000 miles removed from their source, seem,
on reflection, absurd. But there was no absurdity when, as children, we prayed for Sir Francis Drake and Sir Walter Raleigh;
when we heaped execrations on the heads of the Spaniards for
daring to launch an Armada on England when we could not feel
for the Indian dead in the Black Hole of Calcutta. We were West
Indians, and we wore, uncomplainingly, green woolen blazers and
grey flannel trousers to school, not because they were comfortable
(the wool itched and stank in the tropical heat) but, because, on
some decaying street in Liverpool, a British teenager wore the
same get-up.

West Indians, though, had it easy. This is not to say that the
aftermath of slavery was not harsh; that the humiliation of chain
and whip and branding iron was not intense. But there was no
Civil War, no Reconstruction, and there were never enough
whites around to destroy one's sanity. Besides, one was in the
majority, one had a piece of land, and the British, although
racist to the core, were not brutal. They practiced "benign ne-
glect," got drunk daily on gin and tonic, and tried to bugger as
many black youths as they could get their hands on. But it is precisely this experience that now renders West Indians in New
York inane in a time of discontent. Black Americans move, insis-
tently, to understand their ravished psyches, to give specific
meaning to the black experience. West Indians seem to tether, to
recoil from the harsh search for identity, to wash themselves in
abstruse talk of multiracialism. Having been seduced, they have
come to enjoy their seduction. This does not mean that West
Indians have been inactive in the fight for civil rights in this
country. Many have been in the forefront of the drive for civil

rights. But the mass of West Indians in New York are hostile to any movement that trumpets blackness. Their integrationist fantasies are so powerful that they will pick up that standard at the slightest provocation. And so to *dwell* on blackness, on the need to re-examine the world through black eyes leaves many West Indians uneasy. They have, after all, spent their lives trying not to be black. They proclaim their Chinese, Indian, English, or Portuguese blood, but they never give equal time to the glaring African strain. They continue to insist, proudly, that they are a "mixture." When they are confronted with the physicality of blackness, a fact so lasting, so incontrovertible, they take hope in the possible deliverance of their children from this stigma. "Put a little cream in your coffee," the Barbadian mother tells her educated, black, unmarried son, and he knows that she is not talking about beverages.

The Jamaican government with a population 90% black, and with its political leaders mainly black, has banned from that island all men who dare to utter, on public and not so public rostrums, the words "black power." Even *The Autobiography of Malcolm X* is forbidden reading on this island. One would have hoped that Malcolm's struggle to find out who he was, to move from being a petty criminal to the main theoretician for a generation of black men would make compelling reading for Jamaicans. It is inconceivable that the Jamaican government could not see in Malcolm's life an ordeal, an accomplishment, as heroic, as epic as anyone could hope for. Malcolm, born in an affluent, racist country, was poor, black, and illiterate, and he became, as Ossie Davis says, "our black prince." This is certainly a triumphant life, one that proves nothing so much as the achievement of the impossible. This is a life to be studied, to be praised. But the Jamaican government does not think so.

"Massa Day done, Massa Day done," my grandmother used to say, and as children we took up the chant. But Massa Day is still everyday, everywhere in the West Indies, only the "Massas" are not as white as they used to be. For the reign of color continues unabated, and although jet black men politically rule the islands, or administer justice, their adulation of the white mystique is formidable. They can hardly wait to join the clubs that were founded to exclude them, that would, in fact, exclude them now but for their vaunted "positions." Light-skinned West Indians often find their experience in this country numbing. At home, their skins and their minimal education put them in the ruling social class. Here, they are immediately assigned by the white ruling class to the teeming black underclass and their bitterness is profound.

The independence of the West Indian islands raises once again the particular spectre of the West Indian illusion. West Indians in New York love to return home for the celebration connected with their island's independence. But independence for each island is really nothing more than a flag, an anthem, a diplomatic corps that gets rich and even more pretentious, poverty, exploitation of the land by British and American interests, and governments so fatuous that they believe that true independence is the ability to bar the occasional white reporter who says something the ruling class does not like. And the celebrations to the islanders who fly home are an excuse, to put it bluntly, to get drunk, to have a bacchanal, to have "a time and a half." Not many people debate the lack of national consciousness, the search for national purpose, the tenuousness of national solidarity, the slow economic growth, the concentration of wealth in white hands, the future of the Syrians, Indians, Chinese, the building of a nation. Everyone is too busy celebrating independence, and congratulating each other on how it really feels to be free.

It seems obvious to me that because so many black West Indians in New York are confused about their identities, the American black must now export the manifesto of his psychological emancipation. There are very few black people who have not been affected by the virus of white power and elitism. The black American has now decided that, at whatever cost, he must remove those symbols of white superiority that emblazon his world. To do that, he must hold nothing sacred, he must confront the miasma of lies that make up his history. This time he is serious, and his demand is for nothing less than total escape from the psychological trap into which he has been placed. Now he will adore broad noses and thick lips; he will grow his hair long and kinky. He will do this, not because the world will immediately change, but because it is a kind of liberation. One, of course, hates to prophesy. Time rends prophecies, and today's prophecy is tomorrow's irrelevancy. But the battle to rescue black American minds has already been won in this country, and mopping up has begun.

Not everywhere, of course, and not every mind. But this war is essentially over. It is no wonder that the shout for BLACK POWER! BLACK POWER! produced such white hysteria. Blacks were setting their own limits, blacks were defining themselves, and that signified their psychological deliverance from the vise of whiteness.

In New York, the West Indian readily acknowledges his journey from the cane fields to Bedford Stuyvesant to Crown Heights to Flatbush. He is now "at home" to his peers on President Street or Union Street; on Hawthorne or Fenimore. In Harlem he owns many of the beautiful brownstones on Convent Avenue. His children go to Swathmore or Vassar or Boston University. He is now much more than a hen's kick away from poverty. Now, all of a sudden, the black power movement that has been stridently following him around has come home. In April, 1970, rioting broke out in Trinidad, probably the most racially mixed island in the world. Black Power advocates in the armed forces mutinied and joined the anti-government activists. American warships carrying 2000 battle-equipped marines soon appeared off the northern coast of Trinidad; the government began to jail black power leaders on the island and the revolt petered out.But the spectre of armed revolt on those frangipangi islands, and under the banner of Black Power was no small shock to the West Indians in New York. It was as if, no matter where one turned and how fast one ran, one could not escape the threatening panorama of blackness. The older West Indians here did not quite know what to say. They knew of the poverty and the few resources of these islands, but they could not understand these university students who had suddenly taken to the streets. These students are, almost without exception, the sons and daughters of the middle class. They want to find out if there is more to West Indian identity than the limbo pole and some drunken tourist's laughter.

So the travails of the West Indian and the American black

parent have come together. The children of both are in rebellion against their elders and the hypocricies of the age. West Indian parents at home are embarrassed with their children whose speeches about blackness and identity grow more intense, whose manners have suddenly become abrupt. They are furious because their children, in whom they have invested so much, no longer want to continue the charade of West Indian life. And in New York, the progeny of the islanders talk about their "brothers and sisters" and idolize Cleaver and Malcolm.

This is 1970 and it is imperative now that the West Indian and the American black move towards each other. They need each other, not so much out of love, but because of the realities of the age. The liberation of the black psyche is going to be one of the struggles of the seventies; the American black must lead this struggle. It is his experience of flexibility, of energy, of vitality that would not die that must be the West Indian's guiding light. The American black, forced as he was to fashion his identity, knows the perilous journey, the detours and the seductions that lie in the path of self-realization. James Baldwin, now derided and abused, said it eloquently, nearly a decade ago, in *The Fire Next Time:*

> That man who is forced each day to snatch his manhood, his identity, out of the fire of human cruelty that rages to destroy it knows, if he survives his efforts, and even if he does not survive it, something about himself and human life that no school on earth—and, indeed, no church—can teach. He achieves his own authority, and that is unshakable.

It is this man who must carry his message throughout the non-Caucasian world; who must insist to all the befuddled blacks within the Western ambit, that their freedom is not dependent on speaking English like Englishmen.

When I was growing up in St. Vincent, there were two villages caller Massey and Biabou. Both were tiny places sitting rather timorously along a beautiful bay. No one knew where one began and the other ended, and no one cared. My father, when he was confused about what to do, when his options seemed unclear, would say, "My God, I'm between Massey and Biabou." Many West Indians in New York seem to be perpetually between these villages in search of a viable identity. They can find it, I suggest, in that continuum of sensibility that stretches through the Caribbean and Africa and North and South America. They can find it in a community of black men with a not dissimilar past, an agonizing present, and a fantastic future. They will not find it, willy-nilly, when the wind blows.

III

Forward

Tomorrow must be nurtured by new black images and ideals. Out of our black liberation will emerge a spiritual unity, a new nation.

ALMA MATHIEU LYNCH *has worked in the fields of mental health, educational and technical training administration, and management. For two years she operated a planning, research and development office with the people in Harlem, working to introduce the principles of management and technology as a more efficient route to the development of community resources. She is presently making an extensive study of the application of psychological research, data processing technology, and cultural influences on the cognitive and affective domains of black people as an approach to designing a relevant learning system.*

ACKLYN LYNCH: *"I have a natural distate for biographical sketches. My hope is that the reader will wade through our contradictions but recognize the intrinsic value of our attempt to be visionary. Looking into the future is a very difficult job, but we are confident that black people will get the message."*

Acklyn Lynch & Alma Mathieu Lynch

Images of the 21st Century ...Blackness

You, Black man of toil and endless rivers, of visions, dreams of light, of songs and pain. Your cultural imperative is here!

Your cultural imperative is here and the knives forced across your tongues, tongues that when repaired use new words, language not your own, but language that facilitates the decoding process of understanding and arranging the world around you; rearranging the world of Western civilization. But your beauty is in your antenna, "your feel" for the earth, knowledge of sound and rhythm, *your images*, all of which is quantifiable but of which you have not seen fit to extrapolate in the written formula, but you know the formula and you give it out, produce it, like "Trane" or "Bird" . . . it is there and you have not seen fit to reveal its inner workings.

You knew the formula for the atom, you know it now, but you have not classified it for the world around you; you will do it, as Duke Ellington has done it — smoothly at times and, like John Coltrane, often abruptly.

All knowledge is within you. You know why you are poverty-stricken, jobless, despised, and under-educated but you have not yet acted fully on this knowledge. You understand the irrational behavior of those that lie outside of the "inner cell" of knowledge, their irrational actions against you. The awe is about you, for you are the compounded being; you are a force embodying the sky, the sun, the earth and the river.

You must approach true knowledge of yourself and the "Intercellular Sphere" in which you function. Focus and reflect upon these things for your Cultural Imperative is here. We must recognize where we've been, where we are now, and where we're going.

Impact of the Past

Today we are in a cold war with an aggressive Imperialist (money-monger) and that always precludes the sharpening of knives of the so-called "liberal" social institutions of which the mass of people are in contact on a daily basis, knives that may have seemed to become dull with constant methodical use. Knives that were essentially designed in America after the government drove the native population from their soil initially . . . establishing social and educational institutions to complete the job . . . of the new social order of superiority attempting to cushion the reflection of their corruption and criminality . . . non-accidental planning, molding, shaping, and even reconstructing the guiding principles of intellectual inquiry; oh, but the devastating mirror, offers up none but the true reflection . . .

The system into which we were forced attempted to destroy the culture of which we knew, of our language and values, ways we had of looking and thinking about life of which we were characterized, a way of coping with circumstances. Fortunately, however, they were unable to snatch from us our humanistic nature, images, skills, and the symbolism of our collective unconsciousness (we recall the past). Jung calls this the "racial unconscious."

Let us look for a moment at the language of the system which has attempted to destroy us. *Language usually only reflects the normative values of the culture in a symbolic way.* Language as used in the United States of America was imported from the European culture and its idioms as adopted here (for hostile, criminal, and economic exploitational purposes) were built on "greedy," expansionist desires. Take for instance the word "individualism." Individualism translated here means, not just "do your own thing," but your *market value* to outwit others for extensive consumptive gains. Now let us look at how this language was translated into action concerning you. You had and have a market value attached to your person; you were sold once into this country, you brought wealth to this country, and each day since you have not been paid a fair share for your talents, creativity, and heavy labor. "Individualism," here transposed to its hidden meaning, means "exploitation."

Language and Values

Let us look at language and its psychological ramification within the cultural context of this country and how it has affected you. It is well known by social science scholars that "the man" fed upon you psychologically to satisfy his unclean and "sex fantasy" mind, exemplified in his own words as his *unconscious "id."* This unconscious "id" feasted upon your blood and your beauty and he has since made a science of it, called psychoanalysis. Know you this: *the destructive forces within him needs you,* for he has never been capable of integrating his mental, physical (affective), and cultural "self," because he has no substantial culture. Here in this country, your exploiter brought no cultural (moral, ethical, and spiritual) values that could sustain him, for his values are weak and corrupt. This is why he refuses to let you go psychologically, because he attempts to feed off your culture; a culture which he knows to be strong, courageous, and nurturing.

And this, my brother, you had attempted to copy and imitate until you got your eyes back, then your soul broke loose and unleashed the spirit of balance and harmony, as ripples within "the sea" — Body, Mind, and Soul together. All this you know and is in your music, which is the essence of your language and culture. You will not be free until you rid yourself of the vileness the (white) man told you existed within you; lies which you internalized and that taught you, for example, to set up a color caste system which is contrary to your nature of rhythm and balance in all elements of the earth. Lies against your knowledge of who you are and where you came from.

Freedom must come from within, but everybody "talkin' about freedom, ain't goin' there," because the *cultural imperative* of freedom is always in relation to land. If you speak of freedom in context to this country you may be sadly mistaken, as you have no land here, land that you govern and set the rules and regulations of your culture: standards, codes, and goals for your children to follow. Unless you recognize that your brothers and sisters are in Africa and that that is your land and home and unless they (our black brothers) are free from exploitation, what will you be free from or for? A man can never be free away from home. Know you this: *unless a black man is free on his land, he will never be free away from his land*, land which he ordains, governs, enhances. For who shall respect a man who cannot govern his own home, his own land?

Reviewing the past from its political and cultural perspective then, we find that the goal of the governing body of this *continent* was to perpetrate the creation of what is now the wealthiest, highest, industrial and technical "empire" in Western civilization, a world built with your blood and clever hands. This (amorphous) creation was constructed at the cost of corrupting de-humanization of all colonized (exploited) blacks as well as specified numbers of whites who could not be of immediate use.

Let us back up for a second and get the full meaning of the *language of power* as used in Western tongue of which you have been so eager to become a part. Imperialism, i.e., expansionist theory and practice of *super-governments:* in the 20th century this means that empire which dominates and directs United Nations affairs.

Imperialism, translated here and now, means this self-deceptive "home-on-the-range" country taking the lead in the "scramble" for Africa for unscrupulous capitalist reasons just like they take your money from your "sweat" and use it to fight wars for their own economic aggressive ends, not, of course, to protect, feed, or educate you.

Neo-colonialism, another term you have become familiar with, in this country is just another word for protecting their stranglehold on your wealth. Here in the U.S. it was your human resources, i.e., physical strength and mental endurance. In Africa it was your natural resources, i.e., diamonds, gold, uranium, manganese, iron ore, bauxite, copper, petroleum, etc. Neo-colonialism translated means new ways of exploitation through deception. In other words, *phony;* telling you one thing and doing another.

The neo-colonialist program here in the 1960's enacted this new approach to "civilize" us natives and it was called the poverty program. In other circles of the "governing elite" and liberals, it is called *"free security."* Dig that word: they're home "free" because they got you duped. Remember that . . . "free security" 'cause that's another name for the welfare state programs.

This new language of rationalization for their greediness is called sometimes "multi-racialism," you know it as *integration or buffer groups.* This is the language of the dignified smoke screen to placate us and it means the same thing in South Africa, West Africa, the Caribbean, Latin America, Harlem and Mississippi, U.S.A.

What is this country doing in Africa? Land-grabbing — only, this time they sent in different kinds of missionaries than the British, French, Dutch, Belgian, and Portuguese chose. They send in the Peace Corps (God is no longer in the picture). Liberalism and Imperialism are contradictory for how can you justify grabbing from another country and from people's souls? Peace Corps means, make peace before you steal, while you're stealing, and after you've stolen. On what grounds can this be justified and rationalized? Someone is confused, but it is highly unlikely that it is the peoples of the Third World.

This is in essence why social workers and other "do-gooders" are so despised and distrusted by the "little" man in the street, because the people know that they are being softened up, through "incidental benefits," and that these social workers acting as colonial functionaries are only being used by the system to get information that will eventually kill them.

At this point in time this new empire has brought the managerial elites (white and "multi-racial") into an almost complete stalemate in social and educational programming for the masses (they still program robots and functional illiterates). But this mental programming, particularly around self-racial hatred, has been the most dangerous obstacle mentally to the enslaved blacks, until recently, not even second to the physical cruelty and violence that has been consistently applied.

For with the awareness and expectation of acquiring the oppressor's language, (we) the enslaved people concentrated on adopting and imitating this foreign culture and language and were distracted from destroying our chains of slavery. Enslavement became a "state of mind," in addition to the physical threats of survival.

Up to this present day, fear — fear in every sphere of our lives of reaction from the chains of exploitation, fear of achieving, of thinking, of knowing — this mental programming has been carried out mainly by the schools and other social institutions supported and guided from the government's legislation and other official representatives of the social structure (need we forget the missionaries proselytizing a religion of which they never knew or lived by?). The managers of the colonies in their established social sphere are trained to write off the manhood, intelligence, and creativity of the enslaved and are known as social scientists, psychologists, psychiatrists, historians, and other social engineers. These "specialists" attempt to manipulate and shape the scales and measures to subdue and break the oppressed in the name of science. These "scientific" based policies, formulas, and brutalities will tend to increase against the black man *as our level of consciousness expands into action*, for we know that this mental slavery can be liberated — through a correct state of mind.

Pick up any so-called "scientific" book written by these social engineers, historians, and scholars, recorders of their own guilt, and immediately you will recognize their confusion and anxiety in attempting to analyze and program their continued oppressive and aggressive menticide against you.

In one passage they describe you as savage and man-eating; in another you become accommodative, compliant, and lazy; when you flex the slightest muscle, you are then considered violent, militant, and heathen; and now, brothers and sisters, in the

20th century, you are "disadvantaged" and without "family structure," filled with "self-hatred"and "alienated." Oh, but you despised man, when you get connected and comprehend the shallowness of their mental tools and the fallacies in their weak and distorted brains you then will realize that those menticidal engineers and historians are but holding a mirror and reciting a tale of their own empty reflection. Do you not recall the story of "Lady" Macbeth, who continuously and compulsively washed her hands from her memory of blood? Recall that she was never able to resolve and reconcile the hostile and murderous image . . . the memory of blood on her hands; recall that madness was her final end . . . this is the age of the crumbling empire. The youth call it the Age of Aquarius, it is demonstrated in "their" Broadway stage play "Hair" in which they project their decadence and freakish behavior.

It is only when you begin to proceed to understand this so-called "Western culture" that has raped you that you will understand why their scholars refer to us as without "social cohesion," "constitutional endowment," "identity," and overrun with "impoverishment" and "self-hatred." Tell me, you black man, this self-hatred, this lack of "intra-familial affectionate relationships," is that why you procreate? Now, be honest, is this why we steadfastly produce beautiful black babies!

We can say now, in all honesty, that you no longer hate yourself and thus your own brothers more than the oppressor, no longer are burdened with *anxiety about who you are.* No longer feel you are unworthy of love. Your intellectual aspirations are being reached, but there is still hard work to be done, in the minute by minute details of your life, to prevent the reappearance of self-condemnation and its vicious circle that destroy children, our children.

Since this knowledge is within you, you know that the white Western society *has nothing* that we want to be "accepted" or "integrated into." Our group pride and thus our individual pride has *overreached* the "begging stage," our backs and knees no longer face the sky.

Yet, there are those still, whose posterior is.high with nose in the ground, who *praise* this cruel, vile, and murderous imposed

Western culture . . . and those whose father and fathers before them had been beaten to death — stomped submissive heads into the ground . . . and these are the fearful, half-men who have not yet discovered life — nor the secrets of its meaning — those that prefer to be slaves. We have a job to do, see that the least of us are "converted" into the knowledge of life.

HOW MIGHTY IS THE WHITE MAN[1]

After God had made men, the first ancestor of the Europeans tried to imitate him and to create a man too. And so he did. He built many men who looked exactly as they should, *on the outside*. But at the end, when he tried to make their hearts beat, he did not succeed. He had to give up. Therefore, until this day, people say the white man is mighty. He can do everything, even build people. If only he could make their hearts beat!

Kenya

New World Images

We are beginning to move toward knowledge. That knowledge which was always buried within you. You know, but you want to hear it, in the words of your new language.

The shock of your past is beginning to heal. Any man among you, who has been almost irretrievably sick, knows that while he heals, new forces, new images arise and take shape and once he has been mended, new dynamisms are released and he gushes forward with greater energy and force. Likewise, we who have been colonized, who have known the "Black Death" and have been "converted," our bodies and minds have passed through the "waters" of the *baptismal* and our level of consciousness has come full-faced upon a truth. Truth, that often "blinding" glory — we know the meaning of "free security" that the Harvard "few" speak of when they speak of war and revolution in the same breath with blacks, such as Nat Turner and Malcolm X. This knowledge reverberating through the whole of our visceral cell is a call to action.

You are approaching and proceeding now through self-liberation. The depth of your knowledge is now before your eyes and it is unfolding within you. You are overcoming the corruptive influences of Western civilization which excluded you from the activation of your conscious mental achievements of the past four centuries. You will throw off the burden that enslaves you, for it is erected within you.

We are each here for one and the same purpose: to give of ourselves, our thinking, our skills, our awareness, and to learn from one another the nature of building a better tomorrow intellectually, ethically, politically, and morally for all the people. Particularly, we will be fostering the social goals of living together as mutually supporting black people here in this country and on the African Continent, or whereabouts as our wisdom dictates within our cultural context; a people who have not recently been allowed to write their own pages upon the scene of history. Think of the potency this brings to you!

At the beginning of our new history here, toward the advancement of our people, through love, knowledge, and an advanced culture that utilizes technology and science, we may fall prey to the same delusions and weaknesses of bourgeois thinking, which encourages the establishment and upkeep of a privileged caste. Now think and tell me, brothers and sisters, have we not had enough of this, have we not learned this contemptuous system well: a system of selfishness and individualism?

In the real life experience of each of us, every action we take affects our spiritual and physical existence in our new world and this world is the "cortical happening" of mankind. It is here that the sum of our energies and values are finally added together. So it is that we build a new world and a new nation, whether we are discussing the marketing value of fried chicken, soul music, or reducing a basic curriculum in engineering and architecture to its essentials and relevancies to our existence at this time. It is now that you will begin to realize that your "intercellular" (group) spirit will not rest until the needs of the least of us are satisfied. So as we proceed to discuss our structure, legal systems, and codes, let us free ourselves from the mental existence of chains of selfishness, chains of inequality, exploitation and bourgeois attitudes. Let us move toward the sharing of natural and physical resources, toward human dignity. There

is no room in this de-culturalized Western society for individualism as you have experienced it. This is your cultural imperative!
(There are certain realities that we must begin to face.)

World Projections

In the 21st Century, we can expect a change for the black man
to the extent to which the Third World man has extricated himself from the corruptive chains of Western Imperialistic society.
Just as the new born's umbilical cord must be cut for it to survive, likewise the black man must cut the umbilical cord that
ties him subjugatingly to Western society. His total metaphysical
referent must be independent of Western society. We will begin
to develop a new frame of reference which projects our African-
ity; shaped by new guidelines, new values, new goals, and new
structures.

We are in the crucial stage of defining these values, shaping
and creating them out of our own genius; values that will help
us to be in consonance with the Universe of African people
struggling for independence. *You must be appraised that a new
world order is developing.* Third World countries are moving
toward socialism and away from colonizing exploitation. Africa
is a part of that Third World Movement. Currently the Western
Bloc (i.e., U.S., Canada, Europe, Japan, Israel, and Australia)
"exploit the economies of 20 or 30 African countries for the
benefit of monopolistic capital and they influence or control the
policies of these countries to that end."[2] Pierre Jalée gives hard,
cold, and painful data to this fact in his book on the economic
study of the Third World. "Free Security" for the Western Bloc
will be just about over as the masses of black people (over half
the world's population when combined with other Third World
countries) become *very conscious of their strengths* (values and
culture), *their potentials* (natural, human, and physical resources), *and their rights* (equality of human rights).

Running close upon the heels of the 20th century will be a
stepped-up push for political, economic, and educational independence and the socio-cultural evolution of the black masses.

Quest for Liberation

This solid quest for liberation brought on rapidly by police and military repressive actions against our youth will have as its basic thesis the unification of black people. The Western power structure, recognizing this threat both at the domestic and international level, will attempt to "pit" one group of black people against another. This will be done through religion (Muslims versus Christians) and class stratification (middle-class versus poor) and regionalism (Brothers on the Continent versus Brothers in the Americas). The exploiters will at first attempt to use the affluent blacks to promise more "goodies" and contradictory "opportunities" for a few additional zebra-striped brothers. *But you and your sons and daughters will still not get your due process of law.*

But the capitalist exploiters will continue to play the "stock market" as they attempt to multiply their neo-colonialist holdings *which they must take from your African Brothers and Sisters,* if they are to increase your welfare benefits, whether it is in the form of social security or higher wages. The exploiters will continue to play the black politicians against the black masses in urban and rural areas, pay and play "selected informers" among you against those who are most hungry for justice, those who retaliate against brutal attacks and jailings and other forms of unethical behavior.

Political Organization

Political independence demands the organization of a national black political structure which would allow the easy and continuous flow of decision-making and responsibility between our African continent and the outpost here in America. In evaluating our current organizational structures you know that black people are divided into various groups, i.e., FRELIMO, SNCC, CORE, the Muslims, SCLC, NAACP, the Black Panther Party, OAU, etc., all of which compete for the available human and physical resources in our communities. However, side by side they do not possess a unified and consistent political posture. On occasions, they might work together in order to deal with political crises and urban problems, but they have never been able to maintain unity and cohesiveness. It is particularly important, therefore, that we develop an independent political organization that will shape, mold, and express the aspirations and goals of black people outside of the bankrupt capitalist ethic. Due to their serious commitment for eradicating poverty and subsistance living, black people will formulate a plan free from class stratification where Christians, Muslims, and all black organizations will sit down together to write their own policies for governing themselves. We propose the concept of a "cell system" for your consideration. The cell is capable alone, or while interacting with other cells, of performing all the fundamental functions of life, and of functioning as an independent unit.

If we project an arbitrary estimate of the total black population as being 49 million in the U.S. alone, it will be necessary to organize 49 thousand *community cells* that will deal directly with the community's planning needs, goals, and objectives. Each community "cell" will be administered by seven elected officers, comprised of a woman, a youth (under 21 years old), a community worker, an educator, a minister, a professional, and a businessman. These "cells" will also be responsible for maintaining revolutionary discipline, respect for property (personal and social), and the establishment of a social, mutually supporting direction.

At the next level, there will be organized 7000 district "cells" with 7000 persons per district "cell" which will be responsible for education and economic planning, health, and housing needs as they affect urban and rural life. Each district "cell" will be administered by seven officers elected on the same basis as the community "cells." Decisions which could not be settled at the community level must be arbitrated at the district level with emphasis on the exercise of social justice and would be *binding on all black people.*

At the third level, there will be organized 980 regional "cells" comprised of 50,000 persons within the region. They will be responsible for regional planning, consistent with community needs and aspirations. Each regional "cell" will be administered by seven officers elected on the same basis as the community "cells."

Finally, there will be seven conglomerates each comprised of seven million people. These conglomerates will be broken down into Northeast, North Central, Southeast, South Central, Southwest, Mid-west and Far West. Each conglomerate will be administered by a seven-member council. Each of these conglomerates will select one person to represent them on a seven-member National Council.

The flow of decision-making is an important aspect of the cohesiveness of the organizational structure. Lines of communication should be fluid between the various levels of political involvement, and democratic principles must be adhered to, in order that maximum participation be encouraged. Political decision-making and planning responsibility should flow upwards. Priority guidelines, as they relate to coordination of future goals for development, should flow downwards.

Our guidelines should be freedom with responsibility. What do we mean when we refer to freedom? First, there is the freedom of black people to determine their own destiny. Second, there is freedom from exploitation, hunger, and disease. Third, there is personal freedom to live in dignity and harmony with other men. Fourth, there is freedom from alienation. Fifth, there is freedom of creative thought and development as people consistently express their cultural, moral, and spiritual sensibilities.

It is obvious that these freedoms depend on the will of the people being expressed in struggle for social, economic, and political development. Development is a necessary aspect of freedom, but it must be done by the people themselves. It cannot be given to them. It can only come about by their fullest participation in decision-making at all levels. This calls for responsible action in the decision-making process. *Thus, education and leadership remain vital to the future.*

Discipline must exist in every aspect of our lives. And it must be a willingly accepted discipline. For it is an essential part of both freedom and development. The greater freedom which comes from working together, and achieving things by co-operation which none of us could achieve alone is only possible if there is disciplined acceptance of joint decisions. And this involves the acceptance of lawfully constituted authority. It means that if we work in a factory, we have to accept the discipline of that factory. If we belong to a community "cell," we must accept the discipline of that "cell." *This will be the key to the new man in action.*

Basic Concerns of Economic Development

The question of property remains a distinct challenge for the future, since we have been greatly influenced by traditional concepts of real property and personal property. Capitalism is an economic and social philosophy that permits the individual to accrue wealth and establish ownership. In capitalist societies, where private ownership of production is controlled by the ruling class, they generally keep the profits for themselves, totally or in part, thereby increasing their power and wealth. Criteria for success in this system is based on "How much you can get away with by taking from others." They have established a class structure to maintain their own interest. Black people in general are kept as consumers rather than as producers here and on our African continent. This prevents us from being able to control our economic destiny.

Individual ownership of the means of production and distribution must be critically challenged. It is argued that private ownership of production and distribution denies social equality. For when one man controls the means by which another obtains food, clothing and shelter which are essential to life, then there is no equality. *The man whose means of living are controlled by another, must serve the interests of this other regardless of his own desires or his own needs.* As we plan for economic self-sufficiency, we must consider the minimum standards at which our people must live while continuing to improve the quality of their lives.

First, there must be regional considerations depending on

the cost of living and the available resources. The elimination of poverty and exploitation of black people must be our responsibility and not that of our oppressor. We should, therefore, consider as personal property only those things that are necessary for a healthy life as they relate to food, medicine, clothes and shelter. We should minimize the abuses of conspicuous consumption which often enslave us to materialism. There must also be a rigid code which compels us to respect the right of personal property, and crimes against our people will be dealt with harshly within the "Intercellular" System.

Second, beyond mutual responsibility, we must establish the principle of mutual ownership and control as we pool our resources, physical and mental, in order to build an independent future. These resources must be expertly managed by competent scientists and technicians whose political perspective is geared to serving our economic independence. There will be certain areas of consideration crucial for building a Black Nation:

1. The purchase of land for the development of an agricultural base.
2. The development of a banking and insurance industry that will finance and sustain economic growth.
3. The development of a communications industry in order to educate our people to their responsibilities.
4. The development of an industrial sector to meet consumer needs.
5. The development of an efficient transportation system.
6. The development of an armaments industry to provide our people with their defense needs.
7. The development of a mechanism to deal with trade relationships between black people on the Continent and black people in the Americas.
8. The development of an exchange program of "technical and scientific expertise" among African people to meet our developmental needs. There must be a continuous and two-way flow of this expertise.

A United Black Nation could deal with world banking concerns and common market concerns. Individually you're lost when it comes to borrowing. You can't even get a "small" loan without giving up your loin-cloth. Only a unified black people can bring about industrialization for our African continent.

The organization of black people around mutual ownership and responsibility is contrary to *the individualistic approach which has encouraged us to exploit one another.* We recognize that every person has both a selfish and a social tendency. However, our concern must be the deliberate organization of society in such a manner that it is impossible — or at least very difficult — for individual desires to be pursued at the cost of other people, or for individual strength to be used for the exploitation of others. We cannot afford to encourage the further development of a group of institutions which perpetuate a series of privileges belonging to a social minority that controls the development of productive processes. Therefore, our needs and progress will be met on a cooperative basis. Intrinsic to this organization of society is the application of the principle of human equality.

Long Range Planning

Of course various questions will be raised at all levels, *viz.,* what levels of stability can be achieved with this type of social organization and attitude to property at the present level of productive forces? Who will decide whether to produce guns or butter? Who will plan for the planners? The decisions regarding development will depend largely on the attitude of black people toward their own destiny, expressed through the organs that represent the community. The effort to create a stable social structure not based on the present system which encourages individual power-grabbing from others will demand rigorous political and personal discipline. There must always be a clear formulation of the community's aspirations, expressed through the political apparatus. The social structure must be organized in such a way that a constant updating of these aspirations will be feasible. Long range planning is a necessary strategy for development. In decision-making our criteria must be:

1. What will be the impact of our present decisions on our future goals and objectives? This must be understood and clearly stated to all our people.

2. There must be a rapid flow of pertinent information in all levels of our political structure. This would require efficiency in the decision-making process and increase speed in the channels of communication.

3. We must plan precise operations that could be implemented smoothly. We will be able to do this by collecting systematically resource information on the socio-ecnomic environment. This will require knowledge of:
   a) natural and physical resources in the African world;
   b) our industrial growth and development potential;
   c) manpower skills necessary for future development;
   d) national and international political actions, legislation, and policy;
   e) financial institutions and their operations;
   f) transportation, marketing, and trading arrangements;
   h) demographic, statistical, and marketing data;
   i) monetary and fiscal policy.

   This information must be collected and organized systematically and will demand the involvement of most people to be assigned very specific research and technical roles within the community "cell."

To what degree it will be possible to reconcile rigid planning of development needs and goals with certain flexibility to sensitivity of taste in black culture is a question that only experience will answer. However, what we must be concerned with at all times is that there are effective internal forces working to provide more opportunity for individual creative action. Education is crucial to this type of development.

Education

As we move toward the 21st Century, black people will have to set their guidelines for education in specific relationship to their economic needs within their own cultural context. Education will be for all the people and its major task will be how to educate and wipe out illiteracy in the shortest possible time, while building on advanced levels of knowledge and technology and maintaining an independent posture. We will be establishing an indigenous learning environment with our people and our overall goals will be the "wiping out" of ignorance in every form, deceasement of hunger, disease and all related forms of poverty for our people. This will be done by you the people.

You have *rejected* the educational process as taught in the Western schools as the process and information appeared *so contradictory* to what you were experiencing on a daily basis!

You knew that this "school" education was burdened with irrelevant facts and that "street" education was more significant in dealing with the real life of your needs and survival tactics in a hostile world. Therefore, you *refused* to think within the structure of the academia because it was contrary to what you knew to be true at home. The language structure was foreign and different to you. The tonal quality and level and speed of expression within the "school" system was difficult to respond to for they were "cold" sounds and you were used to warm sounds, sounds of rhythm within the speech pattern. Therefore, many among us did not learn to write, to read, to speak this "foreign" language, but more tragically we became passive and "turned off our thinking" *within the confines of the school structure.* But, oh, you were thinking, analyzing and synthesizing the "feel" of this defective school process and you were storing this *knowledge* in your own way within the realm of your value judgments. The contradiction for us now is that we did accept, on a superficial basis that is, the standards which these "so-called" educators said was important for us to learn. Our problem, then, has been that of attempting to measure ourselves against a standard outside of our cultural context for ourselves and our children.

Education must reflect the unification of our social, political, and economic perspectives and values. The Western powers during the twentieth century have moved to an intensification of "specialization" in their educational and training activities.

They have "programmed people's minds" through isolated forms of language where there are few, if any, common bases or even routes for effective communication and this takes away a sense of solidarity or unity. It produces cold, alienated people without human values.

The experiences of black people, conditioned through oppression, require an entirely different design for information and knowledge input. We must develop our own learning systems as there are no educational learning systems applicable to large numbers of the mis-educated population living under conditions of economic deprivation, for over thirty decades, that will motivate you intensely.

Instructional learning systems must develop from a familiarity of our cultural past, that is, our language as used to reflect our cultural solidarity. Our brains analyze and synthesize and "store" knowledge and facts selectively on the basis of social value judgments. We learn only in proportion to the values we place on new information and knowledge as it supports our needs. These values and needs become the organizing factors in perception and take place on a subjective level of ordering. That is, you establish your own parameters often unconsciously projected through your culture where you internalize a position and consciously through your environment. Your environment (school—education—home) usually helps you to classify knowledge in a way that makes it (knowledge) more assessible. So you can see that if your environment, that is, school, education, and home, sets your limits in a discriminating, constraining, self-defeating arena, that is what you will learn. This is why your educators must change and establish a wider cognitive domain from which you can operate to expand your knowledge of "the world" and the logic therein. So you see if you can't read or write you know it is because your education has been designed to limit your knowledge and limit your ordering of the Universe, limit your routes to problem solving. Your new education must deal with your affinity to your culture; its flow and tone must be in line with your historical past, it must be in line with your "affective" ways of dealing with your surroundings, that is, your sensibilities to "naturalness" and then you yourself will move quickly to expand your cognitive domain level.

If the cultural environment is negative, without harmony or balance, exemplified by the exploitation of man by man, then the physical (affective) and mental (cognitive) aspects of your life cannot function (work) together. If you take a look at someone who is said to have no "soul" you know that means that his mind and body are not in harmony. So if you take someone who is said to have no "mind" (unlearned) then you can safely say his cultural integrity is not in line with his sensitivity (affective-physical-body) domain.

Black people, knowing the very essence of life as a unified flow of mind, body and spirit working together will take this knowledge and their creative experiences and cut through the meaningless information and dispense with the traditional western approach to education. Knowing our economic and political directions and aims we will develop universities as multidisciplinary centers of continuity where academic training, work and production will function as a whole unit or cell. The university will have the community and its needs as their centers of focus. Assessing the end results of what we wish to achieve in meeting our needs and values, the student will be guided toward his usefulness on cultural, socio-political, intellectual, and industrial planes. Everyone within the community cell will be in school and will be productive. In this socio-political-educational process, no one will be illiterate. This, as you can see, will require discipline, hard, hard work, and the spirit of love and devotion. Production and service will be the goal of each community cell. Progress depends on you and everyone of us understanding the facts (our consciousness level), mastering our resources, and support by all black people. We will begin to solve our problems of above-subsistence living and advancement for all our peoples when we realize *that the critical component is education.*

At no time has the responsibility of the black professional been as great as it is now. And this responsibility has been betrayed by the decisions of some black professionals and the omissions of others. Some brothers have directly sold us out for personal rewards and advancement; others have remained silent in the face of exploitation and oppression. Our independence (cultural, political, and economic) remains a serious challenge which the trained mind must confront. The black professional has a particular social responsibility to deal with the problems affecting the lives of his people. He cannot stand at a distant horizon and gaze at his people's suffering and plead for objective analysis. He must be immersed in the struggle and join the forces of destiny. He has the responsibility of intelligence which should compel him to develop his people as an independent force on the world stage. He must give to his people their viability and strength in order that they might be in harmony with the universe. The black scientist, doctor, engineer, etc. must be concerned with: 1) Participating in the planning and conducting of a crash education program, i.e., "expertise teams" which will go out and help you when you need expert knowledge or technical skills and *for free with no fees attached;* 2) Building independent black schools to service the educational needs of our students; 3) Providing low cost health and medical services; and 4) Building a viable economic system here and on the African Continent.

The technological input of the last century coupled with our need for rapid industrialization for increased productivity and improved living conditions demands that our educational planning focus on technological institutes. Technology brings about a systematically applied approach to how we organize knowledge about physical relationships for useful purposes. There can be no economic growth without the application of technology to land, labor, capital, and education, now or in the twenty-first century. Today, major large scale U.S. private companies are planning ways of exploiting our Black Continent further through the use of what they call "peaceful" technologies. It behooves us to train our people to systematically reproduce, through established and creative logical processes, manmade hardware.

The criteria of success for participation and productivity within the regional "cell" complex will be at least two years of training within the technical institute beyond secondary school for all black people. Training within the Institute will be directly related to a specific job of which they will work during their training period. Management, servicing equipment, and applying the latest equipment modifications will be essential, in addition to preparing functionally competent technicians. The technical institute should concentrate on: 1) Physical science and related engineering technologies (such as aeronautical and aerospace, architectural and building construction, chemical, electrical, instrumentation, metallurgical, nuclear, printing and publications, etc.; 2) Biological science technologies (Health, as medical laboratory, nursing, etc.; and Agricultural, as livestock production, dairy, diversified farm production and supply services); 3) Combined physical and biological technologies (data processing, mechanization systems, dairy and food processing, environmental control, etc.). The Institute would also offer opportunities for research and development for improving upon the production process and for original inventions.

On the University level, the scholars, in addition to their multi-disciplinary approach to functional concern, will work on basic research problems on the professional, governmental, and basic educational level for the operational and organizational efficiency of the community cell, and on special national and international concerns as voted by the people through the National Council. The University will be concerned with total environments such as health systems, environment and medical forms, transportations systems, legal and taxation systems, managerial and organizational systems, scientific research in medicine, chemistry, physics, etc. The University system will work closely with the Regional Technological Institutes on applied problems and conduct scientific research in manufacturing industry, transportation, forms of engineering, and other concrete problems.

It is projected that all other levels of education will work back from the University level to the fundamental secondary and elementary levels. Every measure of education and science will relate to public service values and therefore we will move away from productivity for profit to productivity for the enrichment of the flow of life for our people. For instance, if we need civil engineers, agricultural economists, doctors, this educational process should be designed to eliminate unnecessary aspects of studies from age two until completion, thereby weeding out much of the irrelevant data that is forced upon us in the present educational system. This means the curriculum will be designed specifically to meet the requirement of that particular skill or expertise. The student will understand the direct relationship between theory and practice, that is, work and study will be merged. Students will be prepared to design and operate complete systems such as public health and mental health systems, tele-communication systems, banking and insurance systems, energy systems, irrigation and electrification systems, transportation systems, education systems, etc. There will be no liberal arts colleges with majors in sociology, psychology, English (Romance languages), history, etc. These subject areas will be mastered in inter-disciplinary work which allows the graduating University student to have the ability and capacity to run a system inherent to the progressive needs of black people.

Emphasis in the community-school system must be on education for self-reliance from the elementary level up through the professional and technical levels. Community-University cells should generate their own income from services rendered. Each worker must be a student and every student must be a worker. There should also be established at the national level black foundations, enjoying the confidence of our people, whose sole responsibility is to acquire necessary funds for educational planning and development.

The school system should operate on a three tier basis. At the first level, students should have a structured learning experience from age two through ten. Emphasis should be on culture and consciousness, creative expression, the development of the problem solving process which creates the foundation for quantitative reasoning, the coding of number systems, and theory and practice of the natural sciences.

The second tier will be the secondary level ranging from the chronological age of ten through sixteen. There the student will be prepared to deal with all aspects of the sciences, physics, advanced mathematics, chemistry, the fundamentals of engineering, and comparative studies of national and international education. The third tier, of course, will be the University and Technological Systems described above.

For every community and district cell in the political structure there should be two secondary and two primary schools. For every regional cell there should be one technical institute and for every conglomerate there should be four universities.

It is the liberated individual who undertakes to build the new society. The liberation of the individual does not follow national liberation. An authentic national liberation exists only to the precise degree to which the individual has irreversibly begun his own liberation.

Death

In a struggle for independence we must recognize we will be traveling along a difficult road, a road that may lead to an early death. No man's death is indispensible for the triumph of freedom. It happens that one must accept the risk of death in order to bring freedom of life. In this struggle we must come to grips with death, with family ties, with man and woman relationships, and with our willingness to sacrifice material gains.

These are serious problems which we cannot sweep under the rug. We must face them squarely, for answers to these questions will determine the extent of our commitment to the struggle or the paralysis which will force us to cop out. Death must be confronted as the ultimate expression of our liberated consciousness. Death must be understood by our family and those who love us. Brother Malcolm and Brother Martin's families dealt with this inevitable dimension of the struggle and their deaths have not paralyzed those who loved them, but rather strengthened their determination to continue the struggle for freedom. Black people are not afraid of death for they have died in wars, at the end of a rope, or from a policeman's bullet. Brother Nat Turner walked boldly to his death and never flexed a muscle. *He died for freedom.* At the other end of the spectrum the junkie challenges death every day when he takes a shot of heroin, but he is willing to gamble on the experience. As people fighting for their liberation, we must begin to reassess death in a positive sense as it reflects an authentic articulation of the struggle.

The Liberated Family

Family responsibilities must be understood in revolutionary terms. Every member of the family must not only participate in the struggle but understand the responsibilities of independence. The new man must be nurtured by the example of disciplined manhood. Black youth must have living heroes to fashion their lives after, and must learn to solve their problems in a collective manner. Black men must feel a sense of group responsibility to deal in council with problems that young people have brought before them. In every community "cell," black men should be organized to handle codes of conduct and new images for black youth and to project the language of authority. Father must come forth and take up the identity card as Father and brother and enforce discipline in the family, nurturing "blood" through acts of love. He must begin to look at his woman with love, patience, and courtesy and he will become the center of all operations within the household.

Criteria for Change

Black people are defining criteria and principles for "international" government around economic independence and the sharing of resources produced by our mutual effort without exploitation of the least of us. This philosophical reference point is based on the worth and human equality of each within our government sphere; people determine the policies and priorities which the leadership will pursue. We project that the government will be based on the sense of the common good rather than on the protection of private property and a class/caste individualistic society. It will be a new and unique political theory. And you will produce it. You must develop and control your own resources.

Black people are already working toward the provision of independent and alternative economic structures; mutual health and medical care, mutually owned housing co-operatives, uniquely designed community learning systems and facilities, all within the cultural context of its people. We will be applying our understanding of recent scientific and technological processes, but it will be on the shoulders of our "natural" creative talent, which has always been based on the *complete integration of mind, body, and soul, dynamically interacting together toward a "spiritual" whole.*

Values

Our new political theory and thus our new social order will be based on our own theoretical formulations developed out of a need for solidarity. We are and will be concerned about loyalties, nurturing an atmosphere of love, and a sense of belonging (all of which have been long since gone in Western society). Love is the driving force towards the unity of our people who have been separated spiritually and physically for a long time. Brother Malcolm maintained that unity between Africans of the West and Africans of the Fatherland will well change the course of history and that we must "return" to Africa philosophically and culturally and develop working unity in the framework of Pan-Africanism.[3]

Brother Stokely Carmichael argues that we must have an undying love for black people which pre-supposes self-love, the fullest appreciation of one's cultural heritage, and awareness of the creative genius of one's people.

Art is an expression of our creative talents and it will provide us with new images for projecting our aspirations. Our language of art will express social truths and will state new guidelines for liberation. The beautiful is that which is free and independent of exploitative control. WE ARE BLACK AND WE ARE FREE; WE ARE BLACK AND WE ARE INDEPENDENT; WE ARE BLACK AND WE ARE PRODUCTIVE. These transcend being Black and Beautiful; being Black and Proud. It gives us a new focus on our destiny.

We are moving toward a "classless" and "casteless" society where social esteem will depend largely on our ability to identify with our cultural group and demonstrate faith in our ideology, our ability to form loving companionships and our ability to commit our energies toward hard work with others. We are still living in dangerous circumstances, but our integrity and our spirit can overcome this. You must only believe in the task at hand, that of the unification of African peoples to bring human and social justice into being through internal personal evolution and revolutionary change. Our philosophy should be born of international liberation for black folks.

Those who continue to work selfishly for their own ends, for themselves, will fall into defeat. Those who resist cooperation, those within our own ranks who continue to exploit you, will become confused and their own deceit will bring them down. Your exploiters will become "tortured" men. The "spasms" of the 21st century, of those colonial imperialists, will become great and you will see more jumping out of the windows than a "little bit," more than in the days of the Wall Street crash which brought on the depression. For your quest for change will be constant and the pressure on the right "veins" will take care of the deceitful system. The power *lies within you!*

Our cultural values are different and unique but the social revolutionary changes in which we are involved will require strong moral character, stamina (physical, mental and emotional), discipline, a strong sense of "justness" and cooperation, commitment and sacrifice and the ability to think, plan and to organize. These qualities are vital, for you will need to be free to conduct short-range and long-range planning in your daily lives. We must establish small group "Intercellular" codes for discipline. Some are:

1. Do not take a single piece of bread *from our folks, the masses.*
2. Keep your eyes and ears open.
3. Speak politely and carry your dignity at all times.
4. Establish and buy only from your community Co-ops.
5. Return everything you borrow.

6. Pay for anything you damage.
7. Do not damage your own neighborhoods or stores within your community boundaries.
8. Men and women must be mutually supporting.
9. Know the enemy within.
10. Always guide and protect the children.
11. Always be of service to our people.
12. Start now to educate five other persons; transferring all the knowledge that you possess which is relevant to community building and the development of skills from a technological vantage point.
13. Reduce the total intake of food stuffs and nurture your body away from negative assaults of drugs and alcohol. Get healthy and "Eat to Live."
14. Develop the body for physical endurance and strengthen it through exercise such as:
    marching under conditions of duress;
    subsisting on short rations for limited periods;
    imposed periods of isolation in small groups;
    developing and carrying out rigorous intiative and endurance tests.

The current strangehold of "law and order" for continued but increased repression here and in Africa will give increased vital strength to our people. Those intermittent *sieges of intimidation against our brother will strengthen our unity and knowledge.*

Obstacles

Internally we must plan and develop routes for dealing with our own "Intercellular" struggles between black peoples, on the local, regional, national, and international levels. We must continue to encourage, develop, and train people with legal minds who can analyze and work through inter-political problems of conflicting community and regional projections, who with respect, could carry the message unselfishly of the importance of unification and liberation, whether in California or Nigeria. There will also be a need to continue training for community "liberation workers" to protect what we are building.

Leadership at all levels of political organizations from National Council to Community "Cell" must be an authentic expression of the peoples' trust. The unity principle in collective leadership must be binding, once there has been free and open discussions on vital issues. However, there is a point when action must be taken and discussion must end. At the point of consensus decision-making there is a collective responsibility of the people to support the decision. This does not eliminate future critical analysis of the problem at hand. Our leadership must always respect these fundamental principles of solidarity.

These images must be carried out by a liberated people. The power lies within you. There is no job that you can't do. The 20th Century has not begun to challenge your ability, knowledge, or sensitivities. We have only begun to portray a "thing" happening, images that you will make a reality. The images we project may seem complex but generally reflect the kind of problems with which we as black people will be faced as we move forward, *acting in our own stead, instead of reacting to* the social order as the materialistic Western society designs for and through us. There must be an "ingression" of the future into the present. A liberated people, a liberated man, a liberated mind remains a fundamental necessity. Liberty or death will become the objective reality of tomorrow. But black people can never die, even though you and I might die like Malcolm or Martin, Patrice Lumumba or Nat Turner. We shall live on and we shall be invincible. We shall conquer what is justly ours.

NOTES

1. African folktale.
2. Pierre Jalée, *The Pilliage of the Third World*, New York, Monthly Review Press, 1968.
3. George Breitman (ed), *Malcolm X Speaks*, New York, Merit Publishers, 1965, pp. 62-63.

Architecture reflects the aspirations of a community.
New black communities must provide group identity
and serve the black political struggle.

JAMES A. CHAFFERS *is a doctoral candidate at*
the Architecture and Urban Design Graduate School
of Architecture and Design, University of Michigan.
He received his Bachelor of Architecture from
Southern University in Baton Rouge, Louisiana, in
1964 and his Master of Architecture from the Uni-
versity of Michigan in 1969. A Woodrow Wilson
Fellow, he is on the architectural faculty at the
University of Michigan and is a member of the
architectural and engineering firm of Nathan John-
son and Associates in Detroit, Michigan. Chaffers
is the neighborhood architect and planner for the
Grass Roots Organization of Workers (GROW), a
struggling community of approximately 15,000 resi-
dents in the central core of Detroit's near west side.

James A. Chaffers

Design and Reality
in the 70's

Architecture is not a virtuoso effort undertaken for the aesthetic gratification of a particular designer, but rather a social responsibility undertaken to enhance the quality of human life.
— Gropius

As an architect, I am concerned primarily with and about the physical environment of man. As a black American, I share a greater concern and a common lot with the continuing struggle of black people in our quest for liberty and equality.

In this era of black consciousness, there are those who will grasp and accept the full meaning of this statement. I can only assume that when it is recognized that a growing majority of black people (far exceeding the population of most nations) is now concentrated in the heart of our major urban centers, locked into racial enclaves devised and maintained to exploit and oppressively restrict the life-chances and choices of black people, that the irrelevancy of defensive attitudes will become apparent. Further, the whole subject of "rebuilding our cities" takes on an added dimension when one considers that the extreme conditions of deterioration in our existing urban environments are most evident within these black enclaves; reflected not only in terms of physical blight, but (far more importantly) in social and human decay as well.

With regard to the struggle of black people, the hour has long since passed for "pimping" and "game playing," and now requires that we reassess our position, critically analyze our strategies and goals, and move forward from there.

With one lone exception, this will not be a recitation of the "facts" of poverty and discrimination evident within the central cores of our nation's urban centers. The growing economic disparity and deplorable conditions of physical blight that characterize the concrete realities of life for the masses of black inhabitants, relative to a dominant white society, have been more than documented elsewhere. Further, most reports (including National Commission findings), from which many statistics and "poverty facts" are derived, emphasize the attitudes and feelings that provided the content for an extremely powerful form of racism, rather than the system of *privilege* and *control* that is inherent in our society's economic structure and which goes more to the heart of the matter.

Starting from the basic premise that physical change is inseparable from a broader community environment, the bulk of my research thus far has been an effort to gain a greater understanding of some of the basic social, economic, and political forces currently active within the urban central core. This ongoing analysis, of necessity, also includes other relevant forces that originate outside this boundary.

Working (sometimes daily) within this context, two points have become increasingly clear. First, the general march of the black movement in the United States, whose history is rooted in the legacy of a black slave system, is steadily gaining momentum. Somewhere within the last fifteen years (according to persons with more age and wisdom than I) it has made a fundamental shift from a struggle for Rights to what is clearly now a struggle for Power. Secondly, because of the worn and deteriorated conditions of the central urban environment and a resulting proliferation of physical rebuilding schemes, a "strategy on housing" may well govern all other strategies among and affecting black people as they move to accomplish other more definable objectives.

In attempting to gauge the broader dimension and deeper meanings of prevailing political issues and attitudes, I found very quickly that I had to address myself to a phenomenon that was not readily comprehensible, or even easily defined. It was only later that I uncovered a relatively short statement of written material that amazingly expresses, almost precisely, the kind of common spirit that I have encountered; one which has (seemingly) infused all aspects of political decision-making within an ever-increasing number of black neighborhoods.

Speaking at Hearings before the Subcommittee On Housing and Urban Affairs of the Committee On Banking and Currency, United States Senate, Milton Kotler spoke of the political interest expressed by a new power in the black communities. As he stated:

> This power is the power of all classes and groups within black communities; common to all, and thus the power of community. Since the interest which this community power seeks is of common value to all groups, it cannot be met by fulfilling the special interest of any one group in that community. Nor is the political interest held in common and expressed in a unity of power in the black community the sum of the interests of particular groups and classes within the community. This additive notion of community does not hold. Were government to meet every special interest of each group in a community — liberal relief for welfare mothers, jobs for the unemployed, business loans for black merchants, better houses for those poorly housed, et cetera — a common interest would still stand unmet: not patronage, but liberty.[1]

Stated in another way, black people are increasingly realizing the ethnic basis and power-oriented nature of American politics; and, of necessity and for reasons of survival, are developing an identity as a group and are beginning to look upon themselves as a power structure among other power structures. The irreversible thrust of this political activity, which is both a national and social struggle, is necessarily aimed at altering the distribution of power and the related dynamics of social change and political reform in our society.

These aims are revolutionary in the sense that: 1) the reallocation of resources in American society necessary to transform the economic and social status of black people is of enormous magnitude; 2) the social system, in part designed to limit black participation in society, will have to be reformed; and 3) the reallocation of national resources and the reform of the social system will have to be executed during a period of rapid and accelerating urbanization (and related technological change) and rising domestic racial tension.[2]

If only to underscore the nature and exercise of power in America, others might also add (and I am inclined to agree), that most workable visions for fundamental and far-reaching changes in the life-chances and -choices of black ghetto residents, and, by necessity, in the overall social and political organization of our cities will come about (short of revolution) only by a complex bargaining process within political mechanisms that sort out and deal with conflicting group interests.[3]

However, I am personally pessimistic about any meaningful resolution of our crisis through this quasi-democratic procedure, mainly because the whole question of racial conflict brings with it basic limits and constraints on the bargaining process. Clearly, one of the most serious of these constraints is profound and widespread ignorance, much of which is self-imposed. I would tend to think that for most Americans, more or less educated, the enslavement of black people for 200 years, their economic and social plight since the Civil War, and the further dehumanizing, destructive impact of life in an involuntary ghetto has little meaning or relevance.

But be that as it may, the reality and continuing existence of massive slum ghetto systems in our nation's urban regions reflect, in a very real sense, the status quo of economic and political power distribution in the American social structure; and it is within this context of unequal resources that most black leaders will have to operate (at least at this juncture) as they address themselves to the unanswered question of how to amass the kind of power necessary to bring about significant advances and revolutionary changes in the life opportunities of the mass of black Americans.

Lest there be any doubt, this critical mass must include those in the most pressing need of rapid development, who also represent the fastest growing section of the black community. These are the black (youth) street force, the ADC mothers, welfare recipients, domestic servants, unskilled laborers, etc., who must be given an opportunity to exercise initiative, to make important and meaningful decisions, and for higher education, if the black community is to be developed.[4]

Implicit in any on-going struggle or movement in quest of long range goals, is the formulation and planned accomplishment of a continuing series of short-range objectives. There is a constantly evolving set of priorities, resulting partly from varying and shifting philosophical reasonings of how best to proceed, and in part from major external influences that have the potential for drastically altering even a loosely defined course of action.

Externalities from the development and eventual implementation of "mass production housing systems," primarily aimed (as a result of mounting social and political pressures) at providing much faster constructed housing shelters at significantly lower cost than presently possible, could be of this magnitude. For it has been proven time and again, that given the increasingly systematic nature of operation and response inherent in a highly industrialized society (system) such as ours, the introduction of a major developmental change in a previously underdeveloped area of our economy, will create repercussions throughout all its parts.

Recognizing that the urban core is made up primarily of black families and individuals of low income who occupy a large and growing number of substandard dwelling units, the pressures will be understandably great from all quarters to have massive numbers of such units built for their consumption; even at the risk of sub-optimizing the need for more houses in the overall priorities of the black movement.

The particular significance that this has for whatever strategy black leadership develops or has already developed with regard to housing, should be rather obvious.

In an effort to bring about "lowest cost housing," most of our funding, research, and attention thus far is being directed at ways and means of depressing the construction and operating costs of the physical structure. To this end, the implementation of a new "industrialized" building technology which would make possible the production of high volumes of housing shelters through a combination of larger standardized building components and mass production techniques (along with substantially improved means and methods of financing), is seen as imperative in order to bring housing within the means of lower income groups.

In my judgment, the decision to seek this basically technical solution is a crucial point, with the end result being that the stress will invariably be on the house as an end in itself; viewed, in the main, as an impersonal product to be measured at the point of consumption. Granted, for some this may be all that is necessary, but the thrust of this whole discussion is that, that portion of the overall black population is a small (and conceivably dwindling) minority, relative to the swelling mass. And in effect, as it stands now, we are really talking about the beginning of yet another cog in this nation's gigantic productive apparatus; where undue emphasis on material success and the "sanctity of private enterprise" (in great part, the causes of *black underdevelopment*) have always taken primacy over human values whenever and wherever conflict has arisen, in pursuit of profit.

It would seem that there has been very little thought, if any, given to a relating of this planned physical change to political and social development in areas of our urban centers where such needs are clearly evident.

This is not to say that the process of physical renewal of the environment offers the total panacea for our urban ills, but, if past and recent history is, in any way, an accurate indicator of what we may expect in the future, then housing programs will be major determinants of any significant shifts in economic and population flows (and resulting political muscle); two of the basic ingredients necessary for the development of a (potentially) better-quality environment. Moreover, it is no secret that "the present day political, economic, and bureaucratic dilemma that the cities of America, and their slum and ghetto-dwellers find themselves trapped in, is due, in part, to public (and private) default on its responsibilities to ensure decent housing."[5] Finally, when one considers the order of magnitude of housing construction that we have set as a concrete goal to attain, its importance to all aspects of future urban growth and development can hardly be overstated.

Given the current state of political activity within black communities, which says, in effect, that any program that merely aims at providing houses (as if that function can be abstracted from their political life) will have no meaning, it is important to realize that there are other approaches to "lowest cost housing" to be considered. Basically, and very briefly, these are:

Economic approach — adjusting certain economic factors to aid the consumer's basic ability to pay;

Performance Design approach — maximization of general benefits from various investment levels;

Social approach — reflect the special needs of particular consumers in the design requirement for housing;

Development Process approach — coordinate the process which generates residential environment for maximum efficiency and cost savings; and

Operational approach — successful application to the "real world" of research output from all forementioned approaches to the problem of housing costs.[6]

When this wider range of approaches is considered, a number of extremely pertinent questions are raised. Is it possible for employment-derived consumer income to be improved so that the gap between housing costs and the consumer's capacity to pay is eliminated? What are the considerations, steps, and relationships that *should* influence the design of housing? How can knowledge of these considerations, steps, and relationships be structured and organized to influence the design in a fully effective and coordinated fashion? What is the clearest, most direct, and complete statement that can be made about performance concepts to be used in the design of housing? What are the elements of such a concept? "Housing for low-income people" may not be the same thing as "lowest cost housing." What special characteristics then, if any, should "housing" for low-income people have? The cost of housing may lay not simply in the way the physical product is organized, but in the way the *process* that produces it is organized. Approaching the housing problem this way, what cost-savings can be realized? Is research available which organizes the relationship between user requirements, activity configurations, and the housing design process?

In light of the obvious merit of all the approaches mentioned earlier, it is probably safe to say that a "technical solution" is being sought partly because of our existing technological resources (with accompanying lobbyist and pressure groups) and ability to operate comfortably and effectively within this sphere; and in part because of our apparent lack of any meaningful quantitative or qualitative data necessary to deal with this problem from other points of view.

> For technology to apply to the real need of people seeking housing, their requirements must be understood. Yet, appropriate studies of activity patterns which may be stated as user needs have not been made, and are not available to be plugged into the housing design and development process. Consequently, it is difficult to specify exactly what it is (beyond the minimum physical requirements) that should be developed in order to provide appropriate housing for any group; particularly for persons of low or moderate income.
>
> The performance criteria for building programs today relate, by and large, to patterns of life assumed appropriate or acceptable for people who can independently afford "good" housing, and fail to allow for more complex living patterns among persons of lower income.[7]

It has also been noted that the scale at which we work is increasing in both size and speed, and opportunities for our cities to grow and evolve gradually, with sympathetic response to the community, have given way to large-scale programs that are attempting to "design" qualities that previously developed through evolution.[8]

Significantly, in a classic understatement, a National Urban Commission concluded that, "we must develop systematic procedures for determining the evolving needs of people."[9]

Again, Kotler speaks more to the point when he says:

> Programs do not succeed by their goals alone, nor by their ingenious mechanism or colossal allocations. They must have a structure of operation that is natural and in compatibility with the aspirations of the people these programs intend to serve.
>
> No technical ingenuity can make up for the "defect of principle," and no enlargement of goal can compensate for unnaturalness of the program operation.[10]

More specifically, programs intended to serve the needs of black people in America must do so in the course of the ongoing black political struggle; any program (housing or whatever) that undercuts the legitimate political aspirations of black people is inevitably doomed to failure.

Given the almost total rule of black communities by outside forces, we must begin to understand that the current revolt of black people, by sheer necessity, will have to be pushed beyond the average white or black man's tolerance for change, and repeated change, and repeated change.

I am under no illusions about "liberty and justice for all" in our society, but I do possess a certain degree of residual hope. And if there is, in fact, a growing and true concern for improving the quality of our urban environment, as expressed by our Presidents, our National Congress, and others less powerful, but equally important, then it is perhaps reasonable to assume that there are those (with resources) who both understand and accept the need for a fundamental reordering of our priorities and processes in urban rebuilding, and who are willing to pursue the development of housing production systems that are compatible with urban realities.

I recognize that this is an omnibus task with a vast range of varying elements and variables to be defined and developed. A great deal of attention, however, must be paid to the emerging (and potentially critical) interrelationships between the aspirations and evolving goals of black people in quest of fundamental change and the "process of mass housing design."

It is my hope that out of such investigation will come clearer directions for the development of a structured means by which the performance requirements of each of these two major forces could be co-ordinated (and conceivably interlocked at some future point) for mutual gain and benefit.

NOTES

1. Kotler, Milton. Institute for Policy Studies, "Hearings before the Subcommittee On Housing And Urban Affairs of the Committee On Banking And Currency, United States Senate, Ninetieth Congress, First Session on Proposed Housing Legislation for 1967" (Washington, D.C. Government Printing Office, 1967).

2. Schuchter, Arnold. *White Power/Black Freedom* (Boston: Beacon Press, 1968), p. 12.

3. *Ibid.*, p. 6.

4. Boggs, James. "The Myth and Irrationality of Black Capitalism." Paper delivered at the National Black Economic Development Conference, Detroit, Michigan, April 25, 1969, p. 5.

5. Schuchter, *op. cit.*, p. 125.

6. Collins, Terry. "taken from a flow diagram of a Low-cost Housing Study, conducted by the Institute for Applied Technology" (Washington, D.C. Government Printing Office, 1968).

7. "Report of The National Commission on Urban Problems to the Congress and to the President of the United States" (Washington, D.C. Government Printing Office, 1969), p. 499.

8. *Ibid.*, p. 499.

9. *Ibid.*, p. 499.

10. Kotler, *op. cit.*

RESOURCES

Abrams, Charles. *Forbidden Neighbors* (New York: Harper & Row, 1954).

Bellush and Hausknecht. *Urban Renewal: People, Politics and Planning* (New York: Doubleday & Company, 1967).

Boggs, James. *Manifesto for a Black Revolutionary Party* (Philadelphia: Pace setters Publishers, 1969).

Chinitz, Benjamin. *City and Suburb: The Economics of Metropolitan Growth* (Englewood Cliffs, N.J.: Prentice-Hall, 1966).

Ewald, William R., Jr. *Environment for Man* (Bloomington & London: Indiana University Press, 1968).

Gamson, William. *Power and Discontent* (Homewood, Ill.: Dorsey Press, 1968.)

Handlin, Oscar. *Fire-Bell in the Night* (Boston: Little, Brown & Company, 1964).

Kain, John. "The Distribution and Movement of Jobs and Industry." Chamber of Commerce of the United States (Washington, D.C., 1967).

Keniston, Kenneth. *The Uncommitted* (New York: Harcourt, Brace & World, Inc., 1968).

Lundberg, Ferdinand. *The Rich and the Super-Rich* (New York: Lyle Stuart, Inc., 1968).

Meier, Richard. *A Communications Theory of Urban Growth* (Cambridge, Mass.: MIT Press, 1962).

Ray, Paul. "A Political Profile of Lansing, Michigan." (M.E.T.R.O. Internal Report No. 11, mimeo).

Schuchter, Arnold. *White Power/Black Freedom* (Boston: Beacon Press, 1968).

Building The American City. "Report of The National Commission on Urban Problems to the Congress and to the President of the United States" (Washingon, D.C. Government Printing Office, 1969).

Don L. Lee

Tomorrow Is
Tomorrow If You
Want One

A black poet must remember the horrors
The good jobs can't last forever.
It shall come to pass that the fury
of a token revolution will fade
Into the bank accounts of countless blacks
and freedom-loving whites.
— Conrad Kent Rivers
The Still Voice of Harlem

This will come in the form of notes. Ideas and non-ideas passing through me like time passes through the year, month, the world. Personal notes will be personal, keeping in mind that I'm a black man first, then poet. Reflections in 24-hour thoughts which both kept me awake and forced me to sleep (my new found ability to sleep four to five hours a night indicated a new maturity). A short preface: I've traveled from coast to coast and half-way around the world, which means that I've been able to communicate with (mainly listened to) brothers and sisters from San Jose, California, to the University of New York; from Sir George Williams University, Montreal, Canada, to Toogaloo College, Mississippi; from Luther College, Docora, Iowa, to the University of Algiers, Algeria, North Africa; from those points and many smaller/larger points in between, I traveled deliberately to give and receive positive/negative messages. Let's view together from a poet's bridge.

Leadership: is not as we knew it. The concept of leadership

has to be redefined; keeping in mind he who controls the image controls the action. I find very little difference between "All the news that's fit to print" and "the World's Greatest Newspaper." The two papers mentioned, and others, are only moderate examples of that which is wrong with this country and I'm sure, if confronted, none of them would acknowledge that neither truth nor the positive interest of black folks is a part of their make-up: America's image makers, developers of myths and the destroyers of weaker men. Crazy is what they called Malcolm X, Stokely Carmichael, and Rap Brown; crazy was their assessment of W.E.B. Du Bois and Paul Robeson; crazy is the adjective used to describe Marcus Garvey, Kwame Nkrumah, Imamu Ameer Baraka (LeRoi Jones), etc. Crazy is crazy only when black people move in an uncrazy way to confront the real craziness of the world; actually crazy is crazy only as the crazy can/will define it.

The new leadership is us. Each one of us. We as a body of one will have to reflect that which should be/that which is necessary. Too often we've assigned roles to our "leaders." We must now assign these roles to ourselves. We must become the Malcolms, Du Bois's and Nkrumahs of tomorrow — do not ask of others what you are not willing to give/do yourself. Reflect that which is necessary. What it means is: 1) are we serious; and 2) what are we willing to sacrifice? Our children are watching us and we must not become the new pimps of tomorrow. The educated pimps.

Tomorrow is tomorrow if we want one. Tomorrow is tomorrow if we can/will define it. To define and legitimize our own existence is the basis of a continuous existence. Europe may be a myth, but it would be very difficult to prove that it is. Congress is one of the most corrupt institutions in the nation, but these are just words if no one believes it; that white boy may be a sissy, a punk, and very unhip, but he is also undeniably the worldrunner. Europeans define what Europe is; those there and those here. Members of Congress define what corruption is; those that are and those that *are*. The white boy may be the euphemisms indicated above, but obviously that doesn't interfere with his running of the world. Our movement is to awaken the consciousness of blackness, of ourselves.

The Closed Societies: NAACP, SCLC, SNCC, The Black Panthers, US, all black fraternities and sororities, CORE and any/most so-called black organizations that are moving to liberate us. First and foremost, we are black men and black women. Human beings. We cannot/must not be forced to become something unnatural, such as organizational robots. Each organization mentioned above demands of its members that they reflect that organization and not necessarily black people. In order to become a part, one has to meet certain prerequisites such as: become *less* black, become *more* black; do not wear a tie, wear a tie; seek integration, seek segregation; change yr/name, do not change yr/name; seek black culture, demean black culture; read only this, read only that; be political, not political enough; power comes out of here, power comes out of there; wear yr/hair this way, wear yr/hair that way; quote this brother, quote that brother; get high, don't get high; formal education, self-education; wear a suit, wear dashikis; bear arms, don't bear arms, etc., etc. The new class division, one group of negroes saying that other negroes are not relevant, and vice versa. We've created such divisions among ourselves that our personalities change as television programs do; this year it's in, next it's out. Our actions move as the group does. I'm not advocating a return to strict individualism (which in itself is just as harmful), but a movement toward combining all efforts which allow and encourage constructive criticism and constructive actions. How can one black person "blackball" another? We must move from ego satisfying pettiness and superficial idealism to the real world. It's popular for individuals/groups to say that they are going to use "the man" (mainly for their own limited personal goals), but if we become products of the realworld, we'll begin to understand that it's very difficult to use/make use of "the man" that uses the world (unless one is equipped to do that — and division is not part of that equipment). It requires all our talents and, most of all, it demands of each of us the willingness to listen, learn, act, and grow.

Actually, we are talking about Nation building, which to

some may seem to be a revolution. But I think at this time we have to stop romanticizing *revolution* and move to *really* under-stand it. In fact, it may be time to stop using the term *revolution* altogether; I think that it has become a misnomer. Especially since white boys have picked it up, and use it as freely as they use drugs — the term has become a legitimate part of the mass media just as the term *black power* has; the next thing u know, Nixon will be talking about revolution. Let's not fool ourselves; if we are talking about a true revolution, that means the death of just about everything in existence that is opposed to the new values which we advocate — which, ultimately means that some of those white boys and girls that consider themselves revolutionary will have to turn around and off their mothers and fathers, and I, for one, do not believe that they will even think about doing that, let alone do it. Check: In the last two years, the only people that have been killed have been black people. There have been no killings of the so-called white revolutionaries, none. At best, Kent State was an accident. And, the most recent killing (murder) in Chicago of Fred Hampton and Mark Clark should serve to clarify this, especially since there were no whites killed during the 1968 Democratic con-vention (which the authorities called a "disorder") and no whites were killed during the "Weatherman" demonstration in Chicago for the "Chicago 8" when they literally ran down that "magnificent mile," damaging everything in sight and putting one of the city's high officials in the hospital. At this time, our priorities are black, black people, *must be*, and our movement is toward building that which will sustain us as a nation. The seventies will be toward developing the ability to maintain and build a nation, and to develop a sophistication for survival.

Institutions: There should be no institutions in the black community that are not controlled by black people. That means that everything from the Catholic church to the public school system must be in the hands of competent blacks. We are talk-ing above reversing a dangerous cycle that has been set up in the black community. The various institutions that now exist must be pushed to the point where they represent and reflect the community which they serve. I can see no reason for all the bars and taverns (and they have become lightweight *institutions* in our community) that are, as you know, in every other storefront in the black neighborhoods. The existence of bars and taverns in numbers in our communities is really a very subtle system of control: keep niggers high and you rule them null and ineffective.

It's a profound comment on our state of being if we can't put an end to the traditional filth that daily threatens our very existence. Just a small suggestion to my brothers that are looking for "action" and are so fixed on inter-city warfare: if you really want to deal, deal with the *Mafia*. As you know, the Mafia is one of the most effective organizations in the world, and to challenge their use of our community can serve as a training ground. But, then again, the Mafia shoots back and most of the frustrated brothers that call for action don't mean against our enemies, but against other brothers. Remember, to move effectively at a mass level we must be in a position to police ourselves and our communities and that calls for *organization*. Yet, we *are* organized. Check: the churches, the black greeks, the countless social clubs, the black women's clubs, the black colleges and universities, and many others that function successfully in the black world. The problem is, is that, in most cases, they are not organized for life but for *death*. However, to those of use who are serious about changing their direction, we may find ourselves putting that suit and tie back on, cutting our hair, cleaning up on speech, learning to smile and, most of all, doing our homework. Physically we have to be where our people are and respect their positions even though we may disagree.

We don't have enough living space; but in our communities, that which is not needed can be found in abundance (another example of space taking is the overpopulation of gas stations; the oil companies occupy just about every corner). We have to start asking ourselves, why is this so? The answers are obvious — we are still being controlled from the outside. Our minds should be thinking about the power of ownership at the community level. It's not enough to replace a white exploiter with a black one. We must move toward true community control and ownership.

Malcolm X talked about history; not only black history, but the history of other people. He understood that there are only six million Jews in this country, but that they wield power way out of proportion to their numbers. How can less than six million be more powerful than thirty million or more blacks? How can so few be so powerful; of course understanding that Jewish power is still not the *real power* (few if any Jews sit on the boards of directors of any of the real power companies in the United States)? But comparatively speaking, the Jewish voice is heard much louder and clearer than the black voice. Two of the main reasons for this is that there exist among the Jewish people a tradition of togetherness, and a system for the continuation of Jewish culture, and a process by which the culture may be disseminated amongst Jews. Most importantly, the Jewish people have developed a *nationalist consciousness* that is interwoven with their *religious reality*.

We find that in *every* urban area where Jews exist today, they continue to build and build, mainly new synagogues and community centers. In most cases, Jewish teachers teach Jewish children. They understand that it is important to get the young mind and keep it. The crucial time, I believe, is between three and six years of age. Jewish doctors attend Jewish patients; Jewish businesses service the Jewish communities, and on and on. This is as it should be. The reason the Jewish people have been able to survive is not only because they are white, too, but because they have developed the institutions that are vital and necessary for survival. They have developed life-giving, life-saving institutions that their own people and other people (mainly black) continuously draw on — they develop the resources that are in demand.

In effect, the Jewish people represent a nation within a nation If all that is not enough — the Jews have moved to build a national state outside of the U.S.A. They understand that total emancipation cannot come about without a homeland of their own. Thus, the State of *Israel*, or, as the Arabs view it, *Occupied Palestine*, came into effect. It is important to understand that even though there may be quiet complaints of anti-Zionism among some Jews, deep down inside each Jew realizes that

Israel must live. We must also understand that Palestine would not have been partitioned off if World Jewry, especially those in the United States, could not guarantee the survival of Israel. Leonard Slater, in his book *The Pledge,* chronicles the efforts of the Jews in this country to see that Israel became and stays a reality. It is commendable to view the type of international network that was built to supply the emerging land with the essentials to help them survive: from machines to make weapons, to brassieres and printing presses; and also how a Jewish underground was trained in this country. Even today we know that *The Jewish Defense League* is more effective than, let's say, the Panthers, and while I revise this article, the young Jews of the League are at *Camp Jedel* for an eight-week seminar and training period to get and keep it together.

Slater also talks about the effective P.R. system that was developed to give Jews popular and favorable publicity at the expense of the *refugees of Palestine,* whom everybody in this country seems to have forgotten — even the big "negroes" under the direction of Bayard Rustin who took out a full-page $8000.00 ad in the *New York Times* Sunday edition to plead with the country to sell weapons to Israel. Yes, these supposed *pacifists* going to the aid of a little U.S.A. in the Middle East but wouldn't think of doing anything for the African Liberation fighters. Damn! But, like I said earlier, the Jews have developed a sophistication for survival and it seems that even some negroes are more concerned about the Jews than themselves.

We have to be in a position to perpetuate and present that which we, as black people, consider most needed to sustain and substantiate us as a nation of people; which means that if we can guarantee our survival here, we guarantee the survival of African People wherever we exist as a world of African people. The reason that most institutions in the black community fail is because the institutions do not have the support of the community in question. Also, the institutions that may be formed in the black community may not necessarily be in the best interest of the community. But there is a beginning. To mention a few: In Chicago, there exists the *Black Women's Committee for the Protection and Care of Our Children.* Here is a group of determined young black women moving to educate and direct the lives of the young people in the community, especially young sisters. They refuse to accept white money, believing that if the community in which they exist cannot, or will not support them, then they need not exist. Although, understanding that that is not enough, they require each staff member to contribute a portion of her salary (all have other jobs) to the upkeep of the center. (By the way, they started off in a storefront and have recently purchased their own building.) Not only do they pay out of their own pockets, but annually they give a benefit and seek monthly pledges from people of the community (which takes care of the main problem — paying off the mortgage). The Malcolm X Liberation University in Durham and its extension in Washington, D.C. move in a similar direction, requiring its faculty members (who also hold other positions) to relinquish 5 to 10 per cent of their annual wages to the support and upkeep of the university. This may seem minor to you, but it's a start. You see, at this level we have people that are involved to give more than just their talents.

The Organization of Black American Culture in Chicago has also moved to tighten up its standing as a permanent part of the community. Each member is required to contribute a portion to the continuance fund which guarantees the year's rent. That which is left, of course, is used to build the library and aid in the various projects of the center. About the most organized and functioning institution in the black community is the Nation of Islam under the guidance and direction of the Honorable Elijah Muhammad. We need not, at this point, say too much except that their weekly newspaper circulation is close to one million; they are building an economic base with Restaurants, Supermarkets, Clothing Stores, Printing Shops, Farms, etc. They are now in the process of building a University-Hospital Complex — in other words, the brothers and sisters of the Nation of *Islam* are moving. You see, by taking care of the basics, we can move on to the specifics.

A man with an ethic, a history, and spiritual guidance is the beginning of a people with an ethic, a history, and meaningful spirituality. I've often come across black people who wander throughout the world thinking they are modern day Meursaults, Raskolnikovs or Frederick Henrys, and have never heard of Bigger Thomas, Harry Ames, or Tucker Caliban. You reflect what/where you are. If a brother moves throughout the world quoting Camus or Dostoievsky, understand, that's where he's at. If he digs Rubenstein and Janis Joplin, that's where he is. To move people from that point, it's necessary that we do it without alienating them. It's not to impress one with one's knowledge, but with one's actions. The values which we believe in cannot necessarily be taught — but may have to be demonstrated. If the ethic, history, and spiritual life you advocate is important, *be it.* Your be-ing it will be the most effective attraction or distraction.

This is the age of power, the power-age. The Vietnam disaster could not exist if the majority of white people in the unitedstatesofamerica did not want it to exist. The United Nations would not be as ineffective as it is if this country didn't want it that way. Brothers Malcolm X, Patrice Lumumba, and Martin Luther King Jr. would be alive if we could have backed up their words. How does one bring down a monster without becoming one? If you see a blackman walking around with a perpetual smile on his face, it's not because he's happy. The basic of power is land. *Land is the only thing that nobody, no-where is making any more of;* we can buy these bell bottoms next year (if they are still in style), buy that Mustang next year — but land is going action-fast and that white boy is hip to it, for he's all over the world taking it. *We're an African people;* that means that our history didn't start in this land, but on the African Continent. This is not to romanticize Africa, for we understand that Africa, in terms of peoples, cultures, languages, religions, total-movement, and life-styles, is as diverse as Europe is. We also are hip to the fact that our African brothers have been through the same type of brain-mis-management that we've been through. However, now is the time to realize that our lot is a common one and that the main weapon used against us is the ability of the enemy to keep us apart and keep us ignorantly talking about each other as if one or the other was some strange space man.

The sixties were the years of search and destroy, the years of the overkill, e.g., the cities and people of the cities. The sixties were the years of police forming nationwide unions and of saying that if the authorities of the cities do not listen to us, we'll make them listen; the years of Vietnam and Songmy and the justification of War Crimes (back to who has the power to define). In the sixties gun selling became big business in the suburbs (the Eisenhower report) along with the systematic assassination of black leaders. The seventies will require a deep, deeper look back into the sixties, with a hope of learning from our mistakes (understanding that future ERRORS may not be so generous). Positive direction is *overneeded*. Realistically being real, the majority of blackpeople in this country view themselves not only as "negroes," but as pure christian-americans, and to forget or to negate that would not only be dangerous, but disastrous.

What about the different voices of the cities and towns? In every major area where blackpeople exist there is at least one voice that overshadows the rest. Why can't these young and old minds come together to define and analyze our position; but most importantly, to direct us as a nation? A black THINK TANK. A man or woman from each (major) black area to come together to pool their resources for the benefit of all black people. One of the main reasons that our enemy is ahead of us is that he *thinks ahead*. It is now known that he knew that "negroes" would be letting their hair grow natural and would start calling themselves black in the sixties. Brothers and Sisters, the only way to move into the seventies is on top. Which means, among other things, coming down off of those ego trips and getting out of those "I" bags. To build a nation, the "I" will have to be *subordinated* so that the *we, us* and *our* can come into existence. We have to start now to move toward the top in the seventies so that we won't be on the bottom in the eighties. Think about it!

Start with the itch and there will be no scratch. Study
*   yourself.*
Watch yr/every movement as u skip thru-out the southside
*   of chicago.*
be hip to yr/actions.

our dreams are realities
traveling the nature-way.
we meet them
at the apex of their utmost
meanings/means;
we walk in cleanliness
down state st/or Fifth Ave.
& wicked apartment buildings shake
as their windows announce our presence
as we jump into the interior
& cut the day's evil away.
We walk in cleanliness
the newness of it all
becomes us
our women listen to us
and learn.
We teach our children thru
our actions.

We'll become owners of the   New World
the New World.
will run it as unowners
for
we will live in it too
& will want to be remembered
as   realpeople.

*Literature is one of the touchstones of a people.
The new black sensibility will shape a literature
whose greatness will rest upon our knowledge of
ourselves and the acceptance of our total humanity.*

LANCE JEFFERS *grew up in Stromsberg, Nebraska,
and in San Francisco. After serving as an officer in
World War II, he received his B.A.* (cum laude) *and
his M.A. from Columbia University in New York
City. His poems have appeared in* Phylon, Freedomways, Black Fire, Black Voices, Beyond the Blues,
and Nine Black Poets. *His short story "The Dawn
Swings In" was included in* The Best American
Short Stories — 1948. *A volume of his poetry is
being published by Broadside Press, and he has
completed a novel entitled* Witherspoon. *He teaches
creative writing at California State College at Long
Beach and black literature at the University of
California at Irvine.*

Lance Jeffers

The Death of the Defensive Posture: Toward Grandeur in Afro-American Letters

The black writer of the seventies will write about black life and black nature with reckless frankness, will write more candidly of his own personal griefs and sicknesses and weaknesses and strengths and raptures, will conceive himself as truth-teller who reveals reality regardless of whom it hurts or disgraces; the Afro-American writer of the seventies will envision his struggle for freedom as inseparable from the struggle of exploited and conscienced men everywhere to alter utterly the condition of oppressed humanity. Finally, the black writer of the seventies will build upon the foundation already laid for the creation of a great Afro-American literature; the outlines of a great literature will begin to emerge clearly, for the black writer of the seventies will explore the continent unexplored of Afro-American nature, will cast aside his traditional defensive posture, will fearlessly explore the infinite complexity of the unexplored continent of black life and black nature in America.

No great body of literature has been created in America either by whites or by blacks. White Americans have not created a great literature because the emotional depth is not there, nor the emotional breadth and empathy that would permit the impassioned rejection of the past-and-present persecution of blacks and Indians. Mark Twain, almost alone among leading white writers (e.g., "The United States of Lyncherdom"), angrily attacks the inhuman cannibalistic dimension of the American character that has found expression in racial persecution; Twain almost alone recognized that that dimension is a crucial key to the understanding of the American character (*The Tragedy of Pudd'nhead Wilson, Huckleberry Finn*); but no white American has written a novel comparable in stature to *A Passage to India* about the black man or the Indian or the Mexican. Because the experience with the Indian and the black man is so very crucial to the inner and outer life of the white American and because the Indian-black experience has been so important in the molding of the white sensibility in America (whether in New Hampshire or New Mexico or Mississippi), the white writer's failure to empathically enter this area of the nation's spiritual life is artistic self-emasculation. To understand, incidentally, this American artistic failure, contrast the sensitivity and grasp and honesty of E. M. Forster's characterization of Aziz in *A Passage to India* with Twain's sentimental characterization of a derooted Jim-in-a-vacuum, and follow that with Hemingway's ancestor worship of *Huckleberry Finn* in *The Green Hills of Africa*.

Or we could go on to point out that the spirituals are the touchstone of all artistic expression in America, and that this is universally unrecognized. If the supreme criterion of art in America is ignored in America to a significant degree by blacks as well as by whites — how can a great literature be created in America? The immeasurable breadth and depth of the slave songs and their superb vision of human life, their magnificently prophetic vision of human life, are unequaled in American arts and letters, impossible to come by in American literary work, though we come very close in Du Bois' great work *The Souls of Black Folk* (the greatest work in American *belles lettres*) and though James Weldon Johnson comes fairly close in *Autobiography of an Ex-coloured Man* (that vastly underrated study of black and human identity); and Richard Wright's great stories "Down by the Riverside" and "Big Boy Leaves Home" suggest the epic grandeur and prophecy of the spirituals. It is the spirituals that the black writer in America must study in order to create a great literature, for the spirituals are un-equalled as art in America.

Why have we failed to create a great literature?

A central answer is that the black writer has been working to significant degree within the framework of his psychological relationship with whites, a relationship in which the element of dependency has been strong; the black writer has worked from a defensive posture *vis-a-vis* the white world. He has thus presented an inadequate and inhibited picture of Afro-American humanity, of Afro-American psychology, of the texture of the Afro-American soul. I am convinced (and two dramas by Ed Bullins — "Clara's Old Man" and "In the Wine Time" — are among the convincers) that the black writer of the seventies will discard the defensive posture. He will move on to explore the unexplored continent of black nature and black life in America. He will explore them without fear, in total frankness; he will explain black life and black nature in terms of themselves.

What is the defensive posture? It is essentially the need to defend black people before the racist hostility of white people, who condemn black people to subhumanity. (And even the definition of defensive posture *seems* to justify it.)

The black writer has known that whites have been eager to believe the worst slanders about blacks, and hence he must be careful, he has felt, to say nothing that would enflame white hostility and white contempt for Afro-America, for the black race. The black writer has felt it necessary to leave the continent of black nature unexplored if exploring the continent meant to throw into the hands of whites anything which they might twist to suit their vision of blacks. All black people in America know that white people as a body regard us as inferior, as not as intelligent as they are (the recent teachers' strike in New York was in essence an attempt to support this thesis), as lacking in their gifts and capabilities and potentialities. We all know that even whites friendly to our aspirations unconsciously (or consciously) consider us their genetic inferiors, and we know that this is a leaden load in the national soul.

Some of us have been startled to stumble upon the idea that

whites who respect the spirituals and blues and jazz consider their creators inferior. Yet whites do consider us inferior, and though we recoil or rage before their view of us, few of us have remained totally indifferent to their view of us; their racial chauvinism has helped to shape our psyche. Moreover, the white nation believes not only in our genetic inferiority but also in the right of whites to rob and murder us, and to shove us down into subservience when we move up. Those of us who have the strength or savvy not to remain shoved are in their view freaks. If this is iniquitously true in 1970, it has been even more overwhelmingly true in the past.

This is the sinister heritage of the white nation. And it is the tragic heritage of the black nation that despite our obvious gifts as a nation, the millions of manifestly superior human beings we have created — from the gifted famous to the poor semi-literate Georgia farmer of superior intelligence and character who is the talented weaver of tales — it is the awful heritage of the black nation that we have been consciously and unconsciously ambivalent about our humanity, about our genetic equality, indeed, our genetic splendor; ambivalent about our right to equality, to nationhood; ambivalent even, many of us, about our right to life, for how else could the white man create in Harlem a vast corps of heroin addicts unless so many of us had doubts about our right to life?

This heritage is a part of our unconscious, and, in seeming paradox, a heavier ill-legacy in the North than in the South, where one is not blinded by "friendly" smiles and pats on the back to the true white sensibility and character structure. (The oppressed as a group are instinctively more responsive to human life and human needs than their oppressors, more responsive to grief and to kindness; and kinder, and more desirous of freedom than oppressors, more committed to freedom than those whose well-being is a parasitical sucking of blood from the deprivation of the oppressed.) From the massive 400-year frontal attack on our belief in our humanity was born the defensive posture of the Afro-American writer.

So that many a black writer has had, like Richard Wright, to fight to live, to fight for the right to a whole conception of himself, has had to fight for the conception of black people as an abundant, inspired, diverse people, glorious in our strength and in our endurance and in our exuberance and in our vitality and in our wit and in our song and in our aggressiveness and in our creativity and in our vividness — and in our mistakenness and in our dishonesty and in our corruption and in our despair: for beauty is the whole, not the part; beauty is the totality of the mosaic, not only the most lovely stones; beauty is Christ's fear and vulnerability and death-wish, not only his strength and revolutionary commitment; beauty is the whole of the human entity. We must accept the totality of ourselves, our total humanity; to deny the existence of our total selves is self-rejection.

The black writer of the past often felt that he had to be a defender of blacks rather than an analyst of blacks; this, he felt, had to be his role, his responsibility. The defensive posture grew from his skin like tragic roses from a rich and threatened soil. But the defensive posture is a crippler, a castrater, and, ultimately, the defensive posture is an evasion of one's own complexity and the complexity of black people, an evasion of the unexplored continent of black nature. The defensive posture is often an excuse for avoiding self-knowledge, and often the defensive posture takes the road toward sentimentality.

The defensive posture has kept us from creating a great literature, for the defensive posture means that writers insist indirectly on maintaining a relationship with their detractors. But the black writers of the seventies will ignore their historic detractors, perhaps regard them with pity, perhaps with indifference and mild contempt. They will not, however, feel threatened by them.

In Kokomo, Indiana, two years ago, a twelve-year-old white boy called a ten-year-old black boy a nigger. "You're a nigger," the white boy charged. "So?" answered the black boy stoutly, indifferently, without a trace of concern or weakness or hurt or anger. A new sensibility is being born, the sensibility of no longer half-believing the detractors' slanders; the sensibility of indifference to one's detractors; the sensibility of whole and undivided self-acceptance. Unthreatened, the black writer will proceed to explore the unexplored continent of black nature and black life, undismayed by what he may find, secure in the knowledge that whatever of evil and whatever of the repugnant he may find, black people in America are a unique and splendid folk; and he will write fearlessly about what he finds, and frankly, knowing that fearlessness and frankness are prerequisite elements in the creation of a great Afro-American literature.

The word "fearlessness" is not used idly, for when a writer shrinks from writing frankly of himself and of his own people, the suspicion is strong that he fears self-discovery. He may fear what he may discover at the depths of himself and at the depths of his people; or, knowing what is there, he may turn from it in fear or revulsion. Assuredly such a timid and fearful attitude is no prescription for great writing. The black writer of the seventies will write from the conviction that self-discovery and psychological freedom are inseparable, from the knowledge that beauty is a wholeness, that beauty encompasses the whole of a person or a people, not only that which one finds attractive. This is the path to grandeur.

And the wholeness of all human life includes hell.

Too infrequently in white American letters does one sense the utter depths of human hell. In Afro-American letters, however, hell is traditionally and passionately captured. Hell is racism, hell is lynching, hell is hunger, hell is poverty; hell is *Big White Fog*, to borrow Theodore Ward's title. The black writer wrestles with this hell, chews and swallows and digests it: hellfire, devil, tail and all. Nor does he succumb before it, as white writers in America so commonly do; the black writer assumes, as the spirituals assumed, the strong possibility of hell's defeat, indeed, the inevitability of the devil's demise. The devil's defeat may not take place literally, or now, and the protagonist may be physically destroyed, like Wright's Aunt Sue and Silas in *Uncle Tom's Children*, but it is a temporary destruction, and the long-run destruction of devil and hell is implied; so much of the work of Wright, like the body of Afro-American fiction, implies man's victory over hell.

Wright's "Big Boy Leaves Home" and "Down by the Riverside" are brilliant examples of the depiction of hell, and stand at the summit of the short story art in America. They are almost alone in their intensity, vision, meaning, their passionate grasp of hell. Wright breathes with anguish the stench that fills American nostrils. He stares with hatred and agony through the windows of comfortable Amerikahaus, curses Amerikahaus, erected as it is on a foundation of sooty black and Indian bones, its bricks cemented with black and Indian blood. This is the hell — the hell black writers stand fast before and challenge — from which the white American writer flees in terror. It is the white writer's failure to face this hell that stunts his growth.

Great writing is a dogged confrontation with the human hell without and the human hell within oneself; great writing is the courage to draw prophetic conclusions from the existence of hell. Thus *Huckleberry Finn,* an uncommonly fine work in which Twain at many points seizes hell's fire in his hands (Huck with his hallucinatory father in the cabin; the counterfeit royalty; the murderous feud), diminishes itself in its failure to depict Jim's hell. Twain never faces the hell of slavery, and Jim is benevolently freed by whites. A basic confrontation with hell is avoided, and Twain evades confrontation with himself. Likewise Hemingway, though he depicts hell in *The Sun Also Rises,* for example, never faces it — for to face it means to see through it and beyond it; to face hell means to face it down, not to succumb to it in despair, as Hemingway does. To face hell means not to collapse because of man's present reality but to face up to the potentialities of man; to face hell means to face up to man's ability to conquer himself, to face up to man's infinite potentialities for health and goodness, for godliness, for creativity, for beauty, for the construction of boundaryless human harmony.

The black writer of the seventies, battling to free his people, will continue the noble tradition of his predecessors: to face down hell and see through it and beyond it in the name of man. But the black writer of the seventies will go even further. He will explore the unexplored continent of himself and his people, will seek out the hidden caves and springs of beauty and hell, will seek out the hell and the complexity within his bones and within the viscera of his people. He has had the courage to stand fast before the American hell; now he will further explore, without flinching, his own nature and the nature of his people, unafraid of what he will find, disregarding the negative response of any man. Self-discovery is painful; the black writer will not shrink from the pain of self-discovery.

Wright's *Native Son* was a first dramatic step toward the black writer's facing black life unashamed and undismayed. The native son is hideous, tigerish, cold, inhuman, monstrous, human: Wright broke the tradition of the defensive posture. Wright's attitude as an artist was that he would tell the truth in defiance of any man's disapproval. Yet at the conclusion of *Native Son* Wright too succumbs to the defensive posture, and Bigger is redeemed; we are left wondering whether this determined freedom-hunter would have yielded at the end, this determined freedom-hunter who, as Professor Trellie Jeffers says, killed a white woman and burned her body so that he could find a tragic freedom. I think that he would have gone to his death cursing, searing with his murderous stare the warden and the guards, would have sat scornfully and enraged in the chair; or I think that his redemption would have been possessed of a rage and a bitterness too galling for even Bigger to bear. (Bigger, at the end of *Native Son*, is less frightening to some than a bitter-to-the-end Bigger would have been.)

Nevertheless, Wright broke through in *Native Son* and in *Black Boy*. He contemptuously threw aside the defensive posture in a way that makes Langston Hughes' *The Ways of White Folks*, a distinguished and important work in its own right, seem pure eulogy. And Wright's "Long Black Song," another study in contempt for the defensive posture, is a finely courageous study of the two sides of black — and human — nature: the heroic, on the one hand, and, on the other hand, the shabby, the weak, and the corrupt. His "Down by the Riverside," a study of the suicidal nature of many blacks, their ambivalence about their very right to live, is also an expression of disregard for the defensive posture.

A second distinguished dismissal of the defensive posture — and probably the finest long fiction by any American author — is *Invisible Man*. Up to the protagonist's speech to the eviction-protesters, this book stands at the summit of American long fiction; it penetrates to the very heart, the nucleus of the American soul. Ralph Ellison's uncertainty comes in the last half of the book. The book's central flaw can be found if one uses the spirituals as the criterion with which to compare it, for there is in the second half of the book the absence of spiritual grandeur — that imprimatur of greatness.

But in the first half of the book, Ellison brushes aside the defensive posture, and Trueblood rises from the center of the earth: human, corrupt, criminal, comic, poetic, weak, foolish, master raconteur, the dregs of the human race, yet somehow redeemed because he insists tenaciously on accepting himself — a strong thing to do, for filth and foolishness and criminality and viciousness and corruption are, expressed or unexpressed, an important part of every human being and of every people. No great literature will be created that does not accept this truth. Thus, man and writer and literature and people must begin with self-acceptance, and writer must begin by writing about life and man and people and nature as they are and not as writer pretends that they are. Trueblood is a dimension of man, as brilliantly conceived and executed a character as exists in literature; Norton and Bledsoe and Trueblood are all dimensions of man.

Probably one reason that Wright created Bigger is that he realized that Bigger the hoodlum is part of all of us, Bigger the killer, the hater, the revenger, the suicide. Perhaps Wright created Bigger because he felt that he was tracing a route to the core of the human soul and to the core of the black soul in America. There is no denying the Bigger-element in black life and American life: he stands there in the shadows, a part of every one of us, menacing and potentially kind, a switchblade in the hand in his pocket, the predator. In writing about this man, Wright was exploring the unexplored continent of black life and black nature in America. Moreover, Bigger represents Everyman, suppressed — Bigger represents the rebel in humanity who will come exploding out and create the New World and the New Man.

Ellison makes the quest and the question even more explicit, and it is this that gives *Invisible Man* its superb body till mid-book, for he asks explicitly, Who am I? This is the question that a great literature must ask of its people. "When I discover who I am," Ellison adds, "I'll be free." And so we shall.

Wright and Ellison, whatever the weaknesses of their big

novels, realized that the defensive posture is ultimately an evasion of the responsibility to explore the unexplored continent; an evasion of the responsibility to find out who we, black people, deeply are.

We know who whites are; we have known that for a long time. But we have evaded to substantial degree the responsibility to explore the unexplored Afro-American continent, the responsibility to find out who *we* are. E. Franklin Frazier gravely undertook in *Black Bourgeoisie* the task of defining a sector of black folk, and paid heavily. But we must emulate his reckless courage and the reckless courage of LeRoi Jones in *Dutchman* and *The Slave* if we wish to create a great literature.

Who are we? The black writer of the seventies will, I am convinced, move swiftly and profoundly to build a great literature which must inevitably rest on honest answers to these questions: Who are we? What kind of civilization have we, black people, created?

We know that European and American civilization is sick with the disease of five centuries' imperialism and genocide. But now the questions are not limited to what kind of civilization *they* have, what kinds of culture *they* have, what kind of human beings *they* produce. Now there are additional questions: what kind of human beings do *we* produce? What is *his* texture, *his* nature, what is at *his* depths? We know the cancers of whites; now the job is to identify and excise our own cancers.

And self-eulogy, however just, however accurate, however deeply true, can easily be an evasion; for it is as if a man, asked to describe himself, describes only that which is attractive about himself, and thus misses that which is also profound and complex in himself. He thus misses part of his mystery, the mystery which, found, not only explains the man but also explains his destiny and gives him the power to alter his destiny.

There are many questions that require honest answers. The following are only a few. Why have we, to a marked degree, turned our backs on the spirituals? Why did black slaves in this country unconsciously or consciously decide to go a different route from that taken by the slave-rebels in Haiti and Jamaica? Why is it that no major novel has been written by a black person about that curse of black life, which affects the entire race in America: racism among ourselves, which is particularly aimed at a very large number of our women? Why are so many of us dishonest and complacent about this curse, which causes incalculable hurt and bitterness to so many; which subtly dislocates numberless lives; which, indeed, subtly dislocates the whole of Afro-American life? (As one example, it is obscene and ignoble that racist rudeness and discriminatory treatment are commonly inflicted upon Africans and darkbrownskin women in certain black institutions of higher learning.)

Other questions: Does the bourgeois aspiration permeate and corrupt vast workingclass sectors of black life? Why do tens of thousands of young black men supinely take their place in the machine of imperialism, just as some of their great-grand-fathers, fresh from slavery, made war against the Indians? (When we answer these questions, we will take the deepest measure of the heroism of Detroit and Watts.) What kind of human beings and what kind of civilization have we created? What kind of human being, what kind of civilization are we going to create in the future? Certainly one of the central tasks of black literature should be to assist in the creation of a New Black Civilization, the New Black Man in America — but first there must be an honest analysis of who we are, what we are, where we have been, what we have been, who we have been. We can prescribe for the future only if we look at ourselves and penetrate into ourselves with the most loving yet the most pitiless kind of honesty. The seventies, I am convinced, will see the powerful emergence of a most relentless kind of honesty among black writers.

The seventies will see the death of the defensive posture. In the seventies the black writer will continue the journey into the vast Afro-American soul, the journey into the unexplored con-tinent (which Du Bois began in that great American literary work, *The Souls of Black Folk*), a journey whose destination is self-discovery and psychological freedom. The seventies will see in Afro-American literature the flowering of the great largeness of soul which characterizes the spirituals and which character-ized Du Bois (that black soul, that world-embracing soul). We shall see in the 1970's the birth of a new prophecy and the building of a grandeur.

The athletic playing field can be a training ground for more than sports. Dr. Pierce studies the offensive mechanisms which, applied on the football field, are also all too often applied in human relationships.

CHESTER PIERCE *was born in Glen Cove, New York, and is a member of both the Faculty of Education and the Faculty of Medicine at Harvard University. Since 1966 he has been co-investigator of a National Science Foundation project on the effects of the environment on men living on American bases in the Antarctic. A graduate of Harvard College (A.B. 1948) and of Harvard Medical School (M.D. 1952), Dr. Pierce is the author of over sixty articles published in psychiatric and medical journals. Among his many other professional activities, He serves as a Senior Consultant to the Peace Corps and the Office of Economic Opportunity. He is Chairman of the American Psychiatric Association's Committee on Academic Education and a member of the Association's Commission on Manpower.*

Chester Pierce

Offensive Mechanisms

In traditional and orthodox teaching of psychiatry, the role of defensive mechanisms is deemed crucial. These mechanisms act to reduce or dilute shame and guilt. They permit the organism to function without being overwhelmed by anxiety. Much of psychotherapy is devoted to understanding and then re-inforcing or loosening defensive mechanisms.

There is, however, no emphasis placed on offensive mechanisms. It is the purpose of this article to introduce the concept of offensive mechanisms, and to discuss this concept in the framework of the violence and aggression it facilitates within the society. Just as in one-to-one psychotherapy the therapist studies anxiety and the resultant defensive maneuvers, the social therapist, as he seeks ways to affect masses of individuals, must study superiority and resultant offensive maneuvers.

For it is from feelings of superiority that one group of people proceeds to brutalize, degrade, abuse, and humiliate another group of individuals. The superiority feelings and the accompanying contemptuous condescension toward a target group are so rampant in our society that it is virtually impossible for any negotiation between blacks and whites to take place without the auspices of such offensive tactics. Thus it happens that this article will consider black-white relations, although it may be true that offensive mechanisms are used generally in many other areas of inter-personal interactions.

Most offensive actions are not gross and crippling. They are subtle and stunning. The enormity of the complications they cause can be appreciated only when one considers that these subtle blows are delivered incessantly. Even though any single negotiation of offense can in justice be considered of itself to be relatively innocuous, the cumulative effect to the victim and to the victimizer is of an unimaginable magnitude. Hence, the therapist is obliged to pose the idea that offensive mechanisms are usually a *micro-aggression,* as opposed to a gross, dramatic, obvious *macro-aggression* such as lynching. The study of micro-aggression by whites and blacks is the essential ingredient to the understanding of in what manner the process of inter-actions must be changed before any program of action can succeed. Our society does not stand in need of new laws or innovative plans as much as it stands in need of eliminating offensive maneuvers from any process of interaction which involves majority and minority citizens. Before detailing some reflections about offensive mechanisms, it is necessary to re-view briefly some medical aspects of racism. For racism to be so witheringly effective, strong offensive maneuvers are mandatory.

Racism

Racism in the United States is a public health and mental health illness. It is a mental disease because it is delusional. That is, it is a false belief, born of morbidity, refractory to change when contrary evidence is presented concerning the innate inferiority of any person with dark skin color. Thus everyone in this country is inculcated with a barrage of sanc-tions which permit and encourage any white to have attitudes and behavior indicative of superiority over any black. Since everyone is involved in this delusion, then by definition it is a public health problem. The extent of the public health involve-ment is judged in terms of other definitions of a public health illness. In the classical mode of such illnesses, racism, besides affecting masses of population, also defies therapy on an one-to-one basis, produces chronic, sustained disability, and will cost large sums of money to eradicate.

There are still other dimensions to the medical description of racism. It is a contagious disease. There may not exist a white or black man in this country who has never had to operate from one side or the other of a line drawn against the black man. For the black man to violate this line, often legally drawn, is to invite the most sinister and ultimate catastrophe. While the white man, even the most indefatigable, non-conforming liberal is liable to have to take advantage of racial prerogative to the detrimental exploitation of some hapless — if unseen — black. Who has not known of relatively immune places such as small Scandinavian villages which seemed relatively bereft of negative racial attitudes until the arrival of a contingent of vociferous, outraged white Americans?

Yet another medical relationship of racism is the fact that it is a perceptual illness. In almost any black-white negotiation each participant views things differently, depending on whether he is white (the offender) or black (the offended). For instance, the psychological hallmark of racism is the altogether too well-known tendency for whites to congratulate themselves, before a black, concerning what marvelous "progress" is being made. To the perception of the white offender, this is true and reasonable. From the vantage point of the black offended, however, this is both untrue and unreasonable. If the black offended then indicates in any manner whatsoever that he is not convinced that congratulations are in order, he is gruffly perceived as at best an ingrate or at worst an ignoramus who refuses to comply to the rules set up by his oppressor. This sparks white animosity and hostility. In turn the poorly understood black is goaded to counter-hostility. It is in this way that the micro-aggressions of offensive maneuvers can accumulate and build to explosive white violence and retaliative black counter-violence.

Offensive mechanisms serve in other ways as a vehicle for the micro-aggressive episodes that come to total up racism. One of the most grisly of these considerations involves the fact that racism is a lethal disease. The offensive mechanisms which assure that the person in the inferior status is ignored, tyrannized, terrorized, and minimized constitute the fabric from which is cut the cloth of statistics that describes the plight of the ghetto citizen. It is a summation of collective micro-offenses by the majority that ignores the fact that a massive commitment is needed to make the ghetto school fail.

Up until now, the education system has succeeded in preparing generation after generation of blacks to accept the docile, passive positions of abused, disenfranchised, second-class citizens. It is a summation of collective micro-offenses by the majority that permits police department after police department to tyrannize black communities. It is a summation of collective micro-offenses by the whites which applies economic terrors to poor blacks who have the temerity to demand what the law provides. It is a summation of collective micro-offenses by the whites to minimize the social importance of any black or any black achievement so that blacks will see themselves as useless, unlovable, unable.

These are the sorts of micro-offenses that lead to the statistical early demise of blacks and to their incomparably higher morbidity and mortality rates. In the psychological perceptions of the black, such deaths are perpetrated, calculated murders by the white offender, whose ever-growing collective micro-aggressions presage more slaughter and even more repression. It is difficult, if not impossible, for a black to understand how a white, particularly a privileged white, can exhibit offensive micro-aggressions without considering himself a murderer. It is axiomatic that the more privileges a person enjoys, the more responsibility he should bear to eliminate the process of offensive micro-aggressions from the confines of his own institutions. It is not the janitor in the hospital who determines the process interactions between black and white. It is the hospital director and the board of trustees and the senior staff.

So much for a psychological fraction of truth about racism as viewed by a black psychiatrist. Racism is a mental health and public health disease characterized by perceptual distortion, contagion, and fatality. The vehicle for these characteristics is the cumulative effect of offensive mechanisms, individually exhibited but collectively approved and promoted by the white sector of this society. I turn now to a more refined description of offensive behavior.

Offensive Behavior

There would be many areas from which a theoretician could command literature to help him understand offensive behavior. As such, one could study the extreme aggressive act, homicide. Or one could look to animal studies, particularly the social behavior of animals. Another route would be to examine what is known about the relationship of endocrine glands to aggression. In political science there is an abundance of information on political conflict and the accession to power or influence. All these sources are illuminated when placed in conjunction with the psychoanalytic literature on aggression, particularly studies on psychosexual development. Nowadays, a student of aggression would have to search for the aggressive component in high school radicalism or campus disorders. Field studies and laboratories (such as those on men living in exotic-stressful environments) are still another source of information about aggression.

To prepare for this article, I felt it of greater importance, however, to observe at first hand how someone is trained deliberately to be offensive. One could elect to observe the training of warriors, for example. I did elect to observe the training of a class of warriors who are in an on-going preparation to be offensively efficient.

Accordingly, I worked last fall as an assistant line coach of the Harvard freshman football team. I had gone to the task with a set of expectations about offensive behavior. Pithy details, like how many feet an end cheated on in order to tighten the defense, occupied my keenest interest. Mundane facts, like whether one uses an inside or outside shoulder block in a given instance, taught me how complicated it is to conduct a good offense. Often I marvelled at the marked improvement to the offense that would accrue from a small change like replacing a brush block with a reverse body block.

Soon I was able to assemble those features of a successful offense that were applicable to both the football warrior-in-training and the school-boy bigot-in-training. Just as the skillful coach teaches his charges certain rules about the offense, the society is unrelenting in teaching its white youth how to maximize the advantages of being on the offense toward blacks.

It is the offense that selects the site of action for the scrimmage. This site is selected with great care and attention. With cunning guile and ruthless artfulness, the offense looks for weaknesses in the opponent and then concentrates its full force on that weakness. The aim is to control in order that one may score. To do this requires deception while carrying out a pattern of plays with the deliberate intention of destroying and demolishing any opponent who chances to present a frustration. Often this guile and deception is most successful when the defense is obliged to accustom itself to your play patterns, since you, the offense, not them the defense, know what your final plan will be. In this way, the offense engages craft in the service of forcing the opponent to take himself out of play. There are critical advantages to the offense. These include, besides selecting the site of action, a knowledge of *when* the play will initiate. Often when this action commences, the best offenders can cheat on the call, so that they are into action, illegally, with such speed and precision that a referee can't disqualify them even if he is suspicious of the action. The emphasis on speed, deception, power, control, and initiative reflects accurately the habitual mode of interchange between whites and blacks. These attributes can be described in terms of specific offensive mechanisms.

In order to make more sense of the offensive mechanisms with attributes of speed, deception, power, control, and initiative, I must first share another insight gleaned from the practice fields, America's laboratory for human relations, where experiments in controlled aggression are usual fare.

One day the coach, a man whom I have admired for a quarter of a century, had me watch a center block a middle guard during a scrimmage. The coach said he, too, would watch the center and middle guard in their head to head contest. At the end of the play, to my amazement, the coach proceeded to instruct a fullback on what he had done wrong. The fullback was at least eight yards away from the skirmish we had agreed to evaluate. Then the coach lined up his offense and demonstrated with himself at the fullback position what the errant youth had done. Finally, he lined them up again and ran the play properly. The freshman fullback, after this demonstration, was able to resume the position and operate in a satisfactory manner.

Later I asked the coach how he knew what the fullback had done since we were watching, specifically and intently, what two other boys were doing. I complained that I could hardly tell what those two had done, much less be able to detect a minor error on the fullback's part. He laughed. He said, "All these years you boys thought I had eyes in the back of my head. I don't. I knew from where the boy was at the end of the play what he must have done. I looked at where he was at, and I knew what must have happened!" This was for me an arresting statement. It defined a professional: one who knew what had to have happened by seeing how it turned out. His intercession defined something else for me. It said that he knew that immediate correction was necessary, easy, and useful. By implication, if such correction was not forthcoming, then this lad would be retarded just a bit in becoming a better offender.

The lesson I learned was that the professional looks at the "end result" of the offensive action and he knows what happened and how it could be made to be a better offensive action, or indeed, if uncorrected, what advantage could go to a shrewd defense. Hence, I decided that one should look to the end of the action of how whites treat blacks to understand what happened. Then one could begin to think about offensive weaknesses which the defense could ferret out.

There are probably many offensive actions that could be delineated in the field of human relations. I will name a few based on what the end result of the action was and which utilize a particular dynamic attribute. After mentioning a few of these offensive mechanisms which deliver micro-aggressive results to a presumed inferior, I will discuss a possible clinical usage that could be made of the concept of offensive mechanisms.

One must bear in mind that the culture makes offensive mechanisms automatic and perhaps almost obligatory on the part of whites. These mechanisms may be seen as conscious, unconscious, or pre-conscious. But to the black, the salient feature is that offensive mechanisms seem automatic. They are ever able to define for whites the way of inter-personal activities with blacks.

Some Offensive Mechanisms

1. "We love you blacks to death." This mechanism is what the clinician can diagnose when a black man feels and perceives at the end of the offense that the white man has said, "you blacks are unappreciative even though we whites love you to death." The varieties of this common offense include the well-used tokenism in which the visible black is displayed before the world as a demonstration of how loving the white man can be. No black should feel unappreciative if a single black is a secretary in the President's office while the remaining 5000 black employees of the company all remain at the most menial level.

The *pat and promise* is also an offense categorized under loving blacks to death. Here the black is made to feel that the good faith registered by white solicitude is sufficient. To demand more is both outrageous and ridiculous from the perceptual view of the white.

Fragmentation and atomization is seen frequently. Every black who is in contact with whites can expect to be called upon for all variety and quality of racial "experiences." Whether he wishes it or not, he is torn apart by a plethora of demands for his time, effort, and attention. These demands are so multitudinous that he is kept from his basic work, whatever it may be, in the service of helping to assuage white consciences. At the same time the collective whites by this maneuver have diluted and neutralized a possibly potent current in the black community. It is essential to the offender that all blacks be divided and claimed by such a multitude of demands that the very number of claims can receive only mediocre and casual attention. If the black rebels against these overtures to fragment and atomize his efforts and strengths, then he, too, can predict long, sorrowful white faces offended by the fact that a black has been unappreciative of their love.

Pacification sounds as if it is too passive to be an offensive variety of the love-you-to-death mechanism. However, to make blacks feel they must be pacific, docile, and accepting requires offensive action of the most intense degree. One type of pacification, seen at its best at academic lectures is the *"glob on,"* in which the speaker almost before he can leave the podium is approached and glued-to by avid whites who wish to talk to him. The speed with which this takes place is proto-typical of the attribute most salient in the offensive mechanism of love-you-to-death. This is the mechanism which depends on blinding speed, once the act is initiated.

All of the offensive mechanisms can occur in overlap, obviously. Some combinations are particularly strong and thus have greater usage by the white offender. The practice field laboratory would predict that a frequent winning combination for the offender is to combine speed with deception. And indeed in white-black relations this turns out to be the case.

2. "You blacks come see us." This mechanism is what the clinicians can diagnose when a black man feels and perceives at the end of the offense that the white man has said, "come see us, at our site of action and we'll help you, if you beg." The offender maneuvers to be sure that the black feels and acts properly humble and humiliated. The black must be put on the defensive. It is gratifying to the white's ego to have an audience with the beggar and to decide whether or not a crumb can be dispensed. If the offended beggar is not properly chastened, the good offender makes sure that the offended knows that reprisals are readily available; this is done quickly. The very best offenders when using this mechanism know how to make the black believe he, the black, must have all the answers to any and all problems. Yet if the black's plans aren't congruent with what the white had in mind, the white offender seizes action by appealing to some other black or white authority. In this way the offended knows he is dispensable, that he must take the defensive. Since these offensive mechanisms are predicated on the satisfying succor they provide to white's esteem and pride, it is no wonder that when the white uses "you blacks come to see us," that the black must be prepared for an onslaught by

deception. It is too gratifying to yield up the offense too readily. Thus the good offender can, by expert deception, keep the poor black returning to beg for an indefinite time. All the while, he the white is enjoying the gratification.

Sometimes at this point in a planned offensive maneuver in football, the speed and deception falter. Here enters the need for raw power, a commodity America has in superabundance!

3. "You blacks are sick." This is the mental offensive mechanism employed by whites when power display is required. At the end of the offensive action, the black feels and perceives that the white has communicated: "You blacks are so sick that we must use all our power to protect you for your own sake." There are obvious parallel usages to the mechanism which the white American doesn't shrink to use when it is convenient, say in Vietnam or Santo Domingo. To accomplish this offense the offended must be made to feel uncertain, unsure, and confused. He is told that he doesn't understand his problem because he is too distorted in his outlook. For example, black men are made to feel masochistic even for accepting the abuse heaped upon them. Never could it be communicated that merely to survive in such a system, to prevail and endure under such duress, defines a resiliency of spirit and an altruistic regard toward protecting one's family as best one can.

When this offensive mechanism is in the hands of a skilled offender, blacks can predict that power pressures are aimed at keeping blacks distrustful and disunified among themselves. For the offender casts grave doubts to the offended about the potentiality of healthy, effective action from any black source.

Once the offended is in this position the final coup is delivered easily. The black is told: control yourself, your sickness is making you lose your temper. The veiled threat, the hidden but clear message in this sort of interaction is that power might have to be unleashed to keep the black from feeling out of sorts about the treatment he receives. For, if the black gets so sick that he expresses anger, the white must display his terrible force.

Here the recipe for a creative, imaginative offense calls for the offender to mix in one of his favorite staples: control. The offensive coach realizes that you can't rely on merely speed, deception, and power. You must be in a position always to control the ball. That is, you must decide what happens next. The attribute of control is associated with the next offensive mechanism.

4. "We're good to you blacks." Here at the end of the offensive action, if the play has been well-executed, the white man perceives and feels that he is still in control. The black man feels and perceives that the white has said: "We're good to you blacks and you should be grateful that we control you as gingerly and humanely as we do."

In order to accomplish this objective every white school child must be taught that he knows more than any black, that he knows how to do everything and anything better than a black and that a black really cannot have an essential idea worthy of attention. The educational system both through formal efforts (like per capita in-put for students) and informal efforts (like the handling of mass media) must make these ideas functionally true. On the obverse, the black child must be inculcated with his own inadequacies, deficiencies, and helplessness. Only if the school system and mass media help actively to make the black as well as the white have these attitudes can the offensive mechanism of "we're good to you blacks" be effective. It is for this reason that the school system and the mass media are the institutions most responsible for initiating and maintaining the *folie à deux* that characterizes race relations in the United States. (*Folie à deux: "double madness"; the presence of the same or similar delusional ideas in two persons closely associated with one another, especially the result of delusional ideas being transmitted from one person to another.*)

With the white offender backed by the power that comes from his group's economic base and the control that comes to him as a result of the way he deploys his school system and mass media, it is easy to be good to blacks. The white can dispense largess, he can define what is best for blacks: what they should do, what they should want, what they should not want. Naturally all this takes place without the benefit of black consultation. Or if black consultation is sought it is unthinkable (for no black, by definition of the oppressors' rules, can have a worthy idea) that the black can truly make a contribution concerning what he needs or wants. Whites always presume to tell blacks what it is like to be black.

After the Black Psychiatrists organized a year ago, and I was elected the first national chairman, a white psychoanalyst — a dear friend — spoke to me on the phone. I timed his "lecture" to me. For twenty-one minutes he harangued about such things as what did I know about poverty since I was never really poor (he has never had schizophrenia but it is all right for him to treat schizophrenia!). He told me in essence that my life was not subjected to racial abuse. I cited the most raw abuses to him, which he conceded he hadn't imagined (since some took place in his home town). I indicated that as I grew older and into greater access to things, the more sad and angry I became. This was especially true when I saw the way decisions are made. Further, I would never presume to tell *him* how it is to be white or what he should do. The rules of our society, however, allowed him to tell me in what must be described as a patronizing lecture, what I should or should not be doing and what was in my own best interest. I presumably should have reacted to such pyschotherapeutic intervention by doing what he said or, in essence, being controlled.

An offensive line coach, the basic science teacher of offensive action, reviewing the interaction just described, would want to know immediately how the offender instituted his play at control. That is, in ball control (which is the name of the game of offense) the critical factors are: *Who initiates the action? Where is the action initiated? When is the action initiated?* In this latter instance my dear friend, and he is still a dear friend (for I'd have no white acquaintances, much less friends, if I withdrew every time I was hit by an offensive mechanism) initiated the action at a site and time of his choosing.

This leads us to consider the last of the offensive mechanisms that we shall discuss. It is the one whose attribute is initiative. As such, to the basic scientist of offensive maneuvers, it must be the mechanism which is most dear to his heart. For the basic scientist in his private field laboratory never ceases to insist that by offense it is meant who, when, where, and how action is initiated.

5. "We whites are right." This offensive mechanism is the most basic. It is of course the one from which spring all the others. And it is the one which most directly testifies to the white that he is superior. As discussed previously the existence of offensive mechanisms stems from the need of whites to reaffirm and reassert feelings and ideas of racial superiority.

At the conclusion of this offensive action, the black man must feel and perceive that the white man has said, "we whites are right, we whites know what we're doing and you blacks are here at our forbearance, for our amusement, entertainment, or other exploitation." I notice in a class I teach that after each session a white, not a black, will come up to me and tell me how the class should be structured or how the chairs should be placed or how there should be extra meetings outside the classroom, etc. The student is on the initiative and sees as his usual prerogative with a black that he must instruct me and order me about and curb my own inclinations and independence. One could argue that I am hypersensitive, if not paranoid, about what must not be an unusual kind of student-faculty dialogue. This I concede. What I cannot explain, but what I know every black will understand, is that it is not what the student says in this dialogue, it is how he approaches me, how he talks to me, how he seems to regard me. I was patronized. I was told, by my own perceptual distortions perhaps, that although I am a full professor on two faculties at a prestigious university, to him I was no more than a big black nigger. I had to be instructed and directed as to how to render him more pleasure! Doubtlessly, the students would be aggrieved to think they came across to me like that and might demand an apology. Yet white America has so structured human interactions that if every time in the next day that a black felt something like I felt from a well-intentioned, well-meaning white, we would have to take time out for literally thousands of apologies. The employ-ment of offensive tactics is so inherent, so intrinsic to all interpersonal relations between white and black, that it is inconceivable to me that well into the next century blacks will not be having these angry thoughts. But can use be made of the study of the description and dynamics of offensive mechanisms, the chief means of racial interaction employed by whites in America?

The Clinical Usage of Offensive Mechanisms

Both a basic science specialist whose laboratory for controlled aggression is a gridiron and a physician whose clinical province is all of humankind are persons who want to know about alternative choices. The football coach spends his life looking for options. The physician spends his life working for treatment possibilities. What are the options or treatment possibilities afforded by a knowledge of offensive mechanisms?

Let me start by saying a few words about a program I'm engaged in. Harvard has discarded the traditional Ph.D. program in clinical psychology. As of a year ago, a new program was instituted entitled "Clinical Psychology and Public Practice." This doctoral program is sponsored conjointly by four separate faculties (education, medicine, divinity, and arts and sciences). As the name suggests, it is our hope that upon graduation our students will not be private practitioners, but public practitioners. There is the expectation that such public practitioners will function often as *change agents* within the society. Their chief concern will be with masses of individuals rather than the therapy of one individual by one individual. This concern grows from the conviction that traditional one-to-one models have failed to be of any essential service value to the great bulk of the nation's population. Further, as matters now stand, there is not a great deal of relevancy to the needs of the black poor and perhaps all non-white and white poor in psychiatric teaching programs. The first applications of the idea of offensive mechanisms will be made by students in Clinical Psychology and Public Practice.

The Street Therapist

There must be developed a group of health workers who could be called "Street Therapists." They might or might not be holders of high academic degrees. The role of the street therapist woud be to conduct supportive-relationship treatment, especially for key individuals in the ghetto as well as to help poor citizens change institutional processes which work now to damage their emotions.

Thus, the street therapist functionally might be seeing a leading community organizer. The relationship between them would be described sometimes as teacher, friend, therapist. The patient would usually not see the street therapist at a given hour or given place. They might elect to meet at 2 a.m. in an all night coffee shop. Compared to traditional therapy there would be much more confrontation and direction, instead of introspection and indirection. There would be more emphasis on actions instead of thoughts or feelings. Environmental manipulation would be commonplace; intrapsychic maneuvering less usual. The orthodox therapist may spend considerable time discussing sexual relations. The informal, direct style of the street therapist may permit drastic reduction of time spent on discussing sexual relations with more time consumed on general social relations.

Paramount in the method of the street therapist will be a knowledge of offensive mechanisms, just as the psychiatrist of the middle-class white never loses sight of the defensive mechanisms of his patient. And just as the psychiatrist remains concerned about his patient's intrapsychic anxiety which molds the patient's defenses, the street therapist stays preoccupied with the conscious feelings that result from the insults, usually of the micro-accumulative variety, that spew forth from white ideas of superiority.

However, the street therapist will not focus all of his effort on such treatment. He will be at home in neighborhood meetings, in bars and barbershops and playgrounds. He will become a consultant to the ever-growing efforts by the poor to organize themselves, to articulate their wants, to negotiate their demands. In this office the street therapist will have much occasion to point out and clarify feelings and "end results" that arise from the accumulative micro-aggressive, micro-assaultive offensive mechanisms set forth, continuously, by the majority.

Thus, the street therapist is truly a doctor since he, in fact, will be a "teacher." The educative applications of knowledge of offensive mechanisms seem limitless. It will be the job of the street therapist to organize and to instruct so that people will accomplish desired and necessary changes. This means people must be politicalized for social action. They must, in the course of whatever social action they undertake, encounter the school system and the mass media. The street therapist helping in the organization will also be teaching and interacting. In the group for which he is an advocate, he will clarify what offensive maneuvers whites use and what effect they are intended to convey.

For his basic science training, the street therapist may have to become a defensive coach so that he can combat the offensive specialist. Once such defensive strategems are devised against micro-agressions, the street therapist must teach them to all his clients.

It is my fondest hope that the day is not far remote when every black child will recognize and defend promptly and adequately against every offensive micro-aggression. In this way, the toll that is registered after accumulation of such insults should be markedly reduced.

What this is saying is that the final clinical application of the knowledge of offensive mechanisms should be to help make each black child an expert in propaganda. That is, he must see what is in his own best interest and decide it for himself while detecting and deflecting the considerable white effort, **via** offensive maneuvers, to make him feel unsure, unwanted, useless, disunited, disaffected, and helpless. In short, he must use his knowledge of offensive mechanisms, taught to him by such creatures as street therapists, to feel himself a respectable, dignified, worthwhile human being despite the murderous social pressures which conspire to make him feel otherwise, and, at the same time, invite his early demise.

Conclusions

The street therapists may or may not be black. But, they will engage in what is urgent and vital. Today race relations are the most pressing concern they could undertake. As street therapists become agents to make people aware of offensive mechanisms, benefits to America would include making each individual more aware of how and why he contributes friction to race relations. Such awareness, often accompanied by discomfort, may lead to better interpersonal interactions and thereby help ameliorate our great domestic problem.

In order for black individuals to both analyze and project propaganda (that is, understanding what is in one's own best interest, which of couse would include domestic tranquility and good international relations), the applied knowledge of how to defense offensive maneuvers is obligatory.

Further, when black groups act, they must know about offensive tactics and strategy. For example, the well-used methodology of "loving-you-to-death" in which the white says: "There are X excellent jobs you can have, because we love you; *but,* you must fill them in two weeks!" The offense has used speed to confuse the defense. The defense must brace for the hidden deception and anticipate such a play as: since you can't fill the jobs you are sick, you are inadequate, you are a failure. The deception is that at the original negotiation, the white knew he had $X + Y$ people to fill the jobs and that the blacks had not a single possibility. The street therapist must make his constituents see these common maneuvers and train them in how to despoil them.

There remain but a few more personal things to be said about offensive mechanisms. In a recent Off-Broadway play, the dying hero wishes that as part of the American dream he had known congressmen and movie stars intimately. During my life I have known congressmen, senators, and movie stars intimately, as well as a wide cross-section of whites from members of the Mafia to members of what people might call America's royal families. Yet despite participating in the American dream, I am so accustomed and conditioned to accepting offensive maneuvers from whites that I can not recall a single instance in which I initiated a contact with a white person. It would be unthinkable for me, for instance, to speak to a white seat companion on an airplane unless the member of the collective offending group first indicated somehow that an action should commence.

It has occurred to me often that those blacks who best adapt to America, whether they are militants or accommodationists, somehow are successful defenders. Another paper could be written on the behavior patterns of the best defenders. It may not be an exaggeration to say that one's adjustment in the United States, if he is black, depends on how practiced he is in anticipating and containing the offense. All one has to do is look at any process interaction in an interpersonal relationship between a black and a white to get abundant evidence of this. I would say regrettably that almost always in this interactional process the black takes the position which could be described as *pro-racist*. He does things which would give comfort, and aid that would sustain and encourage whites to feel superior and his own group to feel inferior. This is true in black to black relations and in white to white relations.

SUMMARY

Offensive mechanisms, the small, continuous bombardments of micro-aggression by whites to blacks is the essential ingredient in race relations and race interactions. An understanding of offensive mechanisms can be enhanced and extended by observing the conduct of experiments in controlled aggression on American playing fields. During the seventies it will be crucial for blacks to become aware of how both blacks and whites project pro-racist attitudes which allow whites to continue to dehumanize blacks. Once the offensive mechanisms are understood, they can be applied usefully to help blacks live better and longer.

Postscripts

Religion, Poetry, and History Foundations for a New Educational System

Margaret Walker

MARGARET WALKER *is Professor of English at Jackson State College, Jackson, Mississippi. She is the author of the celebrated book of poems,* For My People, *published in the Yale University Series of Younger Poets in 1942. Her novel of the Civil War,* Jubilee, *won a Houghton Mifflin Award in 1966. Mrs. Alexander in private life, she is presently working on another novel, more short stories, and a new collection of poems.*

The following speech was delivered at the National Urban League Conference, New Orleans, Louisiana, July 29, 1968, and is reprinted here by permission of the editors of Vital Speeches of the Day.

Members of the Council of Guilds and friends of the National Urban League: I have chosen a subject which I believe vital to our people in this year of extreme crisis: Our Religion, Poetry, and History: Foundations for a New Educational System. Such a subject immediately poses questions and demands a definition of terms. Why do we need a new Educational system? How are the values of a Society formed? What is the role of Religion in a Society? What is the meaning of Poetry? And what is the essential worth of a People's heritage in developing their social consciousness? The answers to these questions should then automatically lead to a set of basic assumptions: one, that the philosophy and aesthetic values of a society are fundamental to the development of certain basic institutions and the social phenomena of that society; two, when these social phenomena and institutions erupt in chaos the basic philosophy must be reexamined and ultimately changed; three, when the society thereby undergoes such violent change the people are morally responsible to create a new set of values on which they can build better institutions for a better society.

Why do we need a new Educational System? We stand today in the throes of cataclysmic social change. We are caught in a world-wide societal revolution that breeds ideological and military conflict between nations. We are impaled on a cross of constant economic problems which automation and cybernation have brought us with the electronic revolution. We are deeply distressed by the conditions of our inner cities. We are equally concerned with the confusing drama on our college campuses which reflects the search of our young people for values different from our own.

Our young people seem to be seething in a boiling caldron of discontent. Like the youth of every generation they want to know and they demand to be heard. Like youth in every age they are the vanguard of our revolutionary age. They are the natural leaders of revolution whether that revolution be of race, class, or caste; whether it is sexual or academic; whether it is political or intellectual. Today the revolution we are witnessing encompasses all of these, for the violence of revolution not only threatens but definitely promises to sweep out every corner of our outmoded existence. Violence today is more than a tool of tyranny, as it has always been, it is also the tool of revolution.

We are not only shedding the old ways of the past. We are overwhelmed by the problems of a new universe. Here in this decade of the 1960's we stand under the watershed of the twentieth century totally unprepared for the innovations of the twenty-first century already rushing headlong upon us. The historical process, of which we are a part, does not necessarily mark off the cycles of man's progress with the man-made dates or hours we have set for change. The life of the twenty-first century has already begun while the debris of the structures in a dying twentieth century crashes all around us.

Our basic institutions of the home, the school, and the church are threatened by the same violent destruction undermining our socio-economic and political system, for they are part and parcel of the whole. Three hundred and fifty years ago, when the American colonies were not yet a nation, a set of built-in values were super-imposed upon the American continent and people by European powers. These values were composed of three basic philosophies: (1) a religious body of belief containing the Protestant work ethic with duty and work as a moral imperative, with the puritanical and Calvinistic aversion to pleasure of secular play, song, and dance, coupled with (2) the economic theories of a Commonwealth only groping for the rising industrialism and capitalism that did not fully emerge until a century later, but which were hidden under (3) the American political dream of Democracy. This democracy was based on the idealism of Christianity which declared all men are brothers and the children of God. Except for the facts of chattel slavery and inhuman segregation the ideal dream might have become a reality. Slavery and Segregation as Institutions contradicted the ideal dream and America developed, instead, a defensive philosophy or rationale for Racism, the fruits of which we are reaping today.

Black people in America have so long borne the stigma of slavery and segregation that every community, black and white, has been warped by this wanton subjugation. For a very long time after Slavery, almost a century in time, the Federal Government gave tacit consent to Jim Crow, and Segregation was supported boldly by law which of course became custom. Now it has been outlawed, but the mark of Cain is still on the land. White America has educated black and white children with a set of monstrous lies — half truths and twisted facts — about Race. Both black and white children, as a result, have been stunted in their mental growth and poisoned in their world outlook. The American white child in the north and south is just as distorted in his thinking as the black child although the expressed manifestations are not the same. The white child has been taught to value Race more than humanity. He has been taught to over-estimate his intelligence and human worth because of race, and at the same time to under-estimate the human worth and intelligence of anyone who is not of his race. The white American is therefore basically ignorant of the cultures of other people, and has no appreciation for any other language, art, religion, history, or ethical system save his own. He is in no way prepared to live in a multi-racial society without hostility, bigotry, and intolerance. He believes that he must convert all people to his way of thinking because he cannot possibly conceive that his way of thinking may not always be right for everyone else. Everyone must dress, think, pray, and amuse himself as he does. Every socio-economic and political system must emphasize or epitomize the values of his mechanistic and materialistic society. He falsely assumes that his values are idealistic and altruistic, that he is democratic and Christian while all others are totalitarian and pagan, yet in all his actions he contradicts his preaching. His every waking hour is spent getting and spending for himself, while denying his brothers any and all of the same rights he claims for himself. Self-righteous and self-centered, he thanks God daily that he is not as other men (meaning other races) are.

On the other hand, our black children have been taught to hate themselves, to imitate people whom they have been taught to believe are superior. Everyday they read in the schoolbooks, the newspapers, the movies, and the television the monstrous lies that deny their existence and denigrate their world. They have been led to believe that we have no black history, no black culture, no black beauty, nor anything black that has value or worth or meaning that is good. They have been told that our world is white and western with a cultural heritage that is Graeco-Roman, Christian in Religion, Protestant in Ethic, and Democratic in politics; that all these things are right and of necessity good and civilized while all the opposites of these are wrong and of necessity evil and savage. The non-western or Oriental world which is colored is therefore primitive in culture, heathen in religion, pagan in ethics, communistic in economics, and totalitarian in politics. This of necessity is evil, anti-Christian, and anti-white, and therefore anti-American. Ancient civilizations and Empires of Egypt, Babylonia, and Persia, ancient cultures and empires of Ethiopia, Karnak, Ghana, Mali, and Songhai, to say nothing of that famous city of Carthage which the Roman orator, Cato, constantly declared must be destroyed; these ancient names are not recited in our history books, nor is the fact that both Asians and Africans and all the

Arab world enjoyed their great Renaissance eras before the Europeans and the Christians. Thus our world has been divided into East and West, into black and white, and given the separate connotations of good and evil. For the most part our people have been gullible and believed the half-lies and the half-truths denying our blackness and wishfully affirming their whiteness by seeking to become carbon copies of white people. But the fact remains that we are living in a multi-racial world in which there are varying cultures, religious beliefs, and socio-economic or political systems and whether we like or dislike it our children must be educated to live in such a world. They must learn to live in a world that is four-fifths colored, nine-tenths poor, and, in most cases, neither Christian in religion nor democratic in ideals.

The struggle of black people in America in this decade of societal revolution must therefore re-emphasize the battle for intellectual emancipation. A new self-concept must be instilled in the black child and a new perspective must be developed in the white child. Moreover, it becomes the awesome task of every well meaning, clear-thinking American, black and white alike, to rectify the wrongs caused by Racism, to change the basic attitudes and twisted facts still erroneously held by Segregationist America, by racists who are white and black. All America must move toward a new humanism with a preoccupation toward providing a full measure of human dignity for everyone. We must create a new ethic that is neither Protestant, Catholic, Jewish, Moslem, Buddhist nor any other ethic narrowed by creed but liberated into respect for the human rights of all men. Our ethic will then become a universal blessing of mutual respect and concern for every living spirit. We need a new educational philosophy in order to achieve this. A knowledge of world religions, world cultures, and all the racial and nationalistic strains that make up the human family will make such an ethic possible. The appreciation of other people and their cultures is predicated upon an understanding of them and understanding is predicated purely upon genuine knowledge. We need a new Educational System. The recent revolution in teaching has been largely electronic, an intellectual revolution is of necessity a revolution in basic ideas.

Our present day system of Education began in the nineteenth century when the scientific revolutions of the eighteenth and nineteenth centuries were charting a new Universe with Newtonian physics. The Einsteinian revolution has outmoded such thinking. We no longer live in the nineteenth century. Even the twentieth century is largely behind us. Yet our religion is still that of the Middle Ages and the Protestant Reformation. What should a creative and spiritually vital Religion do for our Society? Why is the Christian Church in America today derelict in its duty and slow to move its feet toward full integration of all Americans into the mainstream of American life? All America knows that Institutionalized Religion has lost its basic meaning because it has too long been in the employ of Racism that has viciously used the Church and the Christian Religion for selfish ends and vested interests. Segregationists such as the Ku Klux Klan and the Americans for the Preservation of the White Race have so long declared themselves as the true representatives of Christianity, the true American Patriots, and the standard bearers of such nonsense as racial purity and integrity that they have whipped the truth of Christianity — the truth of the brotherhood of man and the fatherhood of God, whipped it senseless beyond recognition. Their lynchropes, their high explosives, boxes of dynamite, long range rifles, and burning crosses are all used in the name of Christ and the Christian Religion. Our burned churches are quite symbolic of racial hatred and spiritual decay. Our people deserve something better than a begging ministry in the employ of a powerful and wealthy hierarchy. The pages of history that tell the true story of Slavery and Segregation are stained with the blood of black men who were crucified by white Christians. No hypocritical white-washing of moribund congregations that are stinking with moral decay will deliver us today. Perhaps it is time for a new avatar. Violently shaken by class, caste, and racial disturbance the Church in America craves a new awakening in which spiritual meaning is reborn and revitalized. Religion in a Society should be the underlying philosophy of the People. It is their way of life, of thought, and of action. It is part of the aesthetic or cultural heritage of the people which undergirds the basic institutions of that society and gives dynamic impetus to all the group action and subsequent phenomena of that society. When the Religion of the People is dead, then they are without vision, without moral imperatives, and without all their aestheic or cultural values. Anything false that is used in the name of Religion is then the opiate or drug by which men lull themselves into a false consciousness, into deadly apathy, and supine complacency. A vital and dynamic Religion is necessary to the cultural advancement of all people. Religious faith is personal, but Religious Institutions are of necessity Social. As such they must serve all the people or they have no value.

Black men, before they came to America, had a religion and ethic that was tribal or communal and that was based on their group participation in rites and ceremonies that gave impetus to their living and moral order to their community. White Puritan Americans at home and abroad as missionaries frowned on this as superstitious nonsense. In America black people lost their ties with Mother Africa but they have neither lost religious faith nor mystical charisma. We are still a people of spirit and soul. We are still fighting in the midst of white American Racism for the overwhelming truth of the primacy of human personality and the spiritual destiny of all mankind. We fight for freedom and peace because we know these are spiritual entities and have nothing to do with guns and money and houses and land. Contrary to the prevailing belief of Racist society, all black men do not necessarily believe that a guaranteed employment of all the people is the highest essence and accomplishment of a society. Artists and the Religious of all nations know this is not so. Wise men are not all bankers and soldiers. Some are philosophers and poets and they too make their religious contribution to society. Some men therefore serve their society with the creative gifts of themselves, neither for money nor fame but for the cause of righteousness and with human integrity for the advancement of all mankind. Whether we remain the test of democracy, the soul of the Nation, the conscience of America, the redemptive suffering people of the world, or the tragic black heroes of a dying society, we know that the essence of life is in Spirit, not in cars, whiskey, houses, money and all the trappings of an affluent society. Call it soul if you wish, but it is our great gift and a part of our black heritage. We declare it worthy to offer on the altars of the world toward the enduring philosophy of a new and necessary humanism.

Our music, and Art, our literature born out of our folkways and folk-beliefs are also part and parcel of this cultural gift and heritage. Like Religion, the Poetry of a People, their Art, Songs, and Literature, come from the deep recesses of the unconscious, the irrational, and the collective body of our ancestral memories. They are indeed the truth of our living, the meaning and the beauty of our lives, and the knowledge of this heritage is not only fundamental to complete understanding of us as a People, it is a fundamental ingredient in the development of our world consciousness. Black people today in America are more than ever before socially conscious, aware of the damage that racism has done to our psyche, the traumatic injury to our children's morale and mental growth. We know the effects of the brutalizing, stigmatizing, dehumanizing systems of Slavery and Segregation under which we have existed in America for three hundred and fifty years.

A new awareness of this black history has taken hold of us in the wake of the riot commission's report that white racism is the creeping sickness destroying America. How, then, shall we diagnose this racism and prescribe for its cure? Will more jobs, better housing, more ballots, and less guns cure racism? Hardly. This is a battle for the minds of men. In the words of one of our greatest thinkers who predicted that the problem of the color line would be the problem of the twentieth century, in the words of that classic, *The Souls of Black Folk*, let us remember that we have three great gifts, a gift of song, a gift of labor or brawn with which we have helped to build a nation, and a gift of Spirit or Soul. Let us stir up the gift of God that is within us and let us create a new world for all Americans. Let us use our heritage of religion, poetry, and history as foundations for a new Educational system. Let us teach our children that we are a great people, that they have a great heritage, and that their destiny is even greater.

It must come as a shock to many of our people living in the

inner cities of America when they read about the deplorable
conditions in the ghettos, to discover that all this abuse directed
against criminals, against dope addicts, against looters and con-
spirators, all this abuse and condemnation directed against those
of us who live in sub-human conditions of black colonies of
the white power structure, all of this is a blanket condemnation
of us as a Race and as a People. What, then, is a ghetto and how
did it come into existence? Must we be blamed for this, too, on
top of all the other Racist hatred and injustice vented upon us?
Who owns all this property and where do the owners live? Do
they value their property more than they value our lives? Is this
why they send the police to protect their property while only
God protects our lives? Is it not true that the ghetto is a black
colony of the white power structure in which we are exploited
with no representation in the political and economic system? Do
the people in the ghettos control their economic and political
lives? Is the money spent in the ghetto returned to the ghetto?
Do the people living in the inner cities run the governments of
those municipalities? Somewhere we must truly place the blame
where it belongs. Poor black people can no longer be the scape-
goats who bear the blame for everything in our society. We not
only must build economic and political power in the ghettoes;
we must change the thinking in the ghettos as we must change
the thinking of all America. We must create a new mental
climate.

Fortunately for many of our people all of us have not been
blighted by ignorance of our heritage. Some of us have come
from homes where all our lives this positive healing process has
existed. While we were simultaneously reading the lies in the
history books at school we were learning our true history at
home from our parents. We have neither the Segregationists'
views of the South nor the racist views of the North about slavery, the Civil War, and Reconstruction. Some of us grew up
reading *Opportunity* and *Crisis* Magazines, reading the *Louisiana
Weekly*, the *Chicago efender*, and the *Pittsburgh Courrier* or
whatever our local newspaper was. We heard the poetry of
Du Bois and James Weldon Johnson and Langston Hughes,
and the music of Roland Hayes, Paul Robeson, and Marian

Anderson. We learned the names of our leaders such as Harriet Tubman, Sojurner Truth, and Mary McCleod Bethune. We knew our great Blues singers and Broadway stars and prize-fighters and Olympic winners. I was delighted to hear Dr. Sam Proctor say at Commencement that he did not need Stokely to tell him he was beautiful, his mother told him that. That is what mothers are supposed to do. But all our children do not know how beautiful they are for all of them have not been so fortunate. All of them do not know that physical beauty is relative according to man-made standards and that what we believe in our minds and hearts is what we are; that we need not become what our enemies wish us to become. We can be what we want to be and most of all we want to be ourselves, and not an imitation of other people.

Contrary to what some of our black brothers believe, this new Educational System must not be one of racial exclusion or this will become another face for racism. This learning must be all-inclusive. Any notions that a wide cleavage in the American people based on race, class, caste, sex, or age — any such notion is unrealistic, naive, negative, and detrimental. Whether black and white Americans are divided by yellow men, red men, or the little green men of Mars, the result can mean nothing but chaos. Shall we divide and conquer? Who will conquer, and who stands to benefit from such cleavage? If any foreign nation can divide us by indoctrination it can also completely destroy us. Some of our black brothers seem confused by the conflict, and the tactics of the struggle seem to cloud the issues. When we were subjected to Segregation by law we sought to become assimilated into the mainstream of American life. We regarded this as a worthy and positive goal. Now some of us seem to have some extreme thinking in the opposite direction. These seem to be appalled with the apparent failure of integration, and disappointed with the slow business of desegregation. Shocked and stung by the ugy face of white racism, they now declare that the sickness of America makes Segregation and Apartheid more to be desired than either desegregation or integration. This is not a clear incentive toward building power in the ghettos nor rebuilding the moral fibre of America. Whatever we have learned from our struggles in the past, at least a few facts should be clear: We fight with faith in the goodness of the future. No matter how troubled we have been, we have not lost our perspective. Our sense of history tells us that our human personality is potentially divine, hence our destiny must be spiritual. These may not seem much but they are enough, if in terms of these truths we teach our children the worth of their human personality, a pride in their heritage, a love for all people in the recognition of our common humanity, and a sense of dignity and purpose in living. They help us realize that freedom, like peace, is spiritual. It is with such tools that we must build our houses for tomorrow.

Just as we minister to the physical needs that are human we must minister to our mental needs that are also human. We must recognize the worth of every living person. All America is crying for this new humanism, for a new educational system, for a new and creative ministry from a new and spiritually vital religion, meaningful and with a genuine moral imperative. A new Space Age of the 21st century craves a vital and new religion to usher in the millenium. A new century promises to erase the color line. A new humanism must prevail. We must find the strength and the courage to build this new and better world for our children. Many of us will die trying in these last years of a dying century, but in the 21st century our progeny will raise their eyes to more than a vision of a brave new world. They will occupy the citadel. There truth will be honored and freedom understood and enjoyed by everyone. Racial justice and understanding will be a prelude to international peace and good will. But we must begin now to destroy the lies, to attack the half truths, to give our children something in which they can believe, to build faith in themselves, love for mankind, and hope for the future. Most of all we must teach them that righteousness is more to be desired than money; for the great possession of money without guiding principles, without judgment,without pride and integrity, such possession is nothing . . . that cars and houses and whiskey and clothes and all the trappings of an affluent society do not dress up empty minds, and ugly hearts, and loveless lives; that meaningless living is without immortality and that it does not give us heroes to honor. Our martyred dead are great because they died for freedom. Our list of heroes is three centuries long, but they are deathless and forever with us. Wisdom and understanding cannot be bought in the Vanity Fairs of the world. Justice and freedom are prizes to be sought and our martyred men of goodwill have already proven they are well worth dying to obtain.

Teach them, our children, that their heritage is great and their destiny is greater. That we are a great people with a great faith who have always fought and died for freedom. Teach them that life and love are for sharing and above all they are never to forget that we are all a part of the mainland, involved with humanity. We are not alone in our beauty and our strength. We are part of all Mankind who thoughout all recorded time have bravely fought and nobly died in order to be free.

Our Religion, Poetry, and History—they are our folk heritage; they are our challenge today to social commitment; they are the foundations of a new education, a new moral imperative, a new humanism on which we base our cultural hope for a free world tomorrow morning in the 21st century.

These things shall be:
A nobler race than e'er the world hath known shall rise
With flame of freedom in their souls
And light of knowledge in their eyes.
They shall be gentle, brave, and strong
To spill no drop of blood, but dare
All that may plant man's lordship firm
On earth and fire and sea and air.
Nation with nation, land with land
Unarmed shall live as comrades free
In every heart and brain shall throb
The pulse of one fraternity
New arts shall bloom of loftier mold
And mightier music thrill the skies
And every life shall be a song
When all the earth is paradise.

The Black Manifesto

This document was presented by James Foreman to the National Black Economic Development Conference in Detroit, Michigan, and adopted on April 26, 1969.

To the White Christian Churches and the Synagogues in the United States of America and to All Other Racist Institutions: Introduction: Total Control as the Only Solution to the Economic Problems of Black People

Brother and Sisters:

We have come from all over the country burning with anger and despair not only with the miserable economic plight of our people but fully aware that the racism on which the Western World was built dominates our lives. There can be no separation of the problems of racism from the problems of our economic, political, and cultural degradation. To any black man, this is clear.

But there are still some of our people who are clinging to the rhetoric of the Negro, and we must separate ourselves from these Negroes who go around the country promoting all types of schemes for black capitalism.

Ironically, some of the most militant Black Nationalists, as they call themselves, have been the first to jump on the bandwagon of black capitalism. They are pimps; black power pimps and fraudulent leaders, and the people must be educated to understand that any black man or Negro who is advocating a perpetuation of capitalism inside the United States is in fact seeking not only his ultimate destruction and death but is contributing to the continuous exploitation of black people all round the world. For it is the power of the United States Government, this racist, imperialist government, that is choking the life of all people around the world.

We are an African people. We sit back and watch the Jews in this country make Israel a powerful conservative state in the Middle East, but we are not concerned actively about the plight of our brothers in Africa. We are the most advanced technological group of black people in the world, and there are many skills that could be offered to Africa. At the same time, it must be publicly stated that many African leaders are in disarray themselves, having been duped into following the lines as laid out by western imperialist governments. Africans themselves succumbed to and are victims of the power of the United States. For instance, during the summer of 1967, as the representatives of SNCC, Howard Moore and I traveled extensively in Tanzania and Zambia. We talked to high, very high, government officials. We told them there were many black people in the United States who were willing to come and work in Africa. All these government officials, who were part of the leadership in their respective governments, said they wanted us to send as many skilled people as we could contact. But this program never came into fruition, and we do not know the exact reasons, for I assure you that we talked and were committed to making this a successful program. It is our guess that the United States put the squeeze on these countries, for such a program directed by SNCC would have been too dangerous to the international prestige of the United States. It is also possible that some of the wild statements by some black leaders frightened the Africans.

In Africa today there is a great suspicion of black people in this country. This is a correct suspicion since most of the Negroes who have left the States for work in Africa usually work for the Central Intelligence Agency (CIA) or the State Department. But the respect for us as a people continues to mount, and the day will come when we can return to our homeland as brothers and sisters. But we should not think of going back to Africa today, for we are located in a strategic position. We live inside the United States, which is the most barbaric country in

the world, and we have a chance to help bring this government down.

Time is short, and we do not have much time and it is time
we stop mincing words. Caution is fine, but no oppressed people
ever gained their libration until they were ready to fight, to use
whatever means necessary, including the use of force and power
of the gun to bring down the colonizer.

We have heard the rhetoric, but we have not heard the rhetoric which says that black people in this country must understand that we are the vanguard force. We shall liberate all the
people in the United States, and we will be instrumental in the
liberation of colored people the world around. We must understand this point very clearly so that we are not trapped into
diversionary and reactionary movements. Any class analysis of
the United States shows very clearly that black people are the
most oppressed group of people inside the United States. We
have suffered the most from racism and exploitation, cultural
degradation and lack of political power. It follows from the laws
of revolution that the most oppressed will make the revolution,
but we are not talking about just making the revolution. All
the parties on the left who consider themselves revolutionary
will say that blacks are the vanguard, but we are saying that not
only are we the vanguard, but we must assume leadership, total
control, and we must exercise the humanity which is inherent
in us. We are the most humane people within the United States.
We have suffered and we understand suffering. Our hearts go
out to the Vietnamese, for we know what it is to suffer under
the domination of racist America. Our hearts, our soul and all
the compassion we can mount go out to our brothers in Africa,
Santo Domingo, Latin America and Asia who are being tricked
by the power structure of the United States which is dominating
the world today. These ruthless, barbaric men have systematically tried to kill all people and organizations opposed to its
imperalism. We no longer can just get by with the use of the
word capitalism to describe the United States, for it is an
imperial power sending money, missionaries and the army
throughout the world to protect this government and the few
rich whites who control it. General Motors and all the major

auto industries are operating in South Africa, yet the white dominated leadership of the United Auto Workers sees no relationship to the exploitation of the black people in South Africa and the exploitation of black people in the United States. If they understand it, they certainly do not put it into practice, which is the actual test. We as black people must be concerned with the total conditions of all black people in the world.

But while we talk of revolution, which will be an armed confrontation and long years of sustained guerrilla warfare inside this country, we must also talk of the type of world we want to live in. We must commit ourselves to a society where the total means of production are taken from the rich and placed into the hands of the state for the welfare of all the people. This is what we mean when we say total control. And we mean that black people who have suffered the most from exploitation and racism must move to protect their black interest by assuming leadership inside of the United States of everything that exists. The time has ceased when we are second in command and the white boy stands on top. This is especially true of the welfare agencies in this country, but it is not enough to say that a black man is on top. He must be committed to building the new society, to taking the wealth away from the rich people, such as General Motors, Ford, Chrysler, the DuPonts, the Rockefellers, the Mellons, and all the other rich white exploiters and racists who run this world.

Where do we begin? We have already started. We started the moment we were brought to this country. In fact, we started on the shores of Africa, for we have always resisted attempts to make us slaves, and now we must resist the attempts to make us capitalists. It is in the financial interest of the United States to make us capitalist, for this will be the same line as that of integration into the mainstream of American life. Therefore, brothers and sisters, there is no need to fall into the trap that we have to get an ideology. We HAVE an ideology. Our fight is against racism, capitalism and imperialism, and we are dedicated to building a socialist society inside the United States where the total means of production and distribution are in the hands of the State, and that must be led by black people, by

revolutionary blacks who are concerned about the total humanity of this world. And, therefore, we obviously are different
from some of those who seek a black nation in the United
States, for there is no way for that nation to be viable if in fact
the United States remains in the hands of white racists. Then
too, let us deal with some arguments that we should share power
with whites. We say that there must be a revolutionary black
vanguard, and that white people in this country must be willing
to accept black leadership, for that is the only protection that
black people have to protect ourselves from racism rising again
in this country.

Racism in the United States is so pervasive in the mentality of
whites that only an armed, well-disciplined, black-controlled
government can insure the stamping out of racism in this country. And that is why we plead with black people not to be talking about a few crumbs, a few thousand dollars for this cooperative, or a thousand dollars which splits black people into fighting over the dollar. That is the intention of the government.
We say . . . think in terms of total control of the United
States. Prepare ourselves to seize state power. Do not hedge,
for time is short, and all around the world the forces of liberation
are directing their attacks against the United States. It is a powerful country, but that power is not greater than that of black
people. We work the chief industries in this country, and we
could cripple the economy while the brothers fought guerrilla
warfare in the streets. This will take some long range planning,
but whether it happens in a thousand years is of no consequence.
It cannot happen unless we start. How then is all of this related
to this conference?

First of all, this conference is called by a set of religious
people, Christians, who have been involved in the exploitation
and rape of black people since the country was founded. The
missionary goes hand in hand with the power of the states. We
must begin seizing power wherever we are, and we must say to
the planners of this conference that you are no longer in
charge. We the people who have assembled here thank you for
getting us here, but we are going to assume power over the conference and determine from this moment on the direction which

we want it to go. We are not saying that the conference was planned badly. The staff of the conference has worked hard and has done a magnificent job in bringing all of us together, and we must include them in the new membership which must surface from this point on. The conference is now the property of the people who are assembled here. This we proclaim as fact and not rhetoric, and there are demands that we are going to make and we insist that the planners of this conference help us implement them.

We maintain we have the revolutionary right to do this. We have the same rights, if you will, as the Christians had in going into Africa and raping our Motherland and bringing us away from our continent of peace and into this hostile and alien environment where we have been living in perpetual warfare since 1619.

Our seizure of power at this conference is based on a program, and our program is contained in the following Manifesto:

BLACK MANIFESTO

We the black people assembled in Detroit, Michigan, for the National Black Economic Development Conference are fully aware that we have been forced to come together because racist white America has exploited our resources, our minds, our bodies, our labor. For centuries we have been forced to live as colonized people inside the United States, victimized by the most vicious, racist system in the world. We have helped to build the most industrialized country in the world.

We are therefore demanding of the white Christian churches and Jewish synagogues, which are part and parcel of the system of capitalism, that they begin to pay reparation to black people in this country. We are demanding $500,000,000 from the Christian white churches and the Jewish synagogues. This total comes to fifteen dollars per nigger. This is a low estimate, for we maintain there are probably more than 30,000,000 black people in this country. Fifteen dollars a nigger is not a large sum of money, and we know that the churches and synagogues have a tremendous wealth and its membership, white America, has profited and still exploits black people. We are also not unaware that the exploitation of colored people around the world is aided and abetted by the white Christian churches and synagogues. This demand for $500,000,000 is not an idle resolution or empty words. Fifteen dollars for every black brother and sister in the United States is only a beginning of the reparations due us as people who have been exploited and degraded, brutalized, killed and persecuted. Underneath all of this exploitation, the racism of this country has produced a psychological effect upon us that we are beginning to shake off. We are no longer afraid to demand our full rights as a people in this decadent society.

We are demanding $500,000,000 to be spent in the following way:

1) We call for the establishment of a southern land bank to help our brothers and sisters who have to leave their land because of racist pressure, and for people who want to establish cooperative farms but who have no funds. We have seen too many farmers evicted from their homes because they have dared to defy the white racism of this country. We need money for land. We must fight for massive sums of money for this southern land bank. We call for $200,000,000 to implement this program.

2) We call for the establishment of four major publishing and printing industries in the United States to be funded with ten million dollars each. These publishing houses are to be located in Detroit, Atlanta, Los Angeles, and New York. They will help to generate capital for further cooperative investments in the black community, provide jobs and an alternative to the white-dominated and controlled printing field.

3) We call for the establishment of four of the most advanced scientific and futuristic audio-visual networks to be located in Detroit, Chicago, Cleveland and Washington, D.C. These TV networks will provide an alternative to the racist propaganda that fills the current television networks. Each of these TV networks will be funded by ten million dollars each.

4) We call for a research skills center which will provide re-

search on the problems of black people. This center must be funded with no less than thirty million dollars.

5) We call for the establishment of a training center for the teaching of skills in community organization, photography, movie making, television making and repair, radio building and repair and all other skills needed in communication. This training center shall be funded with no less than ten million dollars.

6) We recognize the role of the National Welfare Rights Organization, and we intend to work with them. We call for ten million dollars to assist in the organization of welfare recipients. We want to organize welfare workers in this country so that they may demand more money from the government and better administration of the welfare system of this country.

7) We call for $20,000,000 to establish a National Black Labor Strike and Defense Fund. This is necessary for the protection of black workers and their families who are fighting racist working conditions in this country.

8) We call for the establishment of the International Black Appeal (IBA). This International Black Appeal will be funded with no less than $20,000,000. The IBA is charged with producing more capital for the establishment of cooperative businesses in the United States and in Africa, our Motherland. The international Black Appeal is one of the most important demands that we are making, for we know that it can generate and raise funds throughout the United States and help our African brothers. The IBA is charged with three functions and shall be headed by James Forman:

   a) Raising money for the program of the National Black Economic Development Conference;
   b) The development of cooperatives in African countries and support of African liberation movements;
   c) Establishment of a Black Anti-Defamation League which will protect our African image.

9) We call for the establishment of a black university to be founded with $130,000,000, to be located in the South. Negotiations are presently under way with a southern university.

10) We demand that IFCO allocate all unused funds in the planning budget to implement the demands of this conference.

In order to win our demands, we are aware that we will have massive support, therefore:

1) We call upon all black people throughout the United States to consider themselves as members of the National Black Economic Development Conference and to act in unity to help force the racist white Christian churches and Jewish synagogues to implement these demands.

2) We call upon all the concerned black people across the country to contact black workers, black women, black students and the black unemployed, community groups, welfare organizations, teachers' organizations, church leaders and organizations, explaining how these demands are vital to the black community of the United States. Pressure by whatever means necessary should be applied to the white power structure. All black people should act boldly in confronting our white oppressors and demanding this modest reparation of fifteen dollars per black man.

3) Delegates and members of the National Black Economic Development Conference are urged to call press conferences in the cities and to attempt to get as many black organizations as possible to support the demands of the conference. The quick use of the press in the local areas will heighten the tension and these demands must be attempted to be won in a short period of time, although we are prepared for protracted and long-range struggle.

4) We call for the total disruption of selected church-sponsored agencies operating anywhere in the United States and the world. Black workers, black women, black students and the black unemployed are encouraged to seize the offices, telephones, and printing apparatus of all church-sponsored agencies and to hold these in trusteeship until our demands are met.

5) We call upon all delegates and members of the National Black Economic Development Conference to stage sit-in-demonstrations at selected black and white churches. This is not to be interpreted as a continuation of the sit-in movement of the early sixties, but we know that active confrontation inside white churches is possible and will strengthen the possibility of meeting our demands. Such confrontation can take the form of

reading the Black Manifesto instead of a sermon, or passing it out to church members. The principle of self-defense should be applied if attacked.

6) On May 4, 1969, or a date thereafter, depending upon local conditions, we call upon black people to commence the disruption of the racist churches and synagogues throughout the Unted States.

7) We call upon IFCO to serve as a central staff to coordinate the mandate of the conference and to reproduce and distribute *en masse* literature, leaflets, news items, press releases and other material.

8) We call upon all delegates to find within the white community those forces which will work under the leadership of blacks to implement these demands by whatever means necessary. By taking such actions, white Americans will demonstrate concretely that they are willing to fight the white skin privilege and the white supremacy and racism which has forced us as black people to make these demands.

9) We call upon all white Christians and Jews to practice patience, tolerance, understanding, and nonviolence as they have been encouraged, advised and demanded that we as black people should do throughout our entire enforced slavery in the United States. The true test of their faith and belief in the Cross and the words of the prophets will certainly be put to a test as we seek legitimate and extremely modest reparations for our role in developing the industrial base of the western world through our slave labor. But we are no longer slaves, we are men and women, proud of our African heritage, determined to have our dignity.

10) We are so proud of our African heritage and realize concretely that our struggle is not only to make revolution in the United States but to protect our brothers and sisters in Africa and to help them rid themselves of racism, capitalism and imperialism by whatever means necessary, including armed struggle. We are and must be willing to fight the defamation of our African image wherever it rears its ugly head. We are therefore charging the steering committee to create a black Anti-Defama-

tion League to be founded by money raised from the International Black Appeal.

11) We fully recognize that revolution in the United States and Africa, our Motherland, is more than a one-dimensional operation. It will require the total integration of the political, economic and military components, and therefore we call upon all our brothers and sisters who have acquired training and expertise in the fields of engineering, electronics, research, community organization, physics, biology, chemistry, mathematics, medicine, military science and warfare to assist the National Black Economic Development Conference in the implementation of its program.

12) To implement these demands we must have a fearless leadership. We must have a leadership which is willing to battle the church establishment to implement these demands. To win our demands we will have to declare war on the white Christian churches and synagogues, and this means we may have to fight the total government structure of this country. Let no one here think that these demands will be met by our mere stating them. For the sake of the churches and synagogues, we hope that they have the wisdom to understand that these demands are modest and reasonable. But if the white Christians and Jews are not willing to meet our demands through peace and goodwill, then we declare war, and we are prepared to fight by whatever means necessary. We are, therefore, proposing the election of the following steering committee:

Lucius Walker	Mark Comfort
Renny Freeman	Earl Allen
Luke Tripp	Robert Browne
Howard Fuller	Vincent Harding
James Forman	Mike Hamlin
John Watson	Len Holt
Dan Aldridge	Peter Bernard
John Williams	Michael Wright
Ken Cockrel	Muhammed Kenyatta
Chuck Wooten	Mel Jackson

Fannie Lou Hamer   Howard Moore
Julian Bond   Harold Homes

(This list was later revised, more Church representatives were added. — Ed.)

Brothers and sisters, we are no longer shuffling our feet and scratching our heads. We are tall, black and proud.

And we say to the white Christian churches and Jewish synagogues, to the government of this country and to all the white racist imperialists who compose it, there is only one thing left that you can do to further degrade black people and that is to kill us. But we have been dying too long for this country. We have died in every war. We are dying in Vietnam today fighting the wrong enemy.

The new black man wants to live, and to live means that we must not become static or merely believe in self-defense. We must boldly go out and attack the white Western world at its power centers. The white Christian churches are another form of government in this country, and they are used by the government of this country to exploit the people of Latin America, Asia and Africa, but the day is soon coming to an end. Therefore, brothers and sisters, the demands we make upon the white Christian churches and the Jewish synagogues are small demands. They represent fifteen dollars per black person in these United States. We can legitimately demand this from the church power structure. We must demand more from the United States Government.

But to win our demands from the church, which is linked up with the United States Government, we must not forget that it will ultimately be by force and power that we will win.

We are not threatening the churches. We are saying that we know the churches came with the military might of the colonizers and have been sustained by the military might of the colonizers. Hence, if the churches in colonial territories were established by military might, we know deep within our hearts that we must be prepared to use force to get our demands. We are not saying that this is the road we want to take. It is not, but let us be very clear that we are not opposed to force and we are not opposed to violence. We were captured in Africa by violence. We were kept in bondage and political servitude and forced to work as slaves by the military machinery and the Christian Church working hand in hand.

We recognize that in issuing this Manifesto we must prepare for a long-range educational campaign in all communities of this country, but we know that the Christian churches have contributed to our oppression in white America. We do not intend to abuse our black brothers and sisters in black churches who have uncritically accepted Christianity. We want them to understand how the racist white Christian church with its hypocritical declarations and doctrines of brotherhood has abused our trust and faith. An attack on the religious beliefs of black people is not our major objective, even though we know that we were not Christians when we were brought to this country, but that Christianity was used to help enslave us. Our objective in issuing this Manifesto is to force the racist white Christian church to begin the payment of reparations which are due to all black people, not only by the church but also by private business and the United States government. We see this focus on the Christian church as an effort around which all black people can unite.

Our demands are negotiable, but they cannot be minimized, they can only be increased, and the church is asked to come up with larger sums of money than we are asking. Our slogans are:

    All Roads Must Lead to Revolution
    Unite with Whomever You Can Unite
    Neutralize Wherever Possible
    Fight Our Enemies Relentlessly
    Victory to the People
    Life and Good Health to Mankind
    Resistance to Domination by the White Christian Churches
      and the Jewish Synagogues
    Revolutionary Black Power
    We Shall Win Without a Doubt

Basic Tenets of
Revolutionary Black Nationalism

(*Reprinted by permission of the editors of* Mojo.)

1) The right to self-determination is an inherent right of all nations.

2) African-Americans constitute an internal colony of the United States, an oppressed nation situated within the boundaries of the oppressing nation, white America.

3) The struggle for African-American liberation is therefore divided into two main stages: the *survival* and *national liberation* of the black colony (for land and self-government), and the establishment of *revolutionary socialism*, of a black communal society where exploitation of man by man is completely eliminated.

4) For the black captive nation, "race" exploitation has always superseded class exploitation as a general rule; therefore, within the first stage of struggle, the national struggle must supersede the class struggle, and all efforts directed internally should be primarily geared towards the UNITY of all African-Americans, not unity for its own sake, but for the necessity of survival and national liberation of black people.

5) The best way for African-Americans to fight for a true internationalism is through their struggle for national liberation; not as abstract or banal "universalists" who would subordinate our struggle to any "greater" ones which have yet to merit such a gesture, but as concrete internationalists within the form of national struggle.

6) The African-American struggle is intimately tied to the struggles of the "Third World" against imperialism; no people of color will be free to determine their own destiny until all people of color are free.

7) The ties of African-Americans to the mother continent of Africa are therefore manifested not only in the cultural sphere,

in the ancestral roots of our ancient heritage, but in the political sphere as well, in the form of a revolutionary anti-imperialist stance expressed in common struggle against a common enemy.

8) In revolutionary struggle the place of culture is no less important than that of politics and economics — one must give equal attention to all three areas, with politics furnishing the guiding light; to preserve black culture, one must fight for the existence of the black nation.

9) The liberation of Black America and the establishment of a revolutionary black nation-state is only conceivable within the context of total democracy, i.e., *socialism*, existing throughout the entire country.

10) The role of white workers and white radical intellectuals inside the United States is two-fold: to give unconditional support to the just demands of African-Americans for national liberation; to struggle for revolutionary socialism: the elimination of exploitation of man by man and the establishment of a true humanism.

11) With the failure of the forces of Labor to achieve power in the West during the first half of this century, the primary motive force of world history at this juncture has shifted to the peoples of color in the colonies and former colonies and their struggles of liberation directed against western imperialism.

12) Nevertheless, with respect to the international contradiction, Capital-Labor, the forces of Labor will, through revolutionary strategy and tactics consistent with the peculiar characteristics of its condition, ultimately prevail over the forces of Capital.

13) As an internal colony situated within the most powerful imperialist force in history — the United States — African-Americans and their allies have a key strategic role to play in the approaching world-wide revolution: the defeat of imperialism at its very source.

14) With the consolidation of her revolution, Black America has the international duty to both morally and materially aid her brothers and sisters of the "Third World" in the building of a better life for humanity.

— E. Mkalimoto

A Letter from
H. Rap Brown

H. Rap Brown was born and raised in Baton Rouge, Louisiana. He writes in his autobiography Die Nigger Die that "the life story of any negro growing up in america is the story of what has been done to him and how he reacts to that." He entered Southern University in Louisiana at the age of 15. During the summer of 1962 he travelled to Washington, D. C., where he became friendly with a group of young people who were later to be affiliated with SNCC. In 1964 he participated in SNCC's Mississippi Summer Project. By this time he had decided to devote his energies to the community rather than return to school. In Washington, D. C., he worked with the poverty program and as a neighborhood worker and organizer.

In 1966, Brown became director of the SNCC inspired Greene County Project to organize black voters in Mississippi. Since it became apparent the power structure had no intention of including black names on ballots, there was talk of a "Freedom Election," which would create a parallel government. Out of this came the Black Panther Party. Brown was elected Chairman of SNCC in 1967. "Every action that we are involved in is political, whether it is religious, artistic, cultural, athletic, governmental, educational, economic or personal."

After a speaking engagement in Cambridge, Md., Brown found himself in confrontation with law enforcement agents. The following letter was written while he was under arrest at the Parish Prison in New Orleans, Louisiana, February 21, 1968:

Being a man is the continuing battle of one's life. One loses a bit of manhood with every stale compromise to the authority of any power in which one does not believe.

No slave should die a natural death. There is a point where caution ends and cowardice begins.

For every day I am in prison I will refuse both food and water. My hunger is for the liberation of my people. My thirst is for ending of oppression.

I am a political prisoner, jailed for my beliefs — that black people must be free. The government has taken a position true to its fascist nature.

Those who they cannot convert they silence.

This government has become the enemy of mankind.

This can no longer alter our path to freedom. For our people, death has been the only known exit from slavery and oppression.

We must open others.

Our will to live must no longer supersede our will to fight, for our fighting will determine if our race shall live. To desire freedom is not enough.

We must move from resistance to aggression, from revolt to revolution.

For every Orangeburg, there must be ten Detroits. For every Max Stanford and every Huey Newton there must be ten dead racist cops. And for every black death, there must a Dien Bien Phu.

Brothers and Sisters, and all oppressed people, we must prepare ourselves both mentally and physically, for the major confrontation yet to come.

We must fight.

It is the people who in the final analysis make and determine history, not leaders or systems. The laws to govern us must be made by us.

May the death of '68 signal the beginning of the end of this country.

I do what I must out of the love for my people. My will is to fight; resistance is not enough. Aggression is the order of the day.

NOTE TO AMERICA

America, if it takes my death to organize my people to re-
    volt against you,
And to organize your jails to revolt against you,
And to organize your troops to revolt against you,
And to organize your children to revolt against you,
And to organize your God to revolt against you,
And to organize your poor to revolt against you,
And to organize Mankind to rejoice in your destruction and
    ruin,
Then, here is my Life!
But my Soul belongs to my people.
Lasima Tushinde Mbilashaka (We Shall Conquer Without
a Doubt)

Yours in Revolution,
H. Rap Brown

ABOUT THE EDITOR

FLOYD BARRINGTON BARBOUR *grew up in Washington, D. C. He is a graduate of Dunbar High School in Washington, and of Bowdoin College in Brunswick, Maine. He held a teaching fellowship in English from Howard University, and later traveled and studied in Europe. He has written a number of plays which have been performed at Bowdoin College, the Institute for Advanced Studies in the Theatre Arts, the Yale University Festival of One-Act Plays, Brandeis University, and an evening of one-acts at Howard University. An adaptation of his* The Bird Cage *is to be published by Doubleday in* Scenes from Black Playwrights, *edited by Alice Childress. Another play,* Sweet Jesus, *was translated into Dutch by Rosey Pool.*

Barbour has lectured on Afro-American culture at Williams College, Harvard Medical School, Bowdoin College, the University of Pittsburgh, and Howard University. Presently he teaches black literature at the African Studies Center at Boston University and at the Massachusetts Institute of Technology. He is the editor of The Black Power Revolt.

Annotated Bibliography

Ernest Kaiser

Ernest Kaiser is on the staff of the Schomburg Collection, New York Public Library. He is a contributing editor to Freedomways; *his articles and essays have been published in* Black World, Black Expression, Ten Black Writers Respond, *and other publications.*

INTRODUCTION

This bibliography includes the predictions for the general American society during the seventies and after, since blacks are affected by the general trends and changes in American society usually more severely than the whites. It also embraces some visions and projections by blacks for blacks during the 1940's, 1950's and 1960's. And finally, the bibliography contains the visions and predictions by blacks for black people during the seventies, including setbacks and progress. These books should help to round out the picture of what black people can expect and must fight for or against in the seventies.

Books, Chapters from Books,
Pamphlets, Reports, Lecture Series:

Daniel Bell (ed.), *Toward the Year 2000: Work in Progress.* Boston, Beacon Press, 1969. This is the summer of 1967 number of *Daedalus* published by the American Academy of Arts and

Sciences and reprinted in book form. Professor Daniel Bell, chairman of the American Academy's Commission on the Year 2000, summarizes some of the proliferating and challenging literature on the technetronic age of the future in his introduction to this book. In the rest of the book, a group of outstanding experts and specialists take a look at the forces of change in modern society and try to determine how they can best be directed to shape the future.

Theodore L. Cross, *Black Capitalism: Strategy for Business in the Ghetto*. New York, Atheneum Press, 1969. Cross says that true economic emancipation for black people will be achieved only if society satisfies the Negro's need to learn how to mobilize talent for production and marketing in a total economy which will be receptive to his product and services. Cross proposes a 13-point system of attacking the wealth-repressive forces and of reshaping and stabilizing the ghetto economy. He offers a complete blueprint, a total plan of action to abolish ghetto poverty.

Peter Drucker, *The Age of Discontinuity: Guidelines to Our Society*. New York, Harper and Row, 1969. Drucker says that our society now has four discontinuities: a new technology involving a shift in the nature of the raw materials we use; the development of a new "world economy" instead of international economy of separate national units; a new matrix of social and political systems that stand apart from traditional government; and the rise of the "knowledge worker" whose class will dominate our knowledge-centered economy developing out of the capital goods-centered industrial society. And so, he says, we can no longer project the economic or social future on the basis of past data. And future growth and change are uncertain and unpredictable.

Freedom Budget. A. Philip Randolph Institute, 260 Park Avenue South, New York City. This was an economic program projected at the 1966 White House conference "To fulfill These Rights" by A. Philip Randolph. The Freedom Budget proposes an annual federal expenditure of $18.5 billion for ten years to wipe out poverty. The program calls for full employment and a guaranteed income, the rebuilding of our cities, the providing of superior schools for all of our children, and free medical care for all of our citizens.

William H. Haddad, and Douglas G. Pugh (eds.), *Black Economic Development*. Englewood Cliffs, N.J., Prentice-Hall, 1969. This is a symposium held by Columbia University's American Assembly in which the Negro's role in economic life is discussed from many views by over a dozen representatives of public and private agencies. Pugh is a black with the Ford Foundation.

Herman Kahn and Anthony J. Wiener, *The Year 2000*. New York, Macmillan, 1967. Kahn, who has written on thermonuclear war and war escalation, here attempts to present in some detail the anatomy of a predictable "surprise-free future" along with contingent alternative futures, especially for business, in a period of furious technological and scientific innovation.

Nick Kotz, *Let Them Eat Promises: The Politics of Hunger in America*, Introduction by Senator George S. McGovern. Englewood Cliffs, N.J., Prentice-Hall, 1970. A sharp attack on the run-around given the 16 million hungry children and adults by the presidents and their cabinet members and members of Congress, and how the business establishment exploits and produces millions of poor, hungry people every year. Kotz calls for long-range and short-term programs for the alleviation and solution of these problems.

Julius Lester, *Search for the New Land; History as Subjective Experience*. New York, Dial Press, 1969. Here Lester, a young black writer, attempts to look at history since World War II and at change, and to reinterpret many customary American attitudes and views in accordance with his view from the black side of America. Many changes toward Lester's views will have to come in the 1970's.

Claude M. Lightfoot, *Ghetto Rebellion to Black Liberation*. New York, International Publishers, 1968. This book by a black Marxist on the ghetto rebellions discusses black power and the ghetto revolts, the right of armed self-defense and the dangers of calls for "guerrilla warfare," the nature of the increasingly violent and genocidal white racism, the positive features of black nationalism and the pitfalls of black separatism, and finally the necessity for basic society change to achieve full black liberation.

Rayford W. Logan (ed.), *What the Negro Wants*. Chapel Hill, N.C., University of North Carolina Press, 1944. Contributors were W. E. B. Du Bois, Leslie Pinkney Hill, Charles H. Wesley, Roy Wilkins, A. Philip Randolph, W. S. Townsend, Mrs. Mary McLeod Bethune, Gordon B. Hancock, Langston Hughes, George S. Schuyler, S. A. Brown and Frederick D. Patterson. They outlined all of the things the blacks wanted and were fighting on the home front and in World War II to get.

John McHale, *The Future of the Future*. New York, Braziller, 1969. McHale says that the future must be planned and anticipated now or we many face disaster or annihilation. The problems of air pollution, overpopulation, traffic congestion, lack of food, depletion of natural resources, increased leisure and others are taken up here. He gives us an inventory of our options in the future summarizing the research on all of these problems.

Floyd McKissick, *Three-Fifths of a Man*, foreword by Justice William O. Douglas. New York, Macmillan, 1969. McKissick, a black attorney and former National Director of CORE, proposes that we solve our nation's racial crisis with the spirit of the Declaration of Independence and through honest application of the U. S. Constitution. He also wants us to develop black economic power to accompany effective application of our nation's laws. In line with this, McKissick is today developing Soul City in one of the southern states.

Aurelio Peccei, *The Chasm Ahead.* New York, Macmillan, 1969. J. J. Servan-Schreiber, in *The American Challenge* (1968), said that the West European economies, stymied by World War II, were unable to compete now with the advantaged American economy and that West Europe would suffer. Peccei carries Servan-Schreiber's argument even further and declares that America's technological superiority will so widen the trans-Atlantic gap that the whole world will suffer.

Report of the National Commission on the Causes and Prevention of Violence, November, 1969. Superintendent of Documents, U.S. Government Printing Office, Washington, D.C. (Also New York, Bantam Books paperback). This report warns that if the U.S. does not re-order its priorities and attack poverty, dilapidated housing, high unemployment, poor education, overpopulation and broken homes in the black ghettos of our cities together with the white racist attitudes of the majority toward the ghettos — the real causes of crime — then our cities will turn into armed camps with intensifying hatred and deepening division between poor blacks and affluent whites.

Bayard Rustin, "Minority Groups: Development of the Individual," in William R. Ewald, Jr. (ed.), *Environment and Policy: The Next Fifty Years.* Bloomington, Indiana, Indiana University Press, 1968. About the problems of the ghetto, jobs, family, housing, education, poverty, social change, and politics.

David Schoenbrun, "The Challenge of the Seventies." (A series of five lectures at the New School for Social Research, New York City, beginning March 2, 1970.) Schoenbrun, a former radio reporter and the author of several books, asks: why spend fifty billion dollars for an ABM missiles system to protect the country when air pollution may choke us to death? He says that little or no money spent for air pollution, housing and other acute problems of the slums of every city and for the 16 million hungry may result in our destruction from within.

Clarence C. Walton, *Business and Social Progress*. New York, F. A. Praeger. This is a symposium sponsored by the Council for Economic Development in which business leaders, young executives, and outstanding educators discuss current social problems and what business can do to help cope with them.

Aaron W. Warner (ed.), *The Environment of Change*. New York, Columbia University Press, 1969. Here I. I. Rabi discusses "The Revolution in Science"; Jacob Bronowski, "The Impact of New Sciences"; Isaiah Berlin, "The Hazards of Social Revolution"; and Loren C. Eiseley, "Alternatives to Technology," in which he points out that our present system of producing goods and services is only another step in the evolutionary process and that change is coming now in this time of crisis.

Nathan Wright, *Let's Work Together*. New York, Hawthorn Books, 1968. Dr. Wright's thesis is that before black and white can work together, they must each work out their own problems. So this book is concerned with three main areas: those problems which the white people need to deal with; those which the black people must solve for themselves; and those which involve cooperation and unity. He states the problems, discusses them and offers solutions.

Whitney M. Young, Jr., *Beyond Racism: Building an Open Society*. New York, McGraw-Hill, 1969. This is the second reasoned, piogrammatic book on U.S. race relations by the executive director of the National Urban League. If only the Establishment and millions of lukewarm whites would act on his proposals in the 1970's.

————, *To Be Equal*. New York, McGraw-Hill, 1964. Young says here in his first book that the elimination of injustices and inequities is not enough; that a special effort on the part of the entire white and Negro population must be made to help the Negro overcome "the discrimination gap" — the crippling effects that a 300-year legacy of deprivation has produced. He has a plan to overcome all the Negro's problems.

Magazine and Newspaper Articles:

"Black Capitalism: Yes and No" Dunbar McLaurin's article says "yes"; Dr. Andrew F. Brimmer's speech says "no, blacks can make more money by getting jobs in the white business world," *New York Amsterdam News,* Jan. 10, 1970, p. 1+. Louis Martin, in his column in the *New York Courier,* Jan. 31, 1970, says that blacks need both black capitalism and jobs in the white business world. And they will certainly need both in the 1970's.

Robert S. Browne, "The Case for Two Americas — One Black, One White," *New York Times Magazine,* Aug. 11, 1968. Professor Browne of Farleigh Dickinson University and recently of the Institute of the Black World (Atlanta, Ga.), eschews in this article the hard, almost insoluble economic problems involved in black separatism which he espouses. He emphasizes instead the cultural identity and psychological needs of the black group.

Zbigniew Brzezinski, "America in the Technetronic Age," *Encounter,* Vol. XXX, No. 1, Jan. 1968, pp. 16-26. The writer says here that far-reaching innovations will be the result of the impact of science and technology on man and his society. He predicts fantastic changes in man and society as the U.S. and Western Europe enter the technetronic age of computers, automation, cybernetics and telecommunications. The Columbia University professor has repeated his predictions in a recent article in the *New York Times.*

Leo Cherne, "The Next Thirty Years," *New York Times Book Review,* Jan. 18, 1970, pp. 12, 14. Cherne, the executive director of the Research Institute of America, gives a round-up of books about the future of interest to businessmen and economists in the "Business and Economics Supplement." See also Cherne's annual speech before the National Salesmen's Association (Jan. 8 or 9, 1970), giving his predictions for 1970 for the country.

Kenneth B. Clark, "Answer for 'Disadvantaged' Is Effective Teaching," *New York Times*, Jan. 12, 1970, p. 50. Dr. Clark, president of the Metropolitan Applied Research Center, Inc., in New York City, rejects the concept of the culturally disadvantaged children as the teachers' rationale for not teaching them. More effective teaching is the best antidote for deprivation, says Clark, and he wants the promotions and salary increases of teachers and principals tied to the academic performance of their students.

"Free by '63," *New York Times*, Nov. 6, 1961. At the NAACP's annual convention in St. Louis in 1953, Channing Tobias, president of the NAACP's board of directors, called for an all-out drive to end segregation and other forms of racial discrimination by Jan. 1, 1963, the centennial of President Abraham Lincoln's Emancipation Proclamation. Dr. Tobias later organized, with Walter White, NAACP executive secretary, a conference in Washington, D.C., on March 10, 1954, at which the ten-year Fight for Freedom campaign was formally launched with the slogan "Free by '63." The freedom campaign called for a fund of one million dollars a year for ten years. President Dwight D. Eisenhower was the main speaker at the conference. Dr. Tobias died on Nov. 5, 1961.

Hugh M. Gloster, "Negro Colleges Face a Crisis," *New York Times*, Jan. 12, 1970, p. 50. Blacks are 10 per cent of the population but only 3 per cent of the college students, says Dr. Gloster. By 1980, blacks will comprise about 5 per cent of the college students. Black colleges face a crisis today and in the future because one-half of the black college students are now in white institutions. Black colleges cannot compete with the wealthier white institutions now opening to blacks in terms of scholarships, teachers' salaries, and general financial support. And white students do not attend black colleges in large numbers. The trend of black students is away from black southern institutions as blacks migrate North and West.

Vincent Harding, "Fighting the 'Mainstream' Seen for 'Black

Decade'," *New York Times*, Jan. 12, 1970, p. 50. Dr. Harding, director of the Martin Luther King, Jr., Memorial Center and Institute of the Black World in Atlanta, Ga., says that black education in the seventies will be an important part of the political struggle of black people in America against institutionalized racism and oppression and for liberation and a new humanity.

Fred M. Hechinger, "The 1970's: Education for What?" *New York Times*, Jan. 12, 1970, pp. 49, 70. Hechinger says here that the education Establishment of schools and colleges is under attack and is no longer sure of its goals. In fact, the educational goals must be changed and made relevant to the students being educated to work in the different communities.

Robert L. Heilbroner, "Priorities for the Seventies," *Saturday Review*, Vol. LII, No. 53, Jan. 3, 1970, pp. 17-19, 84. Heilbroner's three great priorities or courses of action necessary to restore American society to life and decency are: 1) the demilitarization of the national budget (now $80 billion a year for military purposes); 2) $10 to $15 billion can then be spent annually to abolish poverty which affects whites and blacks; 3) there is a need to rebuild the cities before they collapse on us. It will take $20 to 25 billion a year for ten years to make American cities viable again. This includes housing, health, schools, police, etc. These are the writer's minimal requirements and objectives for America. Four other priorities are the elimination of racism, the winning over of the younger generation, the improvement of our polluted environment, and university work for peace instead of war. But Heilbroner says the power of the vested interests of business and politics and labor in the preservation of military spending is enormous.

"How Earth Can Feed Billions More People," *Muhammad Speaks*, Nov. 21, Nov. 28, Dec. 5, 1969. The Soviet author K. Malin's book is summarized here in a series of three articles. Malin shows that the U.S. economists' cry of overpopulation and the need for birth control is a screen for genocide — Malthus's 1798 theory, long discredited, brought forward in modern dress, appears in books like Paul R. Ehrlich's *The Population Bomb* (1969) [population control or race to oblivion?]. Malin says that these people either do not understand or deliberately distort or minimize the food producing possibilities. If the achievements of science and technology are used properly, he says, the earth can feed billions more people. Food producing possibilities will be simply unlimited. The food supply may be augmented by increasing the quantity of edible plants, increasing the per-acre yield of fodder with chemicals, and by expanding cultivated land. Chemically, all sorts of things can be done: increase edible plant absorption of sun energy; various foods can be made chemically, etc. Seventy-five per cent of the earth is under water, says Malin, and only 10 per cent of the remaining land is cultivated.

Martin Luther King, Jr., "I Have a Dream" (address at the March on Washington for Jobs and Freedom, Washington, D.C., Aug. 28, 1963), *Negro History Bulletin*, May 1968, pp. 16-17. This is Dr. King's famous speech in which he had a vision of whites and blacks living and working together all over the country in the future.

Philip Morrison, "Sciences May Beggar Predictions," *New York Times*, Jan. 12, 1970, pp. 49, 83. Dr. Morrison, a professor of physics at M.I.T., says that in the next third of this century, the various fields of science will probably achieve even more than the great things forecast for them.

"Negroes Nearing Majority in Major Northern Cities," *Focus/ Midwest*, Vol. 5, No. 34, Mar-Apr. 1966, pp. 24-25. This article says that by 1970 it is estimated that Negroes will constitute 40 per cent or more of the population in 14 of the nation's major cities. Some of these are Washington, D.C., Richmond, Va., Gary, Ind., Baltimore, Md., Detroit, Mich., Newark, N.J., St. Louis, Mo., New Orleans, La., and Trenton,

N.J. Cleveland, Ohio and Oakland, Calif., would have black populations of over one-third; and Philadelphia, Pa., Chicago, Ill., and Cincinnati, Ohio, would have black populations of just under one-third. The trend will continue, says the article, over the next decade or so, but the exact rate of increase is unknown. We can also project here that the black population of 22 million will go to about 27 or 28 million and that the black consumer market, now at $30 billion, will go to about $36 billion by 1980.

Whitney M. Young, Jr., "Should There Be Compensation for Negroes?" *New York Times Magazine*, Oct. 6, 1963, p. 43+. In 1963, Whitney Young and the National Urban League put forward a Domestic Marshall Plan for Negroes that would cost $145 billion over 10 years. This more-than-equal treatment or compensatory help for Negroes is needed, said Young, because Negroes suffered a discrimination gap caused by more than three centuries of abuse, humiliation, segregation, and bias. Considered utopian and discrimination-in-reverse when announced, a Marshall Plan for the cities is embraced now by almost everyone.

See also the bibliography on pp. 124-126 of this book.

INDEX